THE FAMILY SILVER

DISCARD

A MEMOIR OF DEPRESSION AND INHERITANCE

The Family Silver

SHARON O'BRIEN

The University of Chicago Press

Chicago and London

SHARON O'BRIEN is the John Hope Caldwell Professor of American Cultures and director of American Studies at Dickinson College. The author of the acclaimed biography *Willa Cather: The Emerging Voice,* she is also the editor of the three-volume Library of America edition of Cather's works.

The University of Chicago Press, Chicago 60637
The University of Chicago Press, Ltd., London
© 2004 by Sharon O'Brien
All rights reserved. Published 2004
Printed in the United States of America
13 12 11 10 09 08 07 06 05 04   1 2 3 4 5

ISBN: 0-226-61664-9 (cloth)

Library of Congress Cataloging-in-Publication Data

O'Brien, Sharon.
    The family silver : a memoir of depression and inheritance / Sharon O'Brien.
       p.   cm.
    ISBN 0-226-61664-9 (alk. paper)
    1. O'Brien, Sharon.   2. O'Brien family.   3. Quinlan family.   4. Irish Americans—
Biography.   5. Depression, Mental—Patients—Biography.   6. Depressed persons—
Family relationships.   7. Children of depressed persons.   8. Elmira (N.Y.)—Biography.
9. Massachusetts—Biography.   I. Title.

CT275.O25A3 2004
973.91'092'39162—dc22

                                                                                    2004000203

To my family—past, present, and future

Remembering is the work of the living.

—MARK DOTY, *Heaven's Coast*

Contents

PART THREE *The Emigrant Irish*

Sources

I came to see the damage that was done
and the treasures that prevail.
　　　　—ADRIENNE RICH, "Diving into the Wreck"

WHEN OUR PARENTS DIE, at first it seems that all the stories we need, and forgot to ask for, have died with them. When my father died I was twenty-nine, unaware that I might need any stories he could tell—about his life, or that of his parents, or of his grandfather Patrick, the famine immigrant who survived the Atlantic crossing from Cork to Boston, found work in the textile mills of Lowell, and made it possible for his descendants to live.

When my mother died, sixteen years later, I had become—so quickly!—a midlife daughter of forty-five. My mother had always been the family story-teller, entrancing her children with tales of the six beautiful, accomplished Quinlan sisters and their autocratic actor father, Handsome Dan, star of min-strel and vaudeville circuits in the late nineteenth and early twentieth cen-turies. As she was dying I wanted still more stories, and now it was too late to ask for them. Sometimes I tried to squeeze them out of her, making my bedridden mother listen to me read family letters from her mother, hoping for a revelation or a new memory, when all she wanted to do was watch *Jeopardy!* or *Hollywood Squares.* When you want your dying parents to talk you can get very selfish.

After my mother's death I felt bereft, an orphan in my mid-forties. All the members of the older generation were gone—no more parents, no more aunts and uncles. No more family history. No protection between me and mortality; my sister, brother, and I were now the older generation, shield-ing my nieces and nephews. I kept saying to myself, "I've lost my link to the nineteenth century"—perhaps an odd expression of grief, but I felt my father and mother had connected me to more than their personal pasts. My father had been born in 1906, my mother in 1909. Their memories of their parents and grandparents carried my story backward in time, broadening it out like a branching river, linking me to those born in the 1840s. My mother's memory of her grandmother—"Grandma Doherty"—carried me and my siblings across the Atlantic to Ireland and the Famine. "Your grandmother came over on a boat, all alone, when she was eight," my mother told us, "her name pinned to her coat so her cousins could recognize her." This story made our Irish past only a heartbeat away.

All the resounding losses of my mother's death reawakened those brought by my father's. These losses challenged me: I didn't want to let death and silence win. "It's too late now," people often say when their parents die. *I wish I'd interviewed my father, asked my mother to write down her stories, saved the photographs, paid more attention, it's too late now.* "It's not too late," I want to tell them, "you can always go back; you can always find or imagine more stories."

I had always been the family historian: the one child who stores the boxes of family photographs and letters, moving them from attic to attic. Now the contents of these boxes were not just mementoes. They were clues. I would become the detective and story-finder I had been before, when I wrote a biography of Willa Cather. I would track down the missing family stories.

At FIRST my search was fueled by personal urgency. When my mother died I was in the middle of a stubborn, nasty, on-and-off depression that darkened my life in my forties and early fifties. I would try many different medications over the years. Finally it seemed the doctors were throwing their hands up when I was told I had "TRD," current shorthand for "Treatment Resistant Depression," depression defined in terms of the failure of medication to make much of a dent in it. This resistant depression—what was it opposing?—also did not respond well to therapy, light boxes, exercise, meditation, acupuncture; it seemed to scorn the whole panoply of late twentieth-century remedies.

Because my unwelcome visitor didn't disappear as the Prozac ads had promised, I had wanted a story to explain what had happened to me; it seemed to me that being subject to human frailty and limitation—un-American attributes, human conditions—required some sort of explanation.

My sister and brother had both had their bouts with depression, and I knew there were genetic sources for the illness. Our mother had struggled with anxiety and phobias, and our father had suffered a devastating depression in the late 1940s. His sister Gertrude had been in and out of hospitals in the 1950s for shock treatments.

Yet such genetic inheritance didn't seem a sufficient story. I wanted to understand how emotional inheritance worked. How could the seeds of depression be passed down through the generations?

Encouraged by psychological theories, at first I cast a critical eye on my parents, looking for an emotional story of origins: how could they have done this and that to me? Surely someone must be to blame! Gradually, as I began to think of my parents as children, themselves shaped by history, culture, and the lives that had come before them, the question of blame disappeared and that of depression's origins broadened. Helped by my training as a teacher and scholar in American studies, I began to see that my family inheritance—of which depression was only a part—had been shaped by Irish history and American culture, forces much larger than the family. I moved from wanting to understand the sources of depression to wanting to understand the family past. I wanted to speak with the dead, and to listen.

I felt as if I were casting a net out into the vast ocean of lost years. I kept throwing the net farther and farther back in time, back to the stories of my grandparents, growing up in the 1880s in Elmira, New York, and Lowell, Massachusetts, in communities of other Irish emigrants and exiles; then going farther back—to the Famine, the devastation that brought my great-grandparents to America in the 1840s and early 1850s.

I found I had become, once again, a biographer. I began to understand how my parents and grandparents had been shaped by history and culture and how a family legacy stretches farther and farther back in time, widening and widening as more and more ancestors flow into the stream coursing toward the self. Instead of just wanting to know where my depression came from, I more and more wanted to know where I came from, and then, where my mother had come from, and my father, and their mothers and fathers, and their mothers and fathers before them.

As I began asking questions of the dead, I found that often they would answer. Sometimes they spoke to me in dreams; sometimes in the fragments they had left behind, stories hidden in gravestones and letters, photographs and wills, houses and deeds, chairs and silverware. Sometimes a story would appear, magically, from a remembered object become luminous with meaning, like the rickety card table in my parents' bedroom, covered with pencil marks and children's scrawls, where my father wrote his business letters, or the fabled Repoussé, the Quinlan family silver, that wove in and out of my mother's stories like a gleaming thread.

As I became more and more a biographer of my own past and my family's, I could draw on the skills I had gained as a biographer of Willa Cather. *Go and find out* is the motto of the mongoose family in Kipling's story "Rikki Tikki Tavi," and that is the biographer's motto too. I began traveling in space as well as time, revisiting Elmira, New York, my mother's hometown and my childhood Eden; Lowell, where my father grew up, and where his grandfather had worked in the textile mills and his father had managed a clothing store; Belmont, Massachusetts, the toney Boston suburb where I grew up and where my parents lived until their deaths; Harvard and Cambridge, where both my father and I had gone to school. I returned to Ireland many times, finally visiting Skibbereen, a little town in Cork where the O'Briens had lived, still remembered as one of the parts of Ireland most devastated by the Famine.

As I cast my net I gathered in my vaudeville actor grandfather's book of clippings, my aunt's hospital records for shock treatments, my mother's books of lists, my father's reading notebook, my aunt Ruth's album books, my aunt Geraldine's teaching records from the Elmira College archives, the hospice nurses' logbook of my mother's dying, a family home movie from 1940, boxes of photographs and letters, the two books my father brought to the hospital to read before his death—*Imitation of Christ* and *Bleak House.*

I found surprising records, too—my father's Harvard file, containing his application letter from 1923, that told me he had once wanted to be a priest; my Radcliffe file from 1963, with *my* long-forgotten application letter that told me I had grown up "in the shadow of Harvard"; records of cemetery plots in Lowell and Elmira that introduced me to relatives I had never heard of, including a great-great O'Brien uncle who fought and died in the Civil War, at Antietam. I haunted historical societies and libraries, looking through crumbling city directories and microfilms of old newspapers, visited the National Archives to find naturalization records, spoke with relatives and old family friends. I attended the Harvard Class of 1927 seventieth reunion in 1997, sitting at lunch with courtly men in their nineties, all of whom had been young with my father—undergraduates in the protected space of the 1920s, still safe from the Depression and the War—now coming together to honor the living and the dead.

"Whatever we had missed," reflects Jim Burden at the end of Willa Cather's *My Ántonia*, "we possessed together the precious, the incommunicable past." The past is particularly precious and incommunicable for the descendants of immigrants and forced migrants to America. We have left the past behind us in Europe or Africa or Asia, and our culture tells us that this is a good thing. When Americans speak about the emigrant past, they traditionally want to tell the story of hope, material success, and positive transformation in America: "I lift my lamp beside the golden door." Such images of light have no room for the darkness of loss or depression. We are a country of the future, not of the past; the break is supposed to be complete, irrevocable.

I can see the visual sign of this break in the genealogies my father and mother tried to create in their notebooks—the family tree only goes back to their parents, the ones born in America. Beyond the birth and death dates of my grandparents is a blank—no names, no stories, no history for those born in Ireland, as if they never existed.

Depression started me on this journey toward the past, and although sometimes I wish I had had a different traveling companion, I am grateful. Like others, I am an inheritor of what seemed, at first, to be incommunicable stories. Searching for them, recovering them, creating them is the story I tell here.

PART ONE   *Looking for Elmira*

For those like us, our fate is to face the world
as orphans, chasing through long years the shadow
of vanished parents. There is nothing for it but
to try and see our missions to the end, as best we can,
for until we do so, we will be permitted no calm.

        —KAZUO ISHIGURO, *When We Were Orphans*

Looking for Elmira

What we call the beginning is often the end
And to make an end is to make a beginning.
The end is where we start from.
                    —T. S. ELIOT, "Little Gidding"

I SAVED THE STRANGEST THINGS after my mother died. Her books of lists I gathered up first, sharing these treasures with my brother Kevin. I took her workbook from her Fear of Flying class, filled with the quizzes she completed to assess her level of terror. I asked the hospice nurses for a Xerox of their daily log book, and they broke rules to give it to me. All the comments the nurses and I made on medication and sleep and bowel movements seemed crucial, like a ship's log, the story of her last journey. I took the fake sheepskin on which she had lain, a supposed remedy for bedsores. I remembered seeing her cradling her head against it, and when I picked it up I could see wisps of her white hair woven through the clumps of wool, so much had shed from the chemo.

I wanted the pink chair she always sat in by the window, doing her cross-word puzzles, reading her books, waiting for one of her children to drive up. The day my mother couldn't get out of bed to walk over to the pink chair must have been the day she realized she was dying.

"I would really like the pink chair," I told Maureen and Kevin, ready for a fight, to throw a fit, whatever it took to get it, sure they wanted it too. My mother's family heritage required siblings to battle over heirlooms; I knew the three of us enjoyed a loving and harmonious relationship, but could that withstand the allotment of the *pink chair*, the jewel in the crown?

"Sure," Maureen said.

"Take it," Kevin said.

I had done everything I could to keep her spirit with me, but it seemed to be ebbing, each day her memory and presence a little further away, each

3

day depression and dryness of soul a little closer. In February, eight months after my mother's death, I decided to return to Elmira, the place of her birth, which I had not visited in thirty-five years. I wanted to combat the depression that was deepening over the winter months. I wanted to go on a pilgrimage.

SHORTLY BEFORE my mother became ill with lung cancer we had been planning a trip back to Elmira together. I had been counting on that journey to lead us together into her memories and my family past. As soon I heard that she had been diagnosed with terminal cancer I flew up to Boston, and I remember as the cab was taking me from Logan airport to Belmont I wondered what would be the first thing I would say to her. When I walked into the living room and saw her sitting, thin and bowed, in her pink chair by the window I went over and we held each other for a long time, not saying anything.

"Now we're not going to be able to go to Elmira."

"I know," she said. "It's not *fair*. Some people live *well* into their nineties." (Just like our mother, the three of us agreed later, to be furious she didn't make it to ninety-five, or at least until a Democrat got elected president.)

Later I asked her if she thought there might be a special place on earth where, after people died, we could find their spirits.

"I don't know," she said slowly, as if this were a new idea for her. "I'd like to think so."

I WAS SURE that place was Elmira. My mother had never really made a home for herself in Belmont, the Boston suburb where she'd lived for more than forty years, so I didn't think I could find her spirit there. It was in Elmira, in the big brown house at 531 West Clinton Street that her father built, that she was truly at home. She lived in that house until she was twenty-seven. After she graduated from Elmira College in 1931 with a degree in Business English, she taught in a series of upstate New York high schools, living in boarding houses in Rochester or Syracuse or Troy, eating the landlady's cooking and starving for home. One Friday afternoon her sister Geraldine, alarmed by her sadness, drove up to Rochester in her new roadster and took her to Elmira for the weekend.

"I didn't want to go back to the boarding house," my mother told me. "I couldn't wait until the summer and I could go home again."

Elmira house, early 1900s

*W*HEN MY MOTHER said the world "El-maah-rah" her upstate New York accent was at its thickest: she drew out the name, her voice caressing the syllables. Elmira had been known as the "Queen City" in the late nineteenth century, and I sometimes wondered if her Irish American parents named her "Regina" for the American town they lived in, as well as for *regina coeli*, the Queen of Heaven. Elmira was the place of my mother's power, her queenship. She was the center of a madcap crowd of girls, her famous "chums," Dot and Nettie and Kel and Gink, girls who stayed together through St. Patrick's elementary school and Elmira Free Academy and then Elmira College, their names familiar to all us kids through our mother's stories, even though we had never met them.

Regina was a dark-haired Irish beauty, dangling boys on a string, surrounded by eager suitors who braved her father's fierce presence to take her to the movie show. Handsome Dan Quinlan would be off on the road with his minstrel troupe or vaudeville act during the school year, but in the summer he was in residence, lording it over the family, keeping track of his daughters' comings and goings. He would usher my mother and her date out of the house, pocket watch in hand, saying "The movie is over at nine

5

o'clock. It is a ten minute walk. I will be waiting for you here at nine-ten precisely, and God help you if you're late." The only boy he ever approved of was her co-lead in the senior play: he'd allow this young man to come over to the house if they were working on their lines. "Quin" her friends called her, and no party or prank was ever complete without her.

In her later years, when she worked at the circulation desk of the Belmont Public Library, my mother entertained her coworkers with stories of her glorious Elmira, just as she had once entranced her children. One day she walked into the staff room to find a New York state map on the bulletin board, the major highways passing Elmira outlined in red magic marker. ALL ROADS LEAD TO ELMIRA, someone had written on a file card.

I AM SURE that after she died, I was looking back toward Elmira with my mother's yearning as well as my own. Most people do not share my magical associations with this now declining industrial city. In my memory and imagination, Elmira is the place of elm trees and sheltering brown houses and the six Quinlan sisters who live in my memory.

REGINA QUINLAN
Elmira, New York

Quinn's such a lively soul, so mischief loving (no, mischief isn't the right word, but it's something like that). She's always doing something real interesting or on the verge of it, and the reason we know this is to be found in her eyes. They fairly dance with her meditated fun and her momentary enjoyment. And then, the way she does things! She accomplishes such a lot without seeming to do a thing.

Regina's high school yearbook photo, 1927

6

Until my grandmother died in the early 1950s, we returned to Elmira every summer, leaving Belmont at the end of June and returning in August to get ready for school. My sister, brother, and I were always awakened in the predawn darkness for the drama of our summer pilgrimage, a two-day journey in the days before the Massachusetts Turnpike and the New York Thruway. "Let's just hope Albany isn't too bad," my father would say: there was nothing worse than being stuck in Albany in the heat, facing an endless line of overhead traffic lights keeping us from the airy freedom of Chemung County.

As we drove through Massachusetts, Worcester and then Pittsfield, we children couldn't wait for our ritual crossing of the New York state line, when we'd poke our heads out the car windows, breathe noisily, and chant "New York State air! Just fill your lungs with it!" On the way back, crossing into Massachusetts, we performed the drama in reverse, pretending to choke, rolling up the windows so we could keep New York's cleaner air in the car.

My father always took the insult to his native state's atmosphere with his usual good humor; this was my mother's moment in the sun. He'd drive us out, spend a few days, and then leave us until the end of the summer. We stayed in the same house where my mother had grown up. My grandfather had died before I was born, so when we pulled into the driveway we entered a world of women. Geraldine, the oldest, taught speech and drama at Elmira College and still lived with my grandmother. Dorothy would come up from Washington, where she worked as a lawyer, and Marion from New York City, freed for the summer from her job as a high school French teacher. When they entered the brown house their professional identities dropped off like fading chrysalises and they became, once again, the Quinlan sisters. My great-aunts Lizzie and Aggie and Lizzie's daughter Rosemary lived a few blocks away, and the tide of women swirled back and forth between the two houses.

Only my aunts Margaret and Ruth were not in attendance. Margaret lived in California, too far for a visit, and ever since Handsome Dan had thrown her out of the house for going to medical school she hadn't felt the same about Elmira. Ruth, the other rebel, had put as much space as she could between herself and her home town: she was then living in Tokyo, vowing never to return. "I had to get out of Elmira," she told me years later. "It would have killed me if I stayed."

As we stumbled out of the car, sticky and irritable from the heat and the journey, aunts streamed toward us in flowery cotton dresses and old lady shoes, cream-colored for the summer. One would cry to my grandmother, still upstairs in her sewing room, "Mother, the O'Briens are here," and then the aunts were calling out "Re-geeee-na" to my mother, which always startled me since my father called her "Jean." The aunts fussed over us, hugging and praising, smelling of talcum powder and fresh lipstick, embarrassing me with kisses.

My grandmother waited on the porch for her kiss: she was wrinkled and old and dressed in black. Once she had caught me playing with the spools of thread in her sewing room and reprimanded me, and ever after she frightened me a little. Her sewing room must have been her sacred place of refuge and creation; she responded to my violation of her sewing box with the sharpness of an artist defending her materials. She crocheted as well, and her white lace doilies covered all the sofa backs and arm rests, bureau tops and tables. After she died the doilies vanished, perhaps sold, perhaps gathered by one coveting sister, and all that remained were the spidery patterns the sun left on the upholstery.

The walk up the porch steps was a long one. But then, after I felt her papery lips brush my cheek, the awkwardness of arrival was over. I had crossed the threshold into my mother's house, and a world opened up. Aunt Geraldine took us down to the college radio station, where we talked into the shiny microphone and made recordings of our voices. Geraldine persuaded my seven-year-old brother to sing "Zip-a-dee-doo-dah," and we can still listen to his rendition on an old 78. *Plenty of sunshine, heading my way!*

Marion made us cooling lemonades and told us stories about her trips to France; Dorothy, the reserved one, stayed in the background, scraping potatoes and setting the table, nourished by the life around her. It was as if we had wandered onto another planet that resembled our own, but in the sky were many suns.

In Belmont we were expected to cultivate the sons and daughters of MIT and Harvard professors, befriending anyone who might be headed for the Ivy League. We were urged to make friends with the class leaders, girls who were "nice" and boys who were "clean-cut." We were not to make friends with any working-class children, not even Irish Catholics. Such people were—my mother's dreaded word—*ordinary*. Choosing playmates and friends was risky: you might bring home scruffy friends whose mothers worked at Woolworth's or whose fathers delivered mail, and have to drop them. But in Elmira the "ordinary" Irish Catholic kids headed for nursing school or the fire department were the daughters and sons of my mother's childhood friends. They lived across the street or down the block. And no matter how strong an attachment we might make to Elmira playmates, we'd be leaving in two months. So here we could play with ordinary children. That was part of the magic spell of Elmira, I now realize: we were on vacation, not just from Belmont but from the demands of upward mobility. This was the summer, a time when rules were suspended and selves were fluid, so we drifted through the long, leisurely days of July and August like leaves carried on the slow, languid current of the Chemung River, on its way from the glens and grottoes of upstate New York to the Susquehanna and the sea.

How wonderful it was just to be ordinary! When my siblings and I circled home at the end of the day, there was no "Who were you with," no sharp-tongued questioning, no scrambled and guilty lying. In Elmira the flow between home and world was as natural and untroubled as the tide.

I have only a few memories of those summers, but like Wordsworth's "spots of time" they are the light-filled landscape of my past, my golden childhood. In my dreams, the house in Elmira is where I return in wonder and longing.

*O*UR BELMONT house was still and dark and quiet, the fragile space of a very isolated nuclear family, a family that had lost its place in the social world of the middle class when my father's depression sent us plummeting economically. "A mausoleum," my sister says. "We grew up in a mausoleum." My parents never "had people over"—the only adult visitors were the occasional relatives, and we knew, without anyone ever saying anything, that we weren't supposed to invite other children over to play.

What was wonderful about Elmira was the sheer number of people streaming in and out of the Clinton Street house. Seven or eight people would be staying there, and our cousins and neighborhood children would come and go. I often heard the six most thrilling words in the English language, "Can Sharon come out to play?" Best of all was the communal freedom of the outdoor bedroom—an airy screened-in porch on the second floor where all the children slept, sometimes joined by a stray aunt who wanted to escape Elmira's nighttime heat.

You could hear mysterious yet soothing sounds as you went to sleep: the drone of the cicadas, the quiet rumble of adult conversation drifting up from the back porch, the hoot of a passing train. Elmira was still an important rail center in the early fifties, and trains traveled through all night: sometimes the whistles would wake me up and send pleasing shivers through my body. Part of me would be flying through the dark with the train, part lying in my cot on the sleeping porch, listening to the comforting breathing of my sister and brother. I'd stay awake for a few minutes, thinking how the stillness the train left behind was so deep and quiet, a clear, cool well, so different from ordinary stillness. Then I'd burrow deeper into my summer quilt and go back to sleep.

In Elmira we'd wake up to the morning sun and the sounds of birds, right beside you in the elm trees, and the clip-clop of the iceman's draught horse, an exciting beginning to the day because it meant you could go outside and see a huge, marbley block of saw-dusted ice under the grape arbor and lay your cheek against its frigid greeting. Then we'd wander onto the back porch where a long, rambling picnic table waited and women drifted in and out, drinking coffee or pouring cereal or munching toast, no one paying too much attention to what you ate because they were so busy talking.

Geraldine, the eldest aunt and family boss, would plan outings to Watkins Glen or Harris Hill, an Elmira Heights attraction where people flew gliders on Chemung Valley updrafts. At least once a week she'd rustle up a picnic expedition to Eldridge Park, Elmira's famed amusement park. We'd ride the wooden horses on the carousel and take paddle boats across the lake, rumored to be bottomless. Grove Park was a daily excursion, just a block away, offering a sandbox, slides, and swings, a covered eating space, and a gazebo where bands played on Saturday nights. Sometimes an aunt took me there; more often my sister did. "I'd push you on the swings till the cows came home." Perhaps this was just an ordinary park, the kind any small town would have offered, but to me it still has all the magical associations the word "grove" calls up—a place where spirits gather, a leafy, sun-dappled, sacred spot.

Belmont had a Grove Park too—a treeless stretch of grass, baseball diamond, jungle gyms, concrete tennis courts. It just wasn't the same.

THERE'S A striking difference between the family photos of the O'Brien children in Elmira and in Belmont. In Belmont we are dressed up and posed, Maureen and me wearing hats and gloves and patent leather shoes, Kevin a suit and tie. We are standing in the driveway or the backyard, depending on the angle of the sun. It is Easter, or a birthday, or First Communion or Confirmation, or Christmas—or, equally celebratory, a Quinlan aunt is visiting. If it's Easter, Maureen or I might be wearing "toppers," baggy short coats that popped up during springtime in the fifties along with the daffodils.

Maureen and Sharon on Easter, late 1940s

If it's winter, we're wearing "storm coats," tank-like belted garments with fake fur collars. My hair is curled—if I'm under twelve there would have been a night of painful sleeping on bobby pins, placed in crosses all over my head, if I'm thirteen I'll have the frizzy perm my mother insisted on to keep me away from long straight hair, the emerging sign of sexual freedom, the "beatnik" look for girls. My mother would have taken the pictures: even though she was baffled by cameras, she was a fierce recorder of our lives. At some point she would have said "everybody outside," and we would have gone out obediently and walked right into our line-up: the three kids, then just Maureen and me—"the girls"—then each one of us alone, or with the visiting aunt.

In the Elmira photos we're freer. Someone—definitely an aunt—is adept at taking action and impromptu shots, and there the three of us are in Grove Park clustered around the hanging bar, or Maureen slouching in a lawn chair with dark glasses, Kevin taking off on his bike, or me hanging from the bars at Grove Park, legs in motion, or triking down the driveway, or playing "Red Light/Green Light" with Kevin in the driveway—me walking toward the aunt-held camera, he pacing away toward Grove Street, both of us ready to stop on a dime when the aunt would say "Red Light" and judge who stopped the quickest. And then there's the one where I see myself before I became shy, sitting in a kid-sized striped folding chair, extending my arm magnanimously as if I were my grandfather reincarnated, about to introduce a vaudeville act.

When I'd visit my parents, by then in my thirties, I'd open the bottom drawer of the secretary and take out the boxes of old photographs. I used to gaze with longing at the Kodak stories of my Elmira childhood, me gazing adoringly at my big sister or lining up with my brother to ride on the carousel at Eldridge Park. I wanted to enter that black-and-white past, slipping into the photographs the way the children in *Mary Poppins* enter the chalk paintings. I wanted, I think, to rescue myself from the months and years of depression that lay ahead.

THOSE SUMMERS were also when my mother was her happiest—perhaps because when she returned to be daughter and sister in Elmira, doted

Maureen, Kevin, and Sharon
in Grove Park, 1948

Sharon in Grove Park, 1948

Kevin and Sharon playing, 1951   Sharon in Elmira backyard, 1949

on by her mother, bossed around by sisters who called her "Regina," welcomed by childhood chums who still called her "Quin," she could relax
her guard, giving her children the freedom to explore the world we were
never allowed in Belmont. Her sisters could take over; she could relax, returning to the landscape of her childhood. And as we explored the huge
brown house, filled with strange, familiar objects, or walked down Grove
Street to the penny candy store, we could feel daring and protected at the
same time.

In Belmont we could step awry and the floor would give way, dropping
us into the whirlpool of our mother's fears or, even worse, the pit of her cold
anger. But here the floor was solid, and we could climb higher and higher,
knowing that if we fell our aunts would be holding the net. Our mother was
surrounded by sisters who told her to let us stay out until dark, eat a second
popsicle, go to the movies with the neighborhood kid pack.

"Now Regina," Geraldine or Marion or Dorothy would say, "just sit back
and have another iced tea, Nell Hagerty is with them and she's almost
seventeen," and she'd say "Oh I suppose it's all right then," and we would
swoop off.

*O*NE COLD night that first February after my mother died I wrote in my journal:

> Something is waiting for me in Elmira. "You can't repeat the past," Nick says to Gatsby, and every time I teach the book I tell my students I agree with him. But now I find myself wanting to say with Gatsby "Of course you can." The past is waiting for me in Elmira, untarnished and whole.
>   I just have to find it.

I'VE DECIDED to go to Elmira. I haven't been there for thirty-five years. It isn't a hard trip to arrange. Elmira College sponsors a center for Mark Twain studies and allows scholars to stay at Quarry Farm, the house where Twain spent many summers. I'm accepted to stay there because Handsome Dan may have been part of Twain's world, and if I discover anything I'll write it up for the archive. My trip will take only four hours: I'll drive up the Susquehanna on Route 15, cutting over to Route 14 after Williamsport. The heroic journey of my childhood has been diminished: this should have been a sign, but I don't want to know that I'm placing too many expectations on this trip.

*C*OMING INTO ELMIRA, I get lost. I see a sign for Eldridge Park, now a "Carousel Exchange" for antique dealers, follow it, and find myself driving down streets I've never seen before, lined with boarded-up buildings, vacant lots, and small, shabby houses. Instead of the mom-and-pop spas where my brother, sister, and I bought red licorice and wooden yo-yos there are chain convenience stores offering lottery tickets, potato chips, and dollar Pepsis. The streets are bare and sun-baked—where are the high elm trees arching over the road, the basket-weave of sun and shade that is Elmira in the summer?

I stop at a Kwik-Way to ask directions. A man with "Jim" written in script and quotation marks over his right pocket begins to give me animated directions to Eldridge Park, realizes you can't get there from here, and winds down. "You're not from here," he says, more an observation than a question. I ask where I can get a map of Elmira and he gives me a complicated route to the downtown Kwik-Way. I pretend to listen.

Eldridge Park will have to wait. At least I have the directions to Quarry Farm the Mark Twain people have sent. As I cross the Chemung River into Elmira a glimmer of the past returns—the river is still here, and yes, here's

Water Street, right where it should be, next to the Chemung. On the way to Quarry Farm I drive through parts of Elmira I've never seen before, the industrial fringes. I pass farm equipment dealers, gear companies, quarries, bus manufacturers. Then I cross Route 17, ascend the hill on Water Cure Road, and find myself in another unknown Elmira world. Suddenly I'm in hill country—little roads lined with Queen Anne's lace and goldenrod, fields of timothy grass, farms and country houses. Did my mother ever come here, ever look down over the Chemung and wonder what lay beyond the horizon?

My room at Quarry Farm overlooks the Chemung Valley. I can see where the river should be but there's no sign of blue. We've had a rainy summer and the water is muddy, the river's course hard to discern. Momentarily the past opens up as I wander through Twain's house—its nineteenth-century character has been preserved, and it has the feel of my grandmother's house on Clinton Street. Rooms wander into rooms, crammed with the panoply of Victorian things, Oriental rugs in russets, browns, cobalt blues, dark oak and mahogany furniture, velvet curtains, books, writing desks, framed photographs and paintings, sideboards, lamps with satin shades, display cabinets for candlesticks, vases, and porcelain boxes. I lift the lids off the boxes but there's nothing inside, not a stray button or piece of forgotten jewelry, not even a scrap of paper.

My bedroom has a full-length, free-standing mirror resting on a dark oak base. I don't like glimpsing myself in its depths: when I'm in depression my face and body seem to belong to someone else, a vague, distracted woman who peers into the glass looking for the healthy self she's left behind her in the past.

I'M GOING to be seeing Kel. Her full name is Marian Kelly McCarthy, but she still goes by her childhood nickname. One of my mother's childhood friends—or "chums," as they called themselves—Kel lives across the street from the old house. Now she's eighty-three, as my mother would have been had she lived; Kel's memories stretch back for most of the century. Her voice was warm and welcoming on the phone. She remembers me as a skinny seven-year-old with bangs; I don't remember her at all.

I leave Quarry Farm at 5:00 so I can be sure to arrive at Kel's punctually at 5:30. We're going to catch the Early Bird special at a local Italian restaurant. I'm often late, partly because of the shyness I can cover but never fully dispel; I tend to put off greetings and hasten farewells. Thresholds are hard for me. But I try to be on time when I'm meeting people who are alone, particularly old women. Their anticipation of company is keen and I don't like to disappoint them by even a few minutes. And, like my mother, they imagine the world of highways, cars, and driving to be perilous: like the ancient mapmakers who filled unknown seas with monsters and whirlpools, housebound elderly women fear the hazards of the road will swallow up their wandering daughters. Even a few minutes' lateness opens up the abyss for them. My mother's terrors used to drive me crazy, but now that she's dead I'm much kinder to her aging compatriots.

As I drive past Grove Park on my way to Kel's, I see the old house for the first time. It seems smaller, diminished. It's painted blue, and the back porch has been blocked off, probably to fill the prosaic need for a laundry room. The back yard, where I'd stare for hours at the Japanese beetles making lacy holes in the grape leaves, has been reduced to a narrow strip of green to make way for a two-story garage, painted the same Colonial blue as the house. The windows are lighted and I see unfamiliar shadows behind the curtains. My grandparents are long dead, and I have no more aunts.

Later I will look up "Quinlan" in the Elmira phone book, just in case. Perhaps there was a sister I never knew about, one so abandoned by her family that she was never spoken of, and perhaps this lost aunt will still be here, ancient but ready to tell me the whole story. But the phone book answers only to reality, not to longing. *Of course there are no more Quinlans, Sharon, how odd of you to think of looking.*

Kel comes to the door and for a moment I am startled. She is my mother's age but she is not my mother. She is a stranger. Then I am past the threshold. We give each other a hug and she says "Well, well, you've made my day."

I am jarred by loss: this is my mother's phrase. Kel fusses over me. She has bought a bottle of wine for the occasion, and I open it for her. We toast my mother. "To Regina!" Kel says, clicking glasses. "My old chum!" "To Regina!" I echo. Kel and I sit in the living room and begin to get acquainted.

Kel wants to help me on my quest. "I wish I could remember more," she says several times during the evening, and those memories she does have she repeats three or four times, as if that way she is giving me more. "None of us will ever forget the day those Oriental rugs arrived, sent by your grandfather," she says. "All the neighbors came around to see them unloaded, and your grandmother had to give house tours for the next month. We'd never seen such splendor."

"Was my grandfather there?"

"Oh, no," she says, with a wave of her hand, adding, "your aunt Geraldine always said he wanted those rugs down before he came home. Kind of a royal arrival."

As Kel tells me about Elmira I find there are not as many people left to talk with as I had imagined. Every so often she mentions someone who would have had wonderful stories about my mother. "But of course she's dead," Kel adds, almost surprised, and then laughs apologetically, as if these numerous deaths were inconveniences Elmira had scattered in the path of my research.

"Almost everyone is dead," she says. But I'm momentarily bringing some of her friends and neighbors back to life, a stand-in for her old chum Regina. As the evening goes on her memories emerge naturally, through association. After dinner Kel lights a cigarette—"It's not going to kill me," she says— and tells me she and my mother would go downtown after school for a "coke and a smoke," and all of a sudden my mother is a teenager in the twenties, off with her chums to sit in drugstore booths, sip cokes through straws until only the ice was left to be chewed, crunched, and swallowed. Cigarette waving, smoke visible in the late afternoon sun, she reveled in the short hours of freedom in between school and home.

When Handsome Dan was in residence the afternoon coke and smoke must have been even giddier, the walk back to Clinton Street slower. "I was afraid of him," Kel confesses, and then, concerned she's offended me, "Of course he was very elegant and wonderful to look at, tall, a great dresser." Later she says simply "I loved your grandmother." My mother has told me the same tale of fear and love: doesn't the story have to be more complex than that?

"What was my grandmother like?"

"She was a wonderful woman," Kel says. "Everybody loved her."

I'm disappointed. I want details.

"Why did everybody love her?"

Kel looks surprised. "Well I don't know," she says. "You just did."

"Did she make you feel safe?"

Kel pauses and nods. "And she doted on your mother," she adds. "The baby of the family."

"Anything else about her?"

"She bought the first radio on the block, and was the first woman in Clinton Street to go to the cinema. Your grandmother told everyone they should go. She thought movies were wonderful."

"Anything else?" I'm glad my Dickinson colleagues who do oral history aren't here. I'm a terrible interviewer.

"Well . . . I remember that when your mother was born, your grandfather was traveling in Europe, one of his tours, and Mrs. Quinlan waited three days before sending him a telegram."

"Why?"

"Well," she hesitates, "your mother was the sixth daughter."

Of course. Handsome Dan had been wanting a son. Someone to carry on his name. My grandmother had waited before sending the disappointing news.

J DRIVE BACK to Quarry Farm down Clinton Street, past the old family house, past the smaller house where my cousins lived—Rosie and Saran and their mother, Rosemary, who boarded dogs and painted landscapes, and their great-aunt Aggie, who lived in a wheelchair because she'd had both her legs cut off by an Elmira streetcar.

I am still depressed and I'm getting afraid: how can depression have followed me to Elmira, my childhood refuge?

I don't want to be driving down Clinton Street in my paid-for Honda Accord. I want to be a small girl walking through a world filled with drama. I want to feel the excited terror I used to feel when we went to visit the Dohertys: Aggie had wooden legs beneath her skirt! Her crabbed fingers would grab me, she'd kiss me and she'd smell like old soap and boiled cabbage! Rosemary's dogs would yap and swirl around me, and I was afraid of their teeth! Rosemary looked like a lugubrious dog herself, a bulldog with heavy dewlap cheeks, and she'd be covered with dog hair and paint stains!

Now I drive past the Doherty house, scarcely glancing at it. Strangers are living there. What's the point of looking?

When I get back to Quarry Farm the phone rings. It's Kel. She wants to know that I've arrived safely. After I hang up the strange room is silent once again, even emptier than before. The phone will not ring again tonight. My sadness seems boundless. This trip is a disaster.

Now I realize I had expected to find more than my mother's spirit in Elmira. I had expected to find my mother.

I knew my mother was no longer at 25 Thayer Road, Belmont. I'd seen the undertakers, dressed in striped pants and gloves and morning coats, carry out her body. I followed them outside, I had to watch the hearse drive off, I had to record every vanishing. I'd helped my sister and brother clean out the apartment and went back my myself, wandering through the empty rooms, sitting on the floor, absorbing the vacancy into my body, taking photographs—black and white—so I could remember what the emptied space looked like.

I knew my mother wasn't at the Belmont Memorial Cemetery. I'd seen her body lowered into the grave. I'd seen the grass grow back over the mound. I'd seen the stonemason add her death date to the waiting hyphen.

I thought I had said good-bye and accepted her death, but now I wonder if my unconscious has been giving me an out. "She could be in Elmira," a voice may have whispered. "That's where you need to go. You will open a door, cross a threshold, and she will be there, holding out her arms to you."

But my mother is not behind the lighted windows on Clinton Street, and she did not raise her arms to greet me when Kel's door opened.

If she's not here there's nowhere else on earth to look for her.

The next morning I write in my journal: "I can't find my past."

Maybe I'm trying too hard to make the past come to life. All day, stubbornly, defiantly, it stays dead. All day I stand outside houses I have tracked down by consulting crumbling Elmira city directories, peering into windows, willing the ghosts to come alive. Nothing.

I stand outside the apartment on West Water Street where my father lived when he was working at the radio station and courting my mother. Did he and my mother walk down to the Chemung on hazy summer days, dreamy with love? The house is shabby, which does not surprise me; I have noticed that the only well-kept Victorian houses in Elmira are the funeral homes.

I stand outside the rooming house where my grandmother lived when she was a sales clerk: it's in a working-class section of town across the tracks from Clinton Street, once Irish, now African American and Hispanic. I know so little about my grandmother's past. I do know that when she was dying my mother paced the hospital corridors because she could not bear to stay in the room with her for too long. I know that she loved bridge and read Shakespeare in a ladies' reading group she organized herself. I know she made my mother feel safe.

I STAND OUTSIDE 531 West Clinton Street. It takes me half an hour to get up the courage to ring the doorbell. An elderly woman answers. "I used to spend summers here when I was a child," I say. "My mother grew up here. I was wondering if I might be able to look around?"

She stares at me, uncomprehending. "I've paid the water bill," she says finally and begins to shut the door.

"I'm not from the water company, I just used to live here and wondered if I could look at the house."

The door shuts.

I go to the Catholic cemetery, across the river in the working-class section of town, hoping for an epiphany, a ghost, a connection. I find a large gravestone with "QUINLAN" alone on the front. On the back are five names: Daniel, Margaret, and then the three daughters: Geraldine, Marion Larkin, Dorothy June.

Of course your mother isn't here, you knew that, didn't you.

*O*N THE way back to Quarry Farm I stop by Eldridge Park. The Ferris wheel and roller coaster have vanished, the filigreed buildings and turrets— vaguely Moroccan, suggesting exoticism and license to law-abiding Elmirans—are boarded up, the paint cracking. The remaining signs ("Funnel Cakes—$1.25") announce false promises, the arrows ("To the Tea Pavilion") point toward nothing. It's raining, and a man in weatherproof yellow sweats is jogging around the lake where there used to be piers, canoes, paddle boats, and ducks. The railroad tracks that once brought amusement seekers here from all over the Chemung Valley are overgrown with scraggly weeds and scrawny wildflowers, and the waiting room is covered with graffiti. The only freshly painted structure is a leftover portable latrine, courtesy of "Ed's Heads," doubtless left by the crew that took down the roller coaster.

I HEAD BACK to Carlisle, driving through a string of small towns in upstate New York and northern Pennsylvania, trying to delay my return. I pass through a town that's having an 1890s festival. There's a light drizzle and the crowd is sparse. A man and a woman in Victorian dress are sitting under a tent, talking to a man in overalls wearing a tractor cap. Someone is trying to organize a taffy pull. Later there will be a parade. I want to stop, I don't want to stop. I'm caught in my depression's paralysis of the will. I keep going because I can't decide.

As soon as I open my door, the empty house washes around me and I know I'm in trouble, on the familiar downward slide into deeper depression. I go upstairs, get into bed, and wait for sleep, wait for the winter to end.

Quinlan family in 1914 (*left to right:* Daniel, Marion,
Dorothy, Geraldine, Ruth, Regina, Margaret, Margaret)

*I*N MARCH, that scummy cold month of beginnings and endings, the ice over my soul begins to crack. I have stopped trying to force life into the past, and so the ghosts can visit, flit by in dreams.

> *I am living in a huge cavern in the ground, not dark but filled with light—not light from a single source, but light that seems to emanate from the walls. I look upward toward the sky. Drifting down are my mother's little notebooks, filled with her lists and jottings. I stretch out my arms to receive them. "This is your inheritance," a dream voice tells me, "this is your mother's writing. It's meant for you. It's a place to start."*

I wake up with that sense you have rarely, that a dream of tremendous portent has been sent to you. I switch on the light and gather up my mother's memo books. I see only a jumble of lists. What does it matter, now, what videos she wanted to see, what Christmas presents she planned to buy, what groceries she needed at the A&P?

I know these little books are precious but I have no idea what they mean.

I put them on the night table and go back to sleep. I feel comforted, as if my mother is saying, yes, you're in the right place, yes, it's all right to look back at the past. It's all right to try to understand where you came from.

Shipwreck

The air was still and cold like the air in a refrigerating room. . . . When kindness has left people, even for a few moments, we become afraid of them, as if their reason had left them . . . it is like shipwreck; we drop from security into something malevolent and bottomless.

—WILLA CATHER, *My Mortal Enemy*

"FEAR IS THE SOURCE OF YOUR DEPRESSION," the psychic said, turning over another Tarot card.

My sister and I were in the Tremont Tea Room in downtown Boston, a place where you can drink tea and get Tarot readings. Maureen wanted to get a reading from Alex, whom she'd consulted before. I tagged along, thinking it must be narcissistically satisfying to have someone devote their full energy, for forty-five minutes, to talking about *you.*

By then I was stuck in the early stages of chronic depression. It was a few months after my mother had died. I'd been in therapy for three years and trying various combinations of medication for two, but this recalcitrant illness kept turning its back on the American recovery story, the "once I was sick but now I am well" narrative that takes the place of Horatio Alger's upward mobility for the ill and suffering. None of the health professionals who'd been keeping me afloat were able to answer the one question I cared about. *When's it going to leave?* I was ready for a psychic to tell me when I would feel better.

I also wanted a good report card. Hadn't I been doing what my therapeutic generation, true to the spirit of capitalism, called "emotional work?" I deserved a pat on the back for going to therapy and reading dozens of self-help books featuring optimistic, reproachful titles (*You Can Heal Your Life! Depressed No More!)* and photographs of smiling, smug authors on the colorful jackets—red and yellow, like fast-food logos.

"That's unusual," Alex said, turning over two more cards. "These are the signs of the parents, but they almost never show up when someone's parents are dead." He frowned, and I waited for the interpretation. Perhaps I was my parents' spiritual inheritor?

"Unless they're controlling you from the grave," he added, turning over some more cards while I tried to look like someone who'd separated from her parents a long time ago.

"Interesting," he said, tapping his finger on a grimy Tarot card showing a woman in a tower, looking out a barred window at a blue-green ocean. Way off in the distance you could see a little sailing ship, but the woman wasn't looking in that direction. She was just gazing at an empty sea. "So, in childhood, who was your jailer?"

I knew only three possible answers: my mother, my father, or my parents. *He's the psychic, let him figure it out.* I shrugged. "I don't know," I said, thinking that I really did not like this man. The rest of the reading picked up a little when Alex got to the more positive stuff, telling me that I was creative and should "write from the heart," because that was how I'd connect to other people's lives, although right then my depression was pretty bad, and I was finding it hard to make out grocery lists and pay bills, let alone write from anything as wizened and despairing as my heart.

"You can't repair forty years of dysfunction in a few months," Alex said encouragingly, briskly dismissing what I had formerly known as my life. "Trust the process," he added, and I went back to my sister's house with my barely passing emotional grade.

ALEX WAS RIGHT about one thing. Fear is often a major source of depression, particularly in women—fear of speaking up, fear of expressing the self fully, fear of not being . . . well, *nice*. And then, fear of what you fear will follow speaking your mind, or not measuring up to what other people expect—abandonment, the ghost that had haunted me and my family for a long time.

When my mother was twelve, her father banished her sister for getting married. My mother told me this story in bits and pieces over the years—she clearly found it painful to talk about—and I've woven together this narrative from the fragments.

In 1916 my aunt Margaret, the second oldest daughter, had just graduated from Elmira College with a major in biology. Without telling her parents, she applied to Johns Hopkins medical school, and when she was accepted, she announced that she would be going, a daring move from a young woman at that time.

My grandfather dismissed Margaret with the famous words, passed down to me by my cousin Bob, "No daughter of mine will go seeking after indecent knowledge." When I first heard these words I suspected that my grandfather's indecent knowledge was sexuality. The body.

The interior of the body was an unmapped territory then, its geography as remote and improbable as the valleys on the other side of the moon. Another Victorian woman traveler might have wanted to go to Madagascar, or Patagonia; did my aunt Margaret want to travel, with her scalpel, into the body?

Dan Quinlan—despite, or maybe because of, his bohemian actor's life—was Victorian to the core when he was at home. Women were supposed to serve men at the dinner table, not cut up their naked bodies in the dissecting lab, and the only knives they should touch were safely part of the family silver. Handsome Dan was the traveler in the family, keeping his two worlds apart: there was his respectable family life in Elmira, and his free, probably sexually free, performing life on the road. Who knew what carefully separated worlds might be shattered if his daughter should enter a secret world and return with knowledge? Margaret had to be stopped, and the power of abandonment was the strongest weapon in the Irish Catholic family's emotional arsenal.

"You have to choose, Margaret," he said. "You can go to medical school, but then you are no longer my daughter."

Margaret went off to medical school, seeking her indecent knowledge. And then, gradually, Dan relented. He even became proud of her. Like many children of immigrants, he valued higher education; unusually, for his day, he wanted it for his six daughters, and supported their attending Elmira College, from which all would graduate in the teens and twenties. Margaret was taking his own child-of-immigrant success story to another level, flying higher. His daughter was going to be a doctor.

One day a telegram arrived at 531 West Clinton Street. Margaret was dropping out of medical school. She had fallen in love with a fellow student—a Protestant—married him, and was having a baby. Handsome Dan banished her again: this time she had sinned against upward mobility, and against his pride.

"It was awful," my mother told me. "My father was raging around the

24

house, saying she was no longer welcome in Elmira, my mother was weeping in the bedroom. I was terrified."

"When did you see Margaret again?"

"Not for years," she said. "Not until she came back to Elmira with her children, and then he acted like nothing had happened."

"So why didn't your mother do anything?"

"There was nothing she could do," my mother said. "Everyone was afraid of him, except maybe for Geraldine. You just walked around the house on tiptoes when he was home." She shook her head.

"What a terrible thing," I said, "abandoning a daughter for getting married." This was as close as I could get to mentioning what my parents had done to Maureen.

"Oh, it is, it is," she said, her thoughts firmly in the past, never recognizing that she had done the same thing herself.

*B*EFORE I CAME to realize how culture and history had shaped my family, and understand the genetic and biochemical sources of depression, I found the psychological and emotional story of depression's origins the most compelling. In my twenties and early thirties—long before Prozac hit the market—I'd trace my depression directly to my mother's doorstep and tell my friends and therapist my own abandonment story, which became my depression's origin myth. "I was twelve," I would begin, "when my mother threw my sister out of the family for getting married."

It was 1958, the era when daughters were supposed to aspire only to be wives and mothers. Postwar America was rebuilding and celebrating the nuclear family, placing women back in the kitchen, the bedroom, and the nursery. Daughters who went to college were supposed to graduate with "MRS." degrees and start their own families. (The pill was a decade away.)

This was not the story in my family. All the children—Maureen and I as well as my brother—were supposed to excel academically, then professionally. Maureen and I both knew that. Marriage? Children? Perhaps some day, but only after we'd gone to graduate school (college would not be enough) and secured prestigious, well-paid jobs. I was slated for medical school because I excelled in science. Kevin would go to law school, and because Maureen liked psychology my parents were promoting business school for her.

"I had as much interest in business school," Maureen would say later, "as in jumping off a roof. At Tufts I joined a sorority, I went to parties, I had dates. After leaving the mausoleum I only wanted to have fun. When I came home with B's at the end of freshmen year—which thrilled me—Dad and Mom scheduled a conference with the academic dean. Why wasn't I getting A's? I couldn't tell them it was because I was fitting studying in around dates and parties."

My sister was living at home and commuting to Tufts, often staying over with a sorority sister—at least that's what she told my parents. She was twenty, I was twelve. I worshipped her. She was glamorous: she wore cashmere sweaters and pearls, long billowy cotton skirts with starchy petticoats underneath, and stockings and red flats. Her books were covered with shiny book covers that said "Tufts University," not "Belmont Junior High School," and inside were complicated subjects like economics and psychology. She had dates and went to dances. Once she was picked up at our house by a blond young man wearing a tuxedo. I was awed.

I learned, through the air, that this young man wasn't suitable—he was Jewish—and then, through the air, that Maureen had dated another unsuitable person, a young man in his mid-twenties (he'd been in Korea) who was starting medical school at Tufts. I wasn't sure why he was unacceptable; later, when I knew the phrase "working-class background," I would understand why the son of French-Canadian factory workers would not have been given parental approval.

*O*NE SATURDAY in January I was in my bedroom, reading, when I heard my mother speak the ominous words, "Sharon and Kevin, come into the living room, your father and I want to talk with you." The living room was the setting for all terrifying pronouncements, punishments, and parental investigations of sin.

I was confused because both of us had been summoned. Kevin and I never collaborated in crime; and besides, only one child could sit in the defendant's chair, the armchair near the bookcase, across the room from the sofa where my parents always sat. Our places were as formally assigned as in a courtroom.

When I got to the living room Kevin had already taken the defendant's chair, assuming, like me, that he must be the guilty one. I sat in the other corner, in the frayed armchair by the fire, the one the cat used as her scratching post.

I looked across the room at my parents, across miles of mustardy carpet, across the coffee table my aunt Marion had sent them when she bought a new one. She'd sent them the sofa, too, when she redecorated; it was pale-green brocade with slippery fabric that felt odd and slinky if your legs were bare. My mother was sitting on the left of the sofa, as she always did, by the light. My father was way over on the right, miles of space in between him and my mother, his face shaded in darkness. My mother's hair was awry, all wispy and out of place, and she kept touching it ineffectually, as if she wanted to run her hand through it but couldn't complete the gesture. My father sat perfectly still, his face expressionless. My parents stayed silent, which was unusual. Usually my mother began the inquisition right away, as soon as you sat down.

Something was terribly, terribly wrong. Perhaps I had committed some crime of which I was unaware, something so monstrous that Kevin had been called in as a witness to my degradation.

My mother cleared her throat and I could see her eyes were shiny. "We have received a letter from your sister. You need to know," she said in a tight, clipped voice, "both of you need to know your sister Maureen has gotten married." My heart beat faster with fear.

Why was I afraid? I was guilty of nothing, and Maureen wasn't either. Getting married wasn't bad, was it? Something momentous had happened, I knew that, something unplanned, because Maureen was supposed to be in college. But not something really *bad*. So why did my mother look so angry and cold, tightening her lips the way she did, and why was my father fading further and further into the darkness so I could hardly see his face? I wanted to walk over and ask him what was wrong, but I never walked over to my parents during a living-room investigation. It would have been like crossing the altar rail at Mass and walking up to the priest. Unthinkable.

"Oh," I said, knowing marriages were supposed to be happy things, "that's great. . . ." My voice trailed off. My mother's face was not mirroring me back; it was closed and pinched and her arms were now folded across her chest. I needed more clues about how to feel and what to say. I had gotten it all wrong.

"What she did, what she did," my mother said, pausing as if there were no words to describe what Maureen had done. "Dropping out of school . . . a mind like hers, a future . . . to get *married*," as if getting married were the worst thing you could possibly do.

"Oh," I said. So night was day, black was white. I'd gotten it all wrong, all the codes had to be switched. Marriage was not a good thing, it was a bad thing. A new brother-in-law was not a person to be welcomed into the family, he was someone who could not even be mentioned by name. "That's awful," I said, now ready to desert my sister to side with my mother.

"Can we go now?" my brother asked.

My mother shrugged. Then my father nodded. Kevin and I went off to our separate rooms and shut our doors. We did not talk about the incident, which affected both our lives, for forty years.

*T*HROUGHOUT THAT whole long winter it seemed that Maureen had indeed dropped off the face of the earth. My parents did not speak of her and I was too afraid to ask where she was. I learned, through osmosis, that she was pregnant, and then that she had had a baby, a little girl she named Maureen.

Kevin later told me that he remembered the arrival of the letter, a thick, crumpled collection of handwritten sheets that my mother would place on top of the high dresser in our parents' bedroom, "the antipodes of Lewis Road," he said. Finally she would throw it out, but my sister remembers some of its contents. "They expected me to pay for some of Kevin's education, and I felt so guilty that I wouldn't be, I included a hundred dollars in the envelope they'd given me for books."

"They didn't keep it, did they?"

"Yes, they did."

I used to think that was demonically selfish, but now I think my parents' keeping the hundred dollars was just sad.

They must have felt like the abandoned ones. We were supposed to be the parents, and one of us had let them down.

*T*HAT DAY in the living room changed my life. It's not just that I would lose my sister for several years, the sister who had mothered me when I was small, taken me to the park, taught me the alphabet, picked me up from my crib in the morning and made me breakfast, during all those times when my father was depressed and my mother couldn't cope. And it's not just that I would fear that the same abandonment lay in store for me if I wanted to have children or get married instead of going to college and graduate school *first*, the way my mother wanted it to be done.

I lost my own inner compass, my understanding of how the world made sense. My mother's icy anger and my father's silent acquiescence—he never interfered in family matters, which he termed "your mother's department"— told me I was wrong to be excited about my sister's marriage. My only choice

Maureen holding Sharon, 1948

was to develop ever more delicate emotional radar to pick up my mother's feelings and desires, which would, for a time, replace my own.

I had to learn new rules. I had to learn what behaviors would be so terrible that some day my mother would be announcing my banishment to my brother, and I would be wandering in the darkness somewhere outside the lighted circle of my family, pressing my nose against the cold glass, seeing them reading by the fire or decorating the Christmas tree, unable to make a sound or raise my hand to knock on the window.

*Y*EARS LATER, when I spoke with my sister about this dark time, I found out that her disowning had not been as total as I had thought, that my parents had been more humane. She had gone to live with Warren's parents in Norwalk, Connecticut, and they had been welcoming; she had spoken with my parents on the phone, and they had visited her in the hospital when the baby was born. But they did not tell Kevin and me about these softenings and reconnections, and I assumed the disowning was complete.

One night, about six months after her daughter was born, my sister showed up at our house with her baby. My father had been the go-between, arranging this reconciling meeting. My mother laughed and cooed at the baby, and she and my sister talked about diapers and rashes and feeding schedules, both agreeing that the little raspberry birthmark on my niece's forehead would go away in time.

That was the most amazing thing—my mother acted like nothing had happened. "They're always so cute at six months," she said as we all gazed at little Maureen, gurgling and kicking her bootied feet on my sister's old bed.

"Aren't they?" my sister said. "Sometimes I just look at her for hours," and my mother nodded.

I hovered in the background, awkward and quiet. I felt shy in the presence of this new sister, who seemed not to notice me and was forming a confusing new alliance with my mother. No one mentioned that my mother had missed the first months of her granddaughter's life, that she had missed my sister's pregnancy, missed being a mother to her twenty-year-old daughter when she needed her.

Neither of my parents ever mentioned what had happened. It was as if Maureen's defiance and their retaliation had disappeared from official family history.

THIS WAS the beginning of seeming normalcy. Maureen lived in a housing project in Belmont. Warren was doing his surgical residency at Boston City Hospital, and they needed to save money. She would visit occasionally, bringing one, then two, then three blond-haired children along, as David and Beth arrived one and three years after Maureen. My parents became doting grandparents, taking the little ones on vacation to New Hampshire, pitching in when Maureen needed a rest. After eight years passed and my nephew Ted was born, my brother-in-law Warren, by then an orthopedic surgeon, was finally allowed in the house: until then, none of us had met him.

When we shared our first Thanksgiving together at 28 Lewis Road, and I was introduced to the father of my nieces and nephews, once again everyone acted as if nothing had happened. No one spoke of the past or mentioned how odd it was to be saying "Nice to meet you" to Warren, who'd been living a mile away from us in Belmont for the last eight years and was the father of my sister's four children, who ranged in age from seven to one.

I *felt* it was odd, but then all the real grownups were laughing and talking and my mother was saying well now she could see where the children got their blonde hair and my father was asking Warren about his residency program, quiet and calm and respectful as he always was, and Warren—who had handled both his exile and his command performance with grace—was calling my mother "Regina," and complimenting her on how young she looked, so I guessed maybe I was wrong. This wasn't odd, this was normal. It must be normal to feel that there was a dark and scary *thing* under the surface and if you just kept talking fast enough and laughing and joking enough, either the thing would go away or you wouldn't notice it anymore.

*W*HEN I WAS in college, I'd entertain my friends with scary mother stories. The most dramatic was the marijuana story, and after I told it they'd say "Sharon, your mother is truly *bizarre*."

I was in high school, and came home one day to find my mother sitting in the sun room, just a few feet away from the front door. This was a bad sign. It meant she had discovered some incriminating piece of evidence while I was at school, gathered on one of her forays into my bedroom, where she'd have checked the closets, the drawers, in between the mattress and the box spring.

"I suppose you know what this is about," she said.

"No," I said, already feeling guilty.

She held out her hand, revealing a brownish, crumbly substance.

I had no idea what she was showing me.

"I found this in your dresser! It's that marijuana, isn't it, you're taking marijuana!"

Later I would, in fact, "take" marijuana. But at that moment I had never seen it: kids at Belmont High School in the early sixties thought it was exciting to drink beer, steal traffic signs, and drape trees with toilet paper on Halloween.

My denials weren't effective until I realized what the substance was: I'd left some orange peel in one of my drawers a few weeks before, hoping it would impart a nice scent, and it had grown dark and crumbly.

When I told my friends this story, it hadn't actually struck me as strange that my mother would search my room while I was out, ostensibly cleaning, but really looking for clues to my secret adolescent life, or that she'd inspect my mail and sometimes open it (that's how she discovered that I'd bought a motorcycle in college, opening an envelope from the Cambridge Police Department containing a summons for an unpaid ticket). That's just how mothers were.

"I wanted to kill your mother," a Radcliffe friend told me a couple of years ago. "She made me so angry." I was shocked and delighted: how liberating, to actually get angry at a mother! You mean you could do this and survive? Once, in therapy, I proudly told my shrink, "I got angry at my mother once."

"How old were you?" she asked, glad to find signs of early rebellion.

"Thirty-four."

A FEW YEARS AGO my brother told me what he remembered about the living-room drama.

"Sharon, I'll never forget what Mom said. Her words are scorched on my memory. *We are now a four-member family.*"

I had forgotten those terrible words.

"And Daddy didn't contradict her?" I asked.

"No," Kevin said. "Dad didn't say anything. I don't remember him contradicting her often. Maybe he was being diplomatic, maybe he was afraid of her, too." He paused. "After that, things weren't the same," he said. "I mean, they got worse."

"Did you worry about us becoming a three-member family? A two-member?"

"Are you kidding? It was like your life hung by a thread. I was so afraid of what would happen if I brought home a bad report card, which to them was anything with more B's than A's. It was as if Mom and Dad might take you to the edge of the world and just drop you off into space."

I looked at my solid, responsible, irreproachable older brother. I couldn't believe what I was hearing. Kevin had always been the good, obedient son, the one who cleaned his room and worked caddy camp in the summers and saved money and went to a good college and never talked back to my parents. He'd never gotten into bad trouble with them, not as far as I knew. He'd never had to explain that an orange peel was not marijuana. He'd gone to law school right after college, he'd done everything right.

"So why was she so scary?"

"It was her voice. You felt like it could bore right through you."

WHEN I WAS trying to understand how abandonment and depression get passed on in families, I came across a book that brought me up short: Alice Miller's *The Drama of the Gifted Child*. When I read that book, like other middle-class, over-achieving readers I've talked to since, I felt that Miller was writing about me.

It's when parents project their "unmet needs and expectations" onto their

32

children and then make their love seem conditional upon performance that the seeds for depression are sown, Miller says. Such children do not seek to find, create, or express their "true selves"—such a venture is far too risky. Rather, they develop "false selves" to gain parental approval. These false selves are not secure, based as they are in the belief that love is a reward for the achievements the parents desire. Miller found that among her depressed adult patients, many had mothers who themselves suffered from depression and who needed to use their children "as an echo, who can be controlled, is completely centered on them, will never desert them."

When Alice Miller describes how the child hides the true self and develops the false self in order to please demanding parents, she reminds us that there is no "fully developed true self hidden behind the false self." What is hidden is the soul material from which the child, one day, might fashion a fuller self. What is hidden are wisps and shadows of authenticity that she may glimpse at times of crisis—or depression—but that are not available to her on a daily basis. "The important point," Miller writes, "is that the child does not know what he is hiding." What she calls the "true self" still exists, she believes, "in a state of noncommunication" because it needs to be protected. Depression accompanies this loss until the child—often the adult child—lets go of the need for her parents' approval and finds needed affirmation in herself.

> Where there had only been fearful emptiness . . . there now is unfolding an unexpected wealth of vitality. This is not a homecoming, since this home has never before existed. It is the discovery of home.

Alice Miller's insights into the connections among parental need, social approval, and adult depression have particular resonance for Americans aspiring to move up in social class, or to maintain middle-class status. My parents wanted only the best for us—the best defined in terms of education and career, and, because of my sister's dismissal, linked with maintaining their approval and love.

In these postmodern times many people question the notion of the "true self," which may seem simplistic or anachronistic; we prefer the notion of shifting, multiple identities. And yet I think there's something to it, provided we think of the "true self" not as a stable, unvarying *thing*, but as a process of growth and expression. Those American parents who assume such growth must be connected to economic success and professional status—an assumption difficult to avoid in our culture—may be, as my parents were, all unknowingly passing on sources of later depression.

LTHOUGH MY family story of abandonment and depression links to larger patterns in American culture, it also has a peculiarly Irish flavor to it. I come from a people for whom abrupt and often unexplained severings of contact were the way to deal with conflict, hurt, loss, and separation. The Irish are great talkers and storytellers, but they prefer silence to speech when it comes to the realm of the emotions. Simply cutting off a family member by not speaking or writing is a common pattern in Irish and Irish American families. Sometimes the black sheep may live only a few blocks away, and yet the silence may endure not just for weeks, but for months or years or decades.

The Irish-born writer Frank McCourt attributes this form of punishment to the importance talk and conversation hold in Irish society. To shun someone, placing her in a circle of silence, is to cut her off from the family's and the culture's lifeblood. It's the cruelest thing you can do. My Jewish and Italian friends don't understand this form of family warfare: "My parents would never cut me off," my friend Andrea says. "I need to be there so we can have something to fight about." And there's the difference: Irish families don't fight openly—there's no shrieking and screaming, no slammed doors, no *noise*. It's all done very quietly—no messy stabbing, just a razor drawn delicately across your skin.

When the six Quinlan sisters were aggrieved they simply ceased speaking to each other, forming shifting alliances with other sisters, to whom they complained about the rest. Over the decades one or two sisters were always on the outs with one or two others; it was hard to keep track. Sometimes sisters went thirty years without speaking, and often the precipitating causes were bizarrely trivial; whatever the spark was, it must have tripped off some frozen, hidden childhood rage or deprivation.

My aunt Ruth boycotted Margaret for two decades because, way back in 1948, Margaret had promised to give her some money to help with dental expenses, and then reneged. Ruth didn't patch things up until the early 1970s, and that was only because she was then shunning Marion and needed an ally. When Marion was dying of breast cancer, Ruth came to the hospital after ten years of silence. She stood in the doorway, gazing at her sister draped with IVs, gasping for breath in the hospital bed. "Ruth must have stood there for two or three minutes," my sister Maureen remembers, "just looking, and then she walked away, without ever speaking. I don't think Marion ever knew she was there." Sixty years of sisterhood drew Ruth to that hospital, and ten years of silence kept her at the doorway. Ultimately she kept faith with the silence, unable to cross the threshold into forgiveness.

WHEN I think of the Quinlans, I wonder if there's some kind of ancient abandonment in my blood and bones, some archetypal form of Irish loss and deprivation behind the vengeful use of silence McCourt mentions.

"Eviction is in the racial memory of the Irish," an Irish friend once told me. "In every family there's a forgotten image of furniture and belongings in the street, right outside the house they couldn't enter anymore." Even safe in America, far away from the British landlords who evicted starving tenants in the nineteenth century, my family has passed along homelessness and abandonment as part of its legacy. All my ancestors came over during the famine years, the late 1840s and 1850s, the time when families would have what they called an "American wake" before someone left, that sure they'd never see the son or daughter again.

Given that my Irish ancestors lost their homes because of poverty and starvation and oppression, not individual choice, I find it absurdly sad that my mother and her family could choose to abandon any of their kin. I've always remembered the line from "The Death of the Hired Man," "Home is the place where, when you have to go there, / They have to take you in," and I've wanted to say back to Robert Frost, *haven't you known any Irish?* The definition of home handed down by the Quinlans, the definition flowing down to other Irish American famine descendants through cultural memory, was: "Home is something that can be taken away from you at any moment."

THE SPRING after my sister left home, I turned twelve. My mother had my picture taken by a professional photographer. He came to the house with his bulky cameras and his tripods and his lights and a folding table for me to sit on. My mother had bought me a new red dress with a white collar, and she'd set my hair on rollers the night before, so my scalp still stung a little from their bristles. "We have to get your hair away from your face," she said, digging a barrette into my head the way mothers do when they want you to look especially tidy. The photographer put a little footrest below the table and escorted me up there and turned my head this way and that while I blinked in the glare of the lights and felt my unfamiliar curls swirl around my face. The photographer took lots of pictures, adjusting my head each time, and then he said "let's try a profile."

I turned my head obediently. "That's it," he said, "hold it," and then I heard the shutter click and then he turned off the lights and I got down from the table and he told me I'd been very good at holding a pose.

I'd forgotten all about those photographs until a few years ago. After my mother died, I was looking through boxes of family memorabilia and saw lots of photographs of myself as a little girl, three or four or five, looking scrappy and elfish and sure of herself, a kid who'd look you straight in the eye and tell you exactly what she would and wouldn't put up with, like the picture of me in a sundress, carrying a baseball mitt.

I kept flipping through them until I saw the photographs from that long-ago session. They're stagy and formal, and the girl is dressed up, every hair in place. The scrappy kid is now the good daughter, headed straight into niceness. I tossed the pictures aside—too inauthentic—and then I saw the profile, the girl looking away from me. I suddenly felt I was getting acquainted with a part of myself, finding a lost sister, someone who could tell me something about where depression comes from.

Sharon with baseball mitt, 1950

Sharon, 1957

Her dress is perfect, her hair is perfect, and yet she is pensive. I want her to turn toward me and speak, but she looks away. As long as she gazes silently into the distance, into the darkness, away from you, she's being honest. She stays in profile because if she turns toward you she won't tell the truth—she'll tell you what you want to hear.

She's the good girl, the one who follows the family plan, the one who assumes the pose. She's getting rewarded for it, and yet she looks inexpressibly sad.

Friends

A Girl Scout is a friend to all and a sister to all other Girl Scouts.

A Girl Scout obeys orders.

—*The Girl Scout Handbook*

I MET ANGIE AT GIRL SCOUT CAMP the summer I was eight. She was a harum-scarum kid from Watertown, the tougher, more working-class town next to Belmont, an ethnic mix of Italians and Armenians that contrasted with Belmont's middle- and upper-class mix of WASPs, Jews, and Irish. Belmont did have a scattering of working-class housing—triple-deckers in Waverley Square and on the North Cambridge line—but most people lived in single-family homes with sculpted lawns and basketball hoops on two-car garages. Watertown was known for its ethnic restaurants, grocery stores where you could buy good cheeses, and a few liquor stores and bars. Belmont prided itself on being a dry town—a sign of respectability and virtue. Belmontians could buy their gin, whiskey, and vermouth for cocktail hour in Watertown and then drive safely back to their quiet, tree-lined streets, with no worries about noisy bars or drunken youths roaming through Belmont Center. Watertown always played Belmont in the Thanksgiving Day football game. The day before the game the *Belmont Herald* would run pictures of the two teams: Watertown players in black shirts bearing names like Antonelli, Ugoletto, and Kazanjian; Belmont players in white shirts with names like Crowley, Reynolds, and Emerson.

Angie was Italian and wore a cross around her neck, which she said gave her great powers to put curses on kids she didn't like. I was relieved that she was at least Catholic, because I wanted to stay friends with her after camp and that would be a persuasive point in her favor. She was a skinny little kid with lots of unruly red hair and sneakers with holes along the side that her mother had mended with tape. I could tell she was poor because she only had one pair of Girl Scout shorts, green with a white stripe down the side,

FRIENDS

which she had to keep washing. And she never got care packages of cookies and brownies from her mother.

Angie used dirty words, even though the Girl Scout creed said we were supposed to be pure in thought, word, and deed.

"I don't give a *turd* for the Girl Scout creed," she said. "The Girl Scout creed stinks," and I would look at her awestruck. I didn't think you could get any more daring than this, but then she said that she didn't give a turd about merit badges, either, and that really floored me, because I was a merit badge over-achiever. I had already earned eight merit badges back in Belmont, and this summer I wanted to add five more of the nature and sport badges that you couldn't get during the year—I was going for the tree badge, the flower badge, the canoe badge, the swimming badge, and the camping badge. The front of my green Girl Scout sash was almost covered in badges, and I wanted to start working on the back.

"You're not working on any merit badges?" It was like someone saying they didn't want to get A's in school.

"Naah, I want to have *fun*," Angie said, rolling her eyes dangerously. "You wanna have fun this summer?"

"Yeah," I said dubiously.

"Let's sneak out after lights out tonight and go shine our flashlights down the john," she suggested, and I said yes because that sounded like a great idea, and then I knew I'd won her friendship for real when I said we should have code names and leave each other messages under a rock. Angie took the name "Red" and I was "Brownie," and each day when we had a plan going we'd leave each other dozens of messages. We were caught a couple of times after lights out, but we just used our cover story, that we had to go to the john, and got off with warnings from the counselors that cemented our friendship even more. "You two always seem to be up to something," they'd say, and I'd thrill to the words "you two," it was so great to have a buddy.

Our greatest coup was the discovery of Waving Rock. We found a large boulder on the edge of Lake Winnepesaukee where you could see the passenger steamer *Mt. Washington* go by every day at 4:00. A birch tree leaned over the rock, and you could push the tree up and down so the whole tree and all its leaves were waving at the boat and the passengers would all wave back. This was *our* rock, we found it, so when the other kids wanted to wave to the *Mt. Washington* too, we charged them ten cents a wave. The counselors found out—someone squealed—and this time "you two" were really in trouble, grounded for two campfires, missing the ghost stories and s'mores, and forbidden to go back to our rock, which the rest of the kids appropriated.

But even our unjust punishment had its appeal. I might have been in Camp Monotomy's equivalent of jail—staying in the counselors' tent with Angie and a counselor during the campfire—but I felt free and dangerous. I was Brownie, and I had a friend. We swore eternal friendship, mixing our spit because blood seemed too scary. "Brownie and Red, forever and ever," we pledged.

"It's so cool you live in Watertown," I said on Leaving Day, when we were sitting on our camp trunks in the field, waiting for our parents to come get us. "We live right near the Watertown line. You can come over and play."

"You can come over and play too," Red said. "We have a tree in my back-yard you can climb, and I have lots of dolls I don't use anymore that we can bury."

"I'll make up a prayer for the burial service," I offered.

"Great. See you back home."

"See you back home."

As soon as I got in the car I was telling my parents about Angie. "I love this camp. I met this really cool girl, and she lives close to us, and we want to play after school."

"Really?" my mother asked. "What's her name?"

"Angie."

"Angie what?"

"Angie De Cicco."

"Oh," my mother said. "Italian. What does her father do?"

Angie didn't have a father, so I had to tell my mother that, and that her mother worked during the days as a cleaning lady at Sancta Maria hospital.

"Where does she live?"

"Watertown."

"Where in Watertown?"

There was a "good" section in Watertown, defined as single-family homes, right near the Belmont line, but Angie lived near the Dairy Queen, which wasn't known as a "good" section—filled with triple-deckers and apartments over dry cleaners and Armenian bakeries.

"I don't know," I lied, trying to conceal Angie's place on my mother's social-class geographical survey map.

"Well. I don't think you'll be seeing very much of this Angie."

And that was it. She didn't say "I forbid you to see Angie," but the disapproving finality in her tone scared me. Somehow, it all seemed fated; I think I'd known all along that Angie and I wouldn't be friends back in the real world.

A few days later Angie called and I said I was busy. She said how about next week and I said I was busy then too, and her voice got small and hurt and when she said good-bye I knew she'd never call me back. After I hung up the phone I told my mother that Angie had called and I wasn't going to see her, and she said that well, it was up to me.

After that I felt slimy and mean and sad. I had betrayed the best friend I'd ever had, and I wasn't sure why, or for what.

LATER, WHEN I was in high school, if I happened to mention I'd seen one of the girls my mother considered "cheap" she'd roll her eyes and look exasperated. Like Mary Lou Gallagher, who chewed gum, wore mascara, and took Business English. Mary Lou was on the vocational track, so she hung out in the basement of the high school with the guys who wore black leather jackets and took shop. She was rumored to have gone all the way with one or two of them, and occasionally the boys in the college track would hoot "Mary Lo-oo-oo" after her when she sashayed through the corridors in her shiny red skirt and spike heels.

Mary Lou had been my friend for a few weeks in fourth grade. I was nine, and this was the spring after I'd abandoned Angie. I was having another try at friendship with a free spirit.

I liked playing with her, liked entering a shabby, messy house filled with exotic cooking smells, lots of little kids, and a distracted mother who smiled absentmindedly and left us alone. I liked roaming the streets with Mary Lou and her scruffy friends, jumping off low-lying garage roofs into snow banks, prying up manhole covers, playing hide-and-go-seek in the cemetery. Then I liked going into somebody's house when their parents weren't home and making anonymous telephone calls: Hello, is Doris there? No, you have the wrong number. Hello, is Doris there? No, you still have the wrong number. Hello, this is Doris, do you have any messages for me? Slam the phone down, giggle and whoop.

Mary Lou dared me to taste the holy water at Our Lady of Mercy. I was sure we'd be struck down by lightening or get our tongues burned when the water turned to holy fire, but it tasted damp and colorless, just like ordinary water. Then I told her I was going to drink the holy water my aunt Margaret had brought back from Lourdes. "I bet you won't," she said. "I bet I will," I said, and I took the bottle (shaped like the Blessed Virgin, with a stopper in the head) over to Mary Lou's house and drank it right in front of her. Then I refilled it with tap water and put it back on the shelf in the dining room where my mother kept it. Mary Lou was impressed.

The world felt bigger when I was with her. To get to her house I'd cross over Grove Street, the dividing line between single- or double-family homes and triple-deckers, camp-going kids and street-hangers, patent-leather respectability and skinned-knee defiance. I can't remember whether my mother simply forbade me to see her anymore, or if she just said "Where have you been, with that Mary Lou Gallagher again?" pronouncing the name with a contempt that hung in the air until I breathed it in and turned it into fear.

"We were just playing, Mom."

"Can't you find someone to play with besides that . . . Mary Lou?"

The next time Mary Lou waited for me after school I told her I couldn't play with her anymore and walked away, headed for the college track.

A FEW months later Kathleen Reilly moved to town. She became my best friend during the last half of sixth grade. She reminded me of my lost friends because she lived on the other side of Grove Street, not far from Mary Lou, and had an amazing free-range mother. Mrs. Reilly was a few years younger than my mother, so she must have been forty-five, but she looked around twenty-eight. She had dyed blonde hair, short skirts and shapely legs, clinging angora sweaters, and a happy laugh. She worked as a secretary and told us racy limericks she picked up at the office, which really blew my mind. *There was a young woman from Crewe, Who encountered a man in a loo. He let out some farts, She checked out his parts, And told him they just wouldn't do.*

Mrs. Reilly was the kind of mother you hoped would come home while you were there, because she'd suggest something fun for us to do, like explore the mysteries of makeup. When we were in junior high, she instructed me and Kathleen to only put eyeliner below *half* the eyelid, and always to sweep *up* with rouge. (These were the days before blush-on.) "Girls," she would say, "buy the best makeup. It's worth the investment. You don't want lipstick that wears off in an hour." Finding a mother who was a makeup mentor shook up my world. Kathleen and I would dress up in Mrs. Reilly's clothes and shoes, applying makeup before her bathroom mirror that I'd wash off before I went home.

I was afraid that I'd have to drop Kathleen, but in seventh grade she had joined me in the accelerated math and science classes—new educational programs supposed to help us catch up with the Russians. (The whole country was still reeling from Sputnik.) I didn't care about keeping up with the Russians, but I was thrilled that Kathleen was accelerated too: that meant that even though her mother was a secretary and her father hadn't gone to college we could stay friends.

*L*OOKING BACK, I can see that my mother's friendship regulation was all about class. Mary Lou was Irish but not the right kind: shanty, not lace curtain. (Kathleen wasn't the right kind either, but getting in with the smart kids meant that she was moving up, and so she squeaked by my mother's radar.) Even though Mary Lou's family lived in Belmont (in a poorer section), they were closer to the kind of Irish who lived in South Boston. Working-class Irish were not the kind of Irish the O'Brien children should be spending time with. These were the kind of Irish my family had left behind, way back in the time of my great-grandparents, the Cullinans and O'Briens and Dohertys who worked in the textile mills of Lowell and the rolling mills of Elmira back in the 1860s. My grandfathers, an actor and a store owner, had already made it out of the laboring class of their immigrant fathers, and then my parents' college education had brought them even higher. My father's depression, job loss, and underemployment made it even more important that we keep associating with the "right" kind of people.

We are supposed to be free of class distinctions in America, unlike those snotty British who are always trying to peg your class origin by your accent, but class is our dirty little secret. We just don't like to talk about it—our preoccupation with class distinctions seems somehow *undemocratic* and we don't want to own up to it. If we move "up" from the working class—the word itself suggests the inferiority of those origins—we're supposed to leave people behind: this is one of the hidden costs of our upward mobility narrative.

In Horatio Alger's *Ragged Dick* the hero leaves his scruffy street buddies behind and finds new friends among the upper class; along the way he changes his clothes, his speech, and finally his name, becoming "Richard Hunter, Esq." by the novel's end. Alger makes him an orphan, a way to

43

demonstrate his self-sufficiency, but the device also allows the author to avoid the possibly troubling subject of the son abandoning his working-class parents or becoming ashamed of them. In the film *Good Will Hunting*, screenwriters Ben Affleck and Matt Damon made the same choice when they made the upwardly mobile Will an orphan. It's okay, the film suggests, for him to leave his working-class buddies behind when he heads for California and an upper-class life, but viewers might have been disturbed if Will had also been cutting ties with his parents. Perhaps making the upwardly mobile child an orphan also makes emotional sense: you can feel isolated and lost in your own family, having to please parents you can't afford to disappoint.

The street gang Ragged Dick must leave behind is composed of Irish ruffians—Micky Maguire and Johnny Nolan. Micky is a street thug and Johnny, although dimwittedly honest, just doesn't posses the drive, smarts, and virtuous smugness the Anglo-Saxon hero enjoys. Alger wrote his books during an era in which Irish Catholics, viewed as an inferior race and associated with blacks by native-born, Protestant Americans, were struggling to "become white." Anti-Irish sentiment was strongest in Boston, where the infamous "No Irish Need Apply" signs appeared in newspaper employment ads and shop windows.

By the time I was growing up in 1950s Belmont the Irish were so well assimilated that I had the luxury of not even knowing I was white, that status had been achieved so long ago. But the history of Boston Irish subjugation still had power: ten years after I walked away from Mary Lou Gallagher, the working-class Irish communities of Charleston and South Boston would erupt in protest against forced busing of their children, which seemed another form of oppression handed down by upper-middle-class WASPs and upper-middle-class Irish Americans like Judge Arthur Garrity, of South Boston busing fame, who lived in Wellesley ("swellsley") and didn't have to think about his own children going to school with black children in Roxbury.

I do not like my mother's snobbery but I have stopped judging it; I have come to understand its origins in her circumstances. It had been hard enough for Irish Catholics like my parents to earn a toehold in a toney Boston suburb. My mother couldn't have her children's friends dragging them down into the world that had been left behind, the world that must have seemed, after my father lost his job, much too close.

The First Time

She must learn again to speak
starting with I
starting with We
starting as the infant does
with her own true hunger
and pleasure
and rage.

—MARGE PIERCY, "Unlearning to not speak"

WHEN I GOT DEPRESSED for the first time I had no idea what was happening, and no words for the experience.

It was the summer after tenth grade.

I was too old for camp, too young for most summer jobs. Some of my friends had found work counseling in summer camps in New Hampshire or waitressing on Cape Cod, but my parents had made it clear I had to stay in Belmont. Perhaps they feared what might happen, now that I was sixteen—in 1961 summer jobs away from home meant suntan oil and browning bodies on the beach, dancing to "The Twist" and "Runaround Sue," wearing shorts and halters; they meant boys, they meant freedom, they meant sex. There was no way I was going anywhere. Look what had happened to Maureen, and she only went to Medford! The only solution? Lockdown.

And so the summer of 1961 introduced me to one of the surefire catalysts for depression: unstructured time. Out of school, I had no tasks to perform, no teachers to wow, no A's to be won. I'd lie in bed as long as I could, submerged in a dark, clotted lake. Sounds were muffled, voices remote; I was living underwater. I had the sense of life going on elsewhere and it grated on me like nasty chalk. I hated the sharp, relentless ringing of the phone. If my mother or father said "Sharon, it's for you," I'd drag myself down the hall and listen to the happy voice of a friend saying "Hey, a bunch of us are going to Wingaersheek beach Saturday, want to come?" I'd say yes because I had nothing else to do, but the trip to the beach would be agony, trying to pass for normal while my friends talked about the great summers they were having, pretending mine was great too. Usually I loved the beach but this summer I hated it. The sun looked down like a fierce hot eye, no place to hide. As soon as we arrived I wanted to be back in the cool dark of my bedroom, but someone else was driving and I was trapped. I'd lie on my stomach and pretend to sleep, or force myself to join the fun. When I got home I'd wash off the sand in the tub, put Solarcaine on my reddened skin, shut the door to my bedroom and dive back into bed, waiting for sleep.

I had no idea what was wrong.

I pulled down all the shades in my bedroom to keep the morning sun out as long as possible, trying to sleep forever, but I'd hear my mother rattling pots as she made breakfast and I knew she'd be calling "Sharon" in what seemed an accusatory voice, but was probably an anxious one. I'd drag myself out to the kitchen, eat breakfast, and slink back into my room, where I'd try to sleep away the day. Sometimes my mother opened my closed door and peered down at me.

—What are you doing
—Nothing, reading. I'm reading
—What are you reading
—A book, I'm just reading
—Why don't you call one of your friends, all you do is spend the day lying there like a bump on a log
—They're busy, everyone's away, leave me alone, Mom, I'm losing my place
   If she doesn't shut the door and leave me alone I'm going to scream thank God the sound of the door closing it's so quiet now

I'd lie back on the bed in the hot, humid Boston summer, listening to the far-off whine of saws and the rumble of power lawnmowers, hoping my mother would leave the house so I could sink down further into the dark lake without sensing her nervous presence somewhere on the shore, calling to me, as she did at the beach, "Sharon, come back in here, you're out too deep."

Perhaps my mother—who had lived through my father's depression—became alarmed. I remember her snapping, one afternoon, "Maybe we need to take you to a psychiatrist," more an attack than a worried suggestion, anger covering the fear. Perhaps she just thought I had a case, maybe an extreme one, of adolescent malaise and sullen apathy. (I remember seeing a book titled *Understanding Your Adolescent* tucked away in the living room bookcase.)

By the middle of July she took charge, dragging me out of bed and sending me to Massachusetts General Hospital as a candy striper. This got me out of the house, but depression, my sly bedfellow, came with me, sitting next to me on the Waverley streetcar, following me to work.

I spent the remaining summer days numbly pushing people in wheelchairs to their destinations in X-ray or Physical Therapy, wishing I had the energy for small talk because the patients looked so small and shrunken in their blue and white striped hospital gowns, their feet white and vulnerable inside their standard-issue slippers. I'd stare at the patients when they didn't notice, wondering what it would be like to spend my life paralyzed in a wheelchair. I thought I would probably kill myself, although I didn't know how I'd bring it off.

At four-thirty I'd leave to catch the subway at Charles Street, the only elevated station on the line. I'd watch the sailboats dotting the river, turning my head so I could get a last glimpse of the white sails scudding across the blue water before the Kendall Square tunnel swallowed us up. Then I'd catch the Waverley streetcar in Harvard Square, depression beside me in the hot summer air.

Sometimes I'd skip the hospital and go to a 10:00 a.m. movie. You could see a double feature at the Uptown for thirty-five cents. I'd stay in the theatre until late afternoon, emerging blinking and stunned from the darkness like some hibernating animal, thrust into a summer light as sharp and bleak as a razor. Then I'd go home and pretend nothing was wrong. What I was suffering from did not have a voice.

——How was the hospital
——Fine, okay, what's for dinner
——Barbara Myers called you, you need to call her back
——Barbara Myers is a jerk

Barbara was a mild, puffy girl with a pockmarked face, even lower in high school social status than me. My mother knew her mother—they'd been Brownie leaders—and I could bet that she had arranged this phone call.

—She wants you to do something with her, you call her back

—I wouldn't be caught dead with Barbara Myers, she is the most boring person on earth

—Suit yourself, go through the whole summer without seeing anyone if that's what you want

*A*UGUST CRAWLED along, me patching together a life out of patient-pushing, daytime movies, candy bars, TV westerns, and my only true consolation, sleep. Sometime that month I'd discovered over-the-counter sleeping pills—*Take Sominex tonight, and sleep! sleep! sleep!*—and on Friday night, facing the horror of the weekend, I'd start taking them and drift till Monday morning in a somnambulist haze. Then, blessedly, Labor Day came, and with it all the new, hopeful signs of school—fresh notebooks, keen Number 2 pencils, glossy blue and white Belmont High book covers. I went back to the safe haven of the classroom, and my spirits lifted.

I DIDN'T NAME this wretched period in my life as "depression" until a few years ago, when I was trying to understand where my midlife depression came from by going back in time. Then those high school summers came back to me, and I realized that this wasn't the usual adolescent moodiness. I was experiencing what the *Diagnostic and Statistical Manual of Mental Disorders* (DSM-IV), the psychiatrists' bible, calls "early onset depression," far more common in girls than in boys, anticipating women's higher ratio of depression. The sources had to have been multiple and intertwining. There was my genetic predisposition to depression, all the genes inherited from the O'Briens and Quinlans just lying in wait for what the psychologists call "precipitating circumstances." My mother's exiling of my sister contributed to the fear both Kevin and I felt during these years, and I was more exposed to parental surveillance since he'd escaped to college. And then there was my rocky journey through puberty and adolescence, made even rockier by my mother's fear that each sign of maturing sexuality meant I'd end up pregnant, married, or even worse . . . *a college dropout.*

We didn't live in a culture then that easily allowed girls to be both pretty and smart, and it was clear what choice I had to make: the roles had been assigned. "Maureen's the pretty one and I'm the smart one," I announced to a family friend when I was a teenager. There were many rewards for being the smart one, and many costs too.

*I*F I'D HAD ANY hopes of being pretty, they were dashed when I started getting pimples. Maureen had escaped this adolescent trauma, but I was in for a long siege. They started popping out all over my face when I turned thirteen. My mother declared total war on acne, a decision I then saw as intrusive and now see as concerned. My father drove us to one skin doctor after another. He'd go for a walk or stroll over to Brigham's for a coffee ice cream while my mother accompanied me into the doctor's office, sitting beside me while he squinted at my face and hummed under his breath.

The skin doctors all seemed to be cousins—pale, lugubrious, nearsighted men whose glasses magnified their eyes alarmingly. Magnification seemed their *raison d'être*—they also possessed magnifying mirrors that transformed my skin into a pocked terrain of hills and craters while they talked earnestly about the biochemistry of acne. I'd stare at my skin's moon surface while they told me about whiteheads and blackheads and hot washcloths. After a while I became convinced that my face had disappeared: when people looked at me they must be seeing only my pimples. After the nearsighted skin doctors popped my pimples with a small metal implement they carried in their vest pockets and applied a cotton ball soaked in a stinging astringent to my reddened face, they recommended twice-daily drenchings of my face in Phisohex, the recommended medicinal soap of the sixties. "And no peanut butter, chocolate, or sweets," they warned.

I hated Phisohex even more than I hated my pimples and sometimes, after days of Phisohexing and following the doctor's grim diet, pasted to the mirror in the bathroom, I'd break out on a rampage, stopping at Henry's Bakery on the way to school and stuffing down six jelly donuts at once or consuming a fistful of candy bars on the way home. Sometimes my mother made chocolate chip cookies, and I'd consume a decent four or five for dessert, and then sneak out during the evening, trying to raise the lid of the cookie jar without a clink, and lift a few more.

Then I'd go to bed and dream of being in a car crash that mashed up my face, so I'd have to have plastic surgery. The kindly plastic surgeon would give me flawless skin and replace my definitively Irish nose, which I thought a huge blemish, with a pert, cheerleadery one. I'd be reborn as the pretty one.

*U*NLIKE MY sister, I began dating occasionally in high school. Each phone call I received from a boy must have sent a stake through my mother's heart. *Not this daughter too! This one is going to go to college and set the*

world on fire, not end up pregnant and married to some man or other. I didn't
like the sound of that boy's voice, I didn't like the way he talked, he sounds
ignorant and common.

She needn't have worried about my taking after Maureen: trained by
church and family, I thought sex was a mortal sin. I had some vague idea
about reproduction and sex based on stray comments from girlfriends, illustrations in a musty old anatomy text I found in the library, and the mysterious pamphlet from Kotex my mother gave me the year I turned eleven. She
tucked it in the bottom of my summer camp trunk along with equally mysterious things called "sanitary napkins" that lay there like fat, flat sausages.

The pamphlet told me something called "menstruation" was coming, and
it had something to do with a uterus, and eggs, and Fallopian tubes, which
looked like graceful fringed flowers. And it had something to do with "fluid,"
which the pamphlet said I was going to "discharge" each month, and that
was why the flat sausages featured something called "absorbency." So I was
prepared for fluid.

I was not prepared for *blood*. The little pamphlets never mentioned the
word "blood."

A few months later, when I began bleeding, I was sure I was dying. My
mother's panicked response confirmed this: "Oh God, and she's not even
twelve, she's not even twelve." All that could mean was that I was dying too
soon, I wouldn't even live to see my twelfth birthday. Then she told me my
period had come, I'd have to go find one of those napkins and put it on, and
I was relieved I wasn't dying but still knew that something pretty bad had
happened much sooner than it should have.

It never occurred to me that my mother's distress had anything to do
with my sister. Now it makes sense: my period arrived just a few weeks
after my mother learned of my sister's pregnancy and marriage, and she
must have feared this sign of womanhood because now I could get pregnant,
now I could follow, if I chose, Maureen's downward path.

After going over the rules for sanitary napkin disposal (wrap them in
paper towels, wrap again in a brown paper lunch bag, deposit in the trash),
my mother said "I suppose you know . . . about the *other thing*."

I knew she was referring to sex. "Yes," I lied, hoping she'd say something more.

"Well, then, I guess that's it," she said, and went back to her ironing.

On the scale of fifties mothers telling daughters about sex, mine was
probably right in the middle. I have a few friends, not many, whose mothers

did a little better, giving them pamphlets on where babies came from. This was not a time for sexual candor. "My mother gave me the babies' pamphlet," my friend Carol said when a bunch of us were talking about fifties mothers. "That was it, until the day before my wedding, when she gave me a tube of KY jelly and said 'Dear, it's really very nice.'"

"That's pretty good, all things considered," Pat said, and we all nodded.

My mother's reticence wasn't surprising. It was the edge in her voice when she said *the other thing* that made me feel that talking about sex didn't just make her feel uncomfortable or embarrassed—it made her angry.

If my mother thought I was an early bloomer, I knew I was late. My girlfriends had all done Spin the Bottle in sixth grade at the mixed "boy-girl" parties I wasn't allowed to attend and had gone to dances in junior high school where they danced with boys. I never got asked. I kept hoping that someday things with boys would work out. I was interested, even though I pretended I wasn't, and had a serious crush on Roger Perry. I sat behind him in home room throughout junior high and still remember the morning in eighth grade when I realized how beautiful the back of his neck was. I had to acknowledge that I was seriously behind schedule one day in tenth grade when I read the "Ask Beth" column in the Boston *Globe*. "Dear Beth," the letter read, "I am sixteen years old and I have never been kissed. Am I behind schedule? Sincerely, Wondering in Medford." I related to that letter: I was sixteen years old and in the same spot. I was no nearer to being kissed than I was to being an astronaut. I knew what Beth was going to say: something consoling, like "Of course not, dear, you're just fine, right in the mainstream."

That's not what she said. "Dear Wondering: Not to worry. Just relax and enjoy your friendships with girls *and* boys. Eventually you'll catch up!" Oh God, I'm a sexual retard. That's what Beth is really saying. *Dear Wondering: you are, in fact, a pathetic failure. When you get kissed, which could be years from now, you'll still be thousands of kisses behind the other girls. Too bad you're wasting the best years of your life sitting home with your parents, sneaking the occasional midnight cookie when you want a real thrill.*

I stared at the *Globe* for a long time. I resolved that I was going to beat "Wondering in Medford." I was going to get kissed first.

𝒯HE FIRST boy to ask me to a dance was Stephen Antonelli. I was in tenth grade and he was in eleventh, so he had the panache of being an older man. Stephen played the saxophone in the band and had a clever, pockmarked face. He was a little shorter than me but I liked him: he had an ironic, downbeat sense of humor, he liked jazz, and he wore black turtle-necks, so he struck me as cool without being too scary. "Great," I said. "I just have to ask my parents."

"Mom, I've been asked to a dance," I said as my parents came in from their Saturday shopping. My mother put down her bags and turned to my father without acknowledging me. "Oh my god, Norb," she said, her voice edged with something more than contempt, something like anger, or maybe even hatred, something dark and vicious and unacknowledged, something that lived down below the surface with the thing that frightened me. Then, I couldn't hear the fear.

She turned back to me. "What's this boy's name?"

"Stephen Antonelli."

"An-to-nelli, he's I-talian. She wants to go out with an Italian!"

My father shrugged his shoulders and said something mild and placating, like "Now Jeannie, there are many fine Italian families in our parish," and my mother gave one of her disgusted sighs.

After my mother said the word "Italian," I could see it painted on the wall in our kitchen, dripping with blood and scum, the name of something obscene. I called Stephen back and said I couldn't go, I'd made a mistake, I was busy.

$\mathcal{M}$OM, I'VE been asked to a dance."

"Who is it this time?"

"Adam Schwartz. He's a junior."

"Jewish boy?"

"No, he's Catholic, isn't it obvious?"

"Don't be fresh with me. Can't you find somebody besides this—Adam Schwartz?"

$\mathcal{T}$HIS TIME I wasn't going to back down. I went to the dance with Adam and he took me to Howard Johnson's afterwards for ice cream, a proper date. When he dropped me off he gave me a goodnight kiss—my first!—and I felt I'd crossed an invisible line. I ran to the bathroom and looked at my face in the mirror, surprised to find that I really didn't look any different. For our next date we went to the Cafe Pamplona in Harvard Square, a funky basement cafe with marble-topped tables and cappuccino, an exotic locale in the early sixties. I was impressed. Then we had a parking double date on Belmont's infamous Somerset Road. We went with Mark and Karen, who had been King and Queen of the Junior Prom. I felt honored by this association with teenage royalty.

I hated the parking date. I waited patiently while Adam explored the territory underneath my bra and panties, kissing me strenuously all the while, sticking his tongue in and out of my mouth with rapid darting motions like a restless lizard. "At least I'm doing French kissing," I said to myself—one more thing to check off my list. *Take that, Wondering in Medford!*

Meanwhile I kept my right arm tensed to push his hand away if he went "too far." I wanted to leave after five minutes but Adam had clamped onto me with unsettling permanence, and Mark and Karen were moaning and breathing heavily in the back seat. I could not ask to go home. This would be sure to anger Adam, who'd already spent ten dollars on dinner, and would let the King and Queen and then the whole school know I wasn't okay about sex. Then Adam changed tactics, putting my hand on his crotch, and I said I had to go home. "My mother's really strict about time," I said, "she'll kill me if I'm not back by midnight," for once telling the truth.

When my mother told me I had to stop going out with Adam I did not protest. We were standing in my parents' bedroom, both of us looking into the full-length mirror. "That Adam Schwartz is Jewish," my mother's reflection said, "and you've been going out with him a lot."

"I guess, what difference does it make," my reflection said.

"I don't want you seeing him anymore," her reflection said.

I left the mirror and went to my room, driven by the coiled-up energy of my mother's fear and my own. When Adam called a few days later to ask me to the graduation dance, I told him I wouldn't be seeing him again. I felt relieved that I wouldn't have to wait in the sunroom for him to pick me up again, my mother hovering in the living room, looking out the windows at each passing car, not speaking to me as I sat in my new dress with my hair curled and sweaty hands, the atmosphere in our house crackling with unspoken words.

A FEW WEEKS LATER school let out, and I got depressed again. I was still jobless. This time my mother enrolled me in a typing course in Boston—she had the same strategy for coping with a depressed daughter as does Esther Greenwood's mother in *The Bell Jar*—and I took the subway in every day to the Copley Secretarial School. There I sat in a small windowless room with six or seven other hopeless girls whose mothers had also decided they had to take typing. I stared at the alphabet soup of the keys and made up nonsense words with the letters in my head ("qwerty," "trew"), repeating them to myself like a mantra when I took the subway home, drumming typing exercises in the air. Sometimes I turned my type-writer words into limericks: anything to pass the time. One limerick could take me all the way from Park Street to Harvard Square. *There once was a fellow named Qwerty, who never would live to see thirty. It's sad but it's trew, he died at twenty-two, and never got old or got dirty.*

Labor Day finally came round again and I went back to school for my senior year, my still unnamed depression lifting like a fog burning off in the sun. I applied to Radcliffe early decision and got in, and knew that in September I'd be living away from home. I couldn't wait.

In the spring my grades slipped a little. For the first time I was getting a little depressed even at school. I slid from first in the class to third, so I wouldn't be giving any graduation speeches. Perhaps my parents were disappointed, but they didn't let me know. I'd done everything they had hoped for, and they were proud. My father still had buddies working for the *Elmira Star-Gazette,* and he persuaded them to print a little news item about me in May 1963. This was my parents' story of me, along with the high school graduation picture of a girl who looks calm, confident, and unreal.

Sharon's high school yearbook photo, 1963

Ex–City Couple's Daughter Honored

Sharon O'Brien, daughter of former Elmirans Mr. and Mrs. Norbert L. O'Brien of 28 Lewis Road, Belmont, Mass., has been awarded an honorary National Merit Scholarship.

Sharon's father was commercial manager of former radio station WESG in Elmira from the time the station opened in 1932 until he received a promotion to an affiliated station in Hartford, Conn., in 1936.

Miss O'Brien, a senior at Belmont High School, was accepted at Radcliffe under the early admissions plan. She expects to major in chemistry and is looking toward a career as a research chemist.

The honorary designation means that Miss O'Brien already has accepted another scholarship, which prevents her from receiving financial assistance from the Merit Program.

Miss O'Brien received an award in recognition of a score of 800 on the College Entrance Board Chemistry Achievement Test taken during her sophomore year.

Last June, she was presented a Phi Beta Kappa Book Award for her superior scholarship and academic promise.

She is a member of the Belmont chapter of the National Honor Society.

Sharon was co-captain of the school field hockey team and played varsity basketball.

She plays the flute in the school band and belongs to the glee club and a capella choir. She also is a member of the French Club and Ski Club.

Sharon was editor-in-chief of the school newspaper.

She is a curved bar Girl Scout and vice president of her parish organization for young people.

When I read this news article—part college admission letter, part c.v.— I was pleased, and did not notice that anything was missing. This person seemed complete and competent. I was proud of her. Look at all those things she'd done! She would have to be the one I'd send off to college, not the girl who couldn't get out of bed.

That other girl couldn't hold a candle to this one.

The Family Silver

A loss of something ever felt I—
The first that I could recollect
Bereft I was—of what I knew not.
—EMILY DICKINSON

EVER SINCE I CAME TO REMEMBER stories I had heard about the Repoussé. Handsome Dan had bought the fabulous, beyond-price silver set during one of his flush periods. "It was exquisite," my mother would say, as she told and retold the story. "Simply exquisite. Shipped from Paris to Baltimore, and then by rail to Elmira." When my mother described the Repoussé's odyssey she seemed to be still marveling that anything French could have found its way to Elmira. After she died I discovered that the Repoussé was not French after all: the Paris purchase must have been one of Handsome Dan's stories.

I am glad my mother never discovered the truth, because the French name and legendary foreign origins made the silver shine more in her eyes. She would evoke the Repoussé lingeringly, worshipping its excess: there were twenty place settings and eighteen implements for each setting, including exotic silverware I'd never seen or heard of: tea spoons . . . grapefruit spoons . . . runcible spoons (an odd combination of fork and spoon that I'd only encountered in "The Owl and the Pussycat") . . . iced tea spoons . . . demitasse spoons . . . butter knives . . . fish knives . . . fruit knives . . . steak knives. Grandest of all, the parade of forks: dinner fork, dessert fork, salad fork, fish fork, pie fork, oyster fork, pastry fork, lobster fork, berry fork! And then the single implements, glorying in distinction—salad servers, carving knives, soup and gravy ladles, sugar tongs, salt spoon, pickle fork, lemon fork, serving spoons and forks, cake cutter. The Repoussé far exceeded the O'Brien family's nightly place setting: a stainless steel knife, fork, and spoon, plus a soup spoon when we were having Campbell's tomato on Friday nights.

When I was a child I thought the family silver was called "Ray Poussay" after its French designer. Now I know it's the French word for "pushed back," referring to the silversmith's method of creating a raised pattern. The word is fitting. On the surface the Quinlans were a family of almost ferocious energy: my mother and her sisters were all spellbinding talkers, inheriting their father's ability to hold center stage. But below the surface, pushed down and back, resentments and silences lingered.

THE REPOUSSÉ seemed to enter the Quinlan family under a curse. Handsome Dan had bought the silver when he was on the road, as he did all the splendors he sent back to Elmira: the Oriental rugs, the Havilland china, the elegant dining room table, the sideboard for displaying his dinnerware. When the silver set arrived in Elmira, my grandmother wept. "She sat at the kitchen table," my mother said, "just sat there and cried."

"Why?"

"They didn't have the money," she said. "My mother was scrimping and saving, and His Nibs goes and spends it all on the silver."

"Why didn't she send it back?"

"She couldn't. Every piece was monogrammed with a Q."

When that wooden crate arrived, unbidden and unannounced, my grandmother would have seen Handsome Dan's love of display, rather than his love of her. Now she had all those glorious place settings, and not enough money to buy the meat and vegetables she would have wanted to spread out on the kitchen table, right there where she was crying.

Of course my grandfather would have had the silver monogrammed: that Q was his sign of possession and status, marking the name he'd chosen for himself and given to our family when he changed his birth name, "Cullinan," to "Quinlan." He must have felt proud, when he chose that Q from the monogram designs, that he had such a distinctive beginning to his last name, far better than an ordinary "C." Monogramming the silver meant marking the identity he'd chosen as surely as did his tuxedo. Stage actors might be looked down upon by respectable society and the Irish thought of as ape-like Paddies, drunkards, or comic buffoons, but Handsome Dan was the Chesterfield of Conversation, the Prince of Interlocutors: he performed elegance and aristocracy. ("There is an evident air of refinement and culture about Quinlan," wrote the *Elmira Star-Gazette*.) Why shouldn't his be the only Irish family in Elmira to have a twenty-place setting of Repoussé? When he invited the town dignitaries to dinner, the rich Protestants who buried their dead in Woodlawn Cemetery (he was destined for St. Patrick's, the Catholic cemetery on the working-class side of the Chemung River), they would know he was a man of substance.

Buying the silver wasn't just about conspicuous consumption. It was about rewriting and reversing Irish history and stereotypes, it was about assimilation, it was about forgetting the Famine. In the late nineteenth century, table manners, etiquette, and elaborate, specialized table settings had

Handsome Dan in tuxedo, late 1930s

increasingly become signs of middle- and upper-middle-class status, a way of separating native-born gentry-class Americans from the flood of immigrants. By creating elaborate household codes, rituals, and dining practices (all those forks!), genteel Americans could mark cultural superiority, distancing themselves from brutish laborers.

In particular, they were drawing cultural boundaries between themselves and the Irish, the first—and largest—non-Protestant immigrant group. An important sign of Irish savagery to both British colonizers and American gentry was primitive eating habits. Relying almost solely on the potato—a result of colonial rule, since pre-conquest Irish had a much more varied diet—the poor Irish cottiers had no need for cutlery, since potatoes could be easily eaten with hands alone. The historian Hasia Diner records that "a listing of *all* material possessions in a parish of 4,000 people in Donegal for 1836 included 243 stools, 8 brass candlesticks, but only 10 table forks, and no other utensils dedicated to cooking or eating." Irish immigrants in the United States were associated with animalistic eating habits—potato eaters who grabbed food with their hands and gobbled in the street, not civilized enough to sit down to a meal and use utensils.

Handsome Dan must have grown up in a household where little attention was paid to the niceties of the table. I doubt that his famine immigrant parents owned a silver set, and they may not even have owned a table. He would have encountered silver place settings during his travels with his minstrel troupes, at hotels and perhaps on trains, and so associated elegant place settings with social mobility. His purchase of the Repoussé signified that the Quinlans had been uplifted and refined, and he insisted on using the Repoussé every night for dinner when he was in residence. The silver erased both the potato-gobbling immigrant stereotype and the memory of the Famine, when the starved dead were found by the roadside, mouths and teeth stained green from the grass.

I can understand why my grandfather bought the silver, and why my grandmother cried: she knew the silver had nothing to do with the everyday needs of a mother raising six daughters. And perhaps she recognized the Repoussé as a stand-in for her wandering husband, who sent her monogrammed Q's instead of himself.

My sister has another take on my grandmother's tears. "Handsome Dan had to have been fooling around on the road," she says. "He bought the silver because he felt guilty." Yes, I can see that too: sending luxurious gifts back to his housebound wife could signify his husbandly duty, and then with a clear conscience he could invite one of the "Dancing Sunflowers" from his minstrel troupe into his bed.

$\mathcal{A}$FTER MY grandparents died my aunt Geraldine, as the oldest sister and curator of the Elmira family home, inherited the silver. For a few years there was peace. Geraldine had been a mother to all her younger sisters, defending them from her imperious father. She had stayed in Elmira, living with her parents until they died, nursing her mother in her last illness. The other sisters either thought it appropriate that she should be the keeper of the silver, or kept quiet about it. They were also, I think, a little afraid of her.

When Geraldine died in an Elmira nursing home, the Repoussé divided the Quinlan sisters instead of uniting them behind the proud Q. Deaths, funerals, and wills had a tradition of bringing out the worst in the Quinlans. Dramas got acted out around the rituals of death that had nothing to do with the visible world and everything to do with the invisible world, nothing to do with the present and everything to do with the past.

When my grandmother Quinlan died in 1953, my aunt Ruth was traveling in Mexico. Geraldine, the new matriarch, sent a telegram bearing the sad news to the American embassy in Mexico City, where Ruth had left forwarding information. After a day or two Geraldine then informed her sisters that Ruth could not be reached, and they went ahead with the funeral—an understandable choice. Geraldine also made out the obituary, and probably no one checked it, so no one noticed that Ruth's name was missing from the list of surviving Quinlan sisters.

Maybe it was an oversight. Most likely it wasn't. Geraldine didn't think much of Ruth, who was her only rival in the family in terms of professional accomplishments and out-and-out dramatic self-presentation. When Ruth discovered that she had been left out of her mother's funeral and obituary, she sent a furious correction to the *Elmira Star-Gazette*: "Miss Ruth Quinlan Sun announces that she was erroneously and maliciously omitted from Mrs. Margaret Quinlan's obituary as a surviving daughter." The editor crossed out "and maliciously" and ran the announcement. Ruth ceased speaking to Geraldine and refused to mention her name, beginning one of the complicated feuds—enforced by silence and shunning—that would mark the six sisters' lives over the years.

My mother worked hard to stay on friendly terms with everyone, but Geraldine's death brought her into the line of fire. During Geraldine's last years and months of illness, my mother had been the one on the scene, traveling frequently to Elmira to see her and handling, along with my father, the selection of her nursing home. My mother loved Geraldine, my father did too, and Geraldine knew it.

In her last months my aunt wasn't thinking about family fairness and equitable distribution; she was thinking about love, and who had been there as a sister when she needed her. And so she made a will leaving her modest estate and the family heirlooms to my mother. "Of course I would have split everything four ways," my mother once told me during one of the rare times when she revisited this painful period. "But they didn't give me a chance."

Ruth, Margaret, and Dorothy—the surviving sisters—sprang into action immediately, sending telegrams to my mother, whom they feared might be about to make off with the family treasures before they got there. One telegram has survived.

WE ARE STRONGLY OPPOSED TO ANY DIVISION OF OUR PARENTS PERSONAL PROPERTY UNTIL THE FOUR SISTERS NOT LIVING IN ELMIRA ARE IN FULL AGREEMENT AS TO SUCH DIVISION STOP GERALDINE QUINLAN KEPT THIS PROPERTY BECAUSE SHE WAS ON THE SCENE AND TOOK UNFAIR ADVANTAGE OF US NOT THERE STOP THE EQUAL RIGHTS OF SURVIVING HEIRS MUST BE SCRUPULOUSLY MAINTAINED STOP

The sisters booked their emergency flights to Elmira—for Geraldine's funeral, and for the four-way division of the spoils. Naturally they wanted their share of the family heirlooms and memorabilia, but they also insisted that Geraldine's estate—perhaps $30,000 in savings—be divided among them too. The lawyers had only been able to find a copy of the will, not the original, so legally my aunt had died intestate, and the sisters insisted on this legality.

They buttressed their case by accusing my parents of trying to increase Geraldine's modest estate by putting her in the second most expensive nursing home in Elmira, not the most expensive. My parents had chosen a small, family-run establishment rather than the more corporate model because they thought it was the best. "I couldn't talk to them about it," my mother said. "I couldn't believe they would think those things of me. And of Norb." Yes, my father must have been in on it too—"it" being some nefarious scheme the sisters couldn't quite define. He'd made a few trips to Elmira by himself to take care of things when my mother was working, and now his involvement became suspicious. I still have a carbon copy of a letter he sent the Quinlan sisters later, patiently, and with remarkably little anger, describing the fairness of his dealings, and reminding them that they'd been kept informed all along. Only in his conclusion does the hurt emerge.

> I can't refrain from one personal observation: that it is a source to me of mystification, disappointment and regret that this family could not credit me with good intentions in all of this, and could not grant me the benefit of the doubt.

Geraldine's choice of my mother as heir must have hurt and enraged the other sisters. Quarrels over wills are rarely quarrels about money and heirlooms; more often they're about ancient hurts and slights and deprivations nursed in silence for years. After their parents died, Geraldine came to represent family, home, and the past. When she expressed her will that my mother inherit, it was as if she were anointing one "loyal" sister and disinheriting the rest.

What *is* mystifying and sad is the lack of trust among these sisters, their instant assumption that my mother would want to keep everything for herself. To stop this imagined threat, they chose to resort to the aggressive and distancing medium of the telegram—unnecessary in the early 1970s, when any of them could have picked up a phone. But useful, because what they all really wanted to say was STOP.

The four sisters met after the funeral to split up the heirlooms. My mother kept her hurt feelings inside, keeping the peace. It was easy to split the money four ways, and easy to divide the Oriental rugs—each sister went away with three. The Repoussé was different. No sister could allow another to have the whole set, so they broke it up. Ruth, recorder of the division, wrote out everyone's separate portion. The twenty place settings dissolved as grapefruit spoons separated from salad forks, iced tea spoons deserted steak knives, serving spoons left their mates. My mother received

1 ladle
1 serving spoon
4 dinner forks

4 dinner knives

4 teaspoons

4 soup spoons

4 salad forks

4 demitasse spoons

1 pair sugar cube tongs

Each Quinlan returned to a different part of the country with her share of the spoils, and for many years afterward they continued to resort to quarreling and exile and then to writing each other out of their wills or diminishing each other's portions. Those who stayed friendly would inherit an ally's silver if she died before they did; others would be left out in the cold. The Repoussé was hidden, diminished, and passed on from favored sister to favored sister, circling around the family like a slow-moving silver snake. No one really knew where it all was, and no one, as far as I know, ever used it to eat with.

Eventually the silver was divided between the last two surviving sisters, my mother and my aunt Ruth. Ruth had by far the larger portion: she had repaired an ancient quarrel with Margaret and had decided to cultivate a relationship with Dorothy, and so she received their Repoussé shares.

After Ruth's death, my mother's first concern was with finding the Repoussé. I still remember returning from the funeral and seeing her frantically rummaging through Ruth's closets and drawers and boxes, after a while saying "She's done something with it, I know she's done something with it." I had rarely seen her this distraught; it was as if she were looking for a lost and necessary piece of her past.

A few weeks later Ruth's executor found the silver in Ruth's safe deposit box, wrapped in grey velvet cloth. He sent it to my mother, but even the receipt of the long-awaited Repoussé didn't seem to satisfy her. "There's something missing," she kept saying, "I know there's something missing." Her response made me think of Emily Dickinson's poem about the existential deprivation we experience as human beings—"A loss of something ever felt I." There was no way the Repoussé could satisfy that yearning for a wholeness that does exist on this earth.

WHEN MY MOTHER was thinking of her own death and making her list of "Valuables" in her memo book, she gave the Repoussé first place—before the Corning glass bowl, Beleek china, Waterford glass, bone china

Repoussé forks

Repoussé forks with monogram

cups and saucers, silver flatware, Hummel Madonna, and even the revered Havilland china. "Should be kept in family," she wrote at the end of this list.

Now I have the Repoussé, the whole set; when my mother died we did not quarrel over possessions. I've taken the knives, forks, and spoons out of their pearly velvet shrouds and put them in the kitchen drawer, mingling fought-over treasures with humbler utensils. When people come to dinner, I mix ornate Repoussé with simple stainless. My friends all know the story and someone will hold up a Q-inscribed fork: "So this is the fabled Repoussé."

Handsome Dan

Dan Quinlan is an Elmira boy and next year he will wear a diamond stud that will cover his whole shirt front.

—Elmira Star-Gazette, 1891

He's a smasher, he's a masher,
This handsome young man
In the center of the first part
As he flirts his satin fan.

He's a hustler, he's a bustler
A Jim dandy minstrel man,
He's no chestnut gag exploder
Be diamond Happy Dan.

—Elmira Star-Gazette, 1892

WHEN I FIRST STARTED THINKING about depression as an emotional inheritance that rolled down through generations, I traced my own straight back to Handsome Dan's doorstep. He'd been the dark influence on my mother's life, and she'd turned her inheritance over to me. But it was hard to have it out with him. He died in 1940, five years before I was born, and the stories and legends about him were so fragmentary, trying to fight him or blame him was like trying to grapple with air. And even if I could have confronted him, I knew he'd never take responsibility for any of the emotional havoc he'd wreaked on the family.

"I bet old Dan was never depressed a day in his life," I said to Maureen.

"No," she said. "He just passed it on."

MY MOTHER told me he'd been known as "Handsome Dan," and sometimes she referred to him that way, always with a biting tone that said she thought he was full of himself. Sometimes she called him "His Nibs" when she was describing his demanding temperament or his sense of entitlement. "His Nibs wanted to be waited on hand and foot." "His Nibs would come and go as he pleased." "His Nibs would sit in state in the living room, watching our comings and goings." According to her, he'd been a famous minstrel show interlocutor, but I didn't really believe her until I looked up his name in the card catalog at the Lincoln Center Drama Archive, expecting a blank, and found QUINLAN, DANIEL (1873–1940) and a file full of photographs and clippings. He wasn't famous enough that we'd still know his name today, but he was one of the best-known figures in minstrelsy during the late nineteenth and early twentieth centuries. Constantly on the road, sometimes away from Elmira for two or three years at a stretch, Dan crisscrossed the country with his minstrels and, later, toured Europe with his vaudeville act.

My mother gave me his scrapbook before she died, and I'd pore over it, trying to glimpse the man behind the minstrel's mask. He proved hard to find. Most of the clippings are reviews of his minstrel performances. His own voice comes through only occasionally, filtered through an interviewer or in the transcript of an after-dinner speech to the Elks. But his "own voice" wasn't a private one: he was always aware of the audience, and he spoke the flowery prose of nineteenth-century sentiment and oratory. *That sublime creation of a Supreme Being which we call Life, becomes vibrant with periods of joy, sorrow, laughter, tears, love, home, and family. . . . As time roams from one decade to another, all normal people crave the occasional hour with the Muse, the Goddess of song, music and dance.*

His photographs are staged publicity shots: Handsome Dan in profile, framed in oak with a golden name plate; Handsome Dan in whiteface posed with his blackface partner for his vaudeville sketch *The Traveling Dentist;* Handsome Dan dressed in fringed buckskin, looking like Buffalo Bill.

The one photo where he lets you in a little, even though it's also a pose, is the striking vision of Handsome Dan as a man of color. This image is not minstrel-show blackface: burnt-cork-blackened cheeks, widened white lips. "He looks like he's about to play Othello," a friend of mine observed. He looks like a prince—a light-skinned black man to whom deference is due, dressed regally in his white shirt, jacket with satin lapels, and shiny satin breeches. He's looking straight at the camera, his gaze challenging, aristocratic, entitled. He's not only handsome, he's sexy, and he seems very pleased about that.

Handsome Dan as man of color, early 1900s

The photograph was taken in New Orleans, the city of racial mixing, octoroon balls, and Creole culture. Maybe he's dressed for Mardi Gras, or a ball in the French Quarter, or an evening of cross-race play-acting? More likely he's dressed for the stage—I don't know.

Ever since I discovered this photograph in a box of old family papers, I've felt he's looking straight at me, out of the past, saying *I defy you to figure me out.*

*Y*OU WERE born in 1863 to John Cullinan and Bridget Larkin, both recent immigrants from Ireland. Your mother died three years later giving birth to your brother Thomas, and you remember her only as a white, comforting light that you could only see from the corner of your eye. Your father still spoke with a heavy Cork accent; he worked in the rolling mills, the night shift, and would come home tired and angry and drunk. If you were going to do one thing in your life, it was to be different from him. Sometimes he beat you, but he never beat Thomas, who was frail and quiet and sweet and looked a lot like Bridget.

Your father married again, and then his temper improved but his drinking didn't, particularly after he opened the saloon. You wanted to stay in school but he made you go to work in the rolling mills when you were twelve, so you never went beyond a fifth-grade education. You were ashamed of your father—of his obvious Irishness, his lack of refinement, and most of all, his illiteracy. You left the rolling mills to work on the railroad when you were fourteen, riding the rails as a brakeman. This was better, you were on the move, but you weren't satisfied. You had dreams of greatness.

More than anything, you wanted to stay in school, and you resented your father for making you quit. When the reporter asked you, "Dan, where did you receive your education?" and you answered "Travel. Travel was my alma mater," you were putting on a good front. The honest part of the interview was when you said "The school room is to me but the dream of childhood days." Your mark of pride, you told this young newspaperman from the *Crawfordsville* (Indiana) *Register*, was when people said of you: "He must be a college-bred man." Like Gatsby you practiced elocution: you wiped all trace of Cork and Kerry out of your mouth, and you decided that all your daughters were going to college to make up for the education you didn't get.

Your brother Thomas worked in the rolling mills too, but he wasn't strong enough for the work, and you helped him get a job as a telegraph operator on the Tioga railroad. Thomas is one person I'm sure you loved more than yourself. The newspaper says you stayed by his bedside while he was dying of tuberculosis—he was only twenty-nine—and that you were holding his hand when he died. When you started your scrapbook you used the Tioga Railroad Company's telegraph log, the one that had three pages filled with his handwriting. You must have dreamed about the future together, boys back in Elmira, and you were connecting his story with yours.

Three months later your father died too, and that's when you changed your name—Daniel Cullinan became Daniel Quinlan. I used to think this was your way of separating from your illiterate father and reinventing yourself in the great American tradition, but it's more complicated than that. Both names are from the same Irish root, so you were keeping your ethnicity and a connection to the past. You were just sprucing up the name a bit, giving it the distinctive "Q" you liked to flourish in your handwriting and would later place on the family silver.

You began your scrapbook with the first reviews of your performances: they're your birth announcement. There are two clippings announcing your wedding—"The Well-Known Minstrel Wedded to One of Elmira's Famous Belles" and "A Popular Couple Married in the Presence of an Immense Crowd"—and the birth announcement for Geraldine, because she was the first. No more personal records, no birth announcements for your other daughters, no records of their six graduations from Elmira College. You liked the headlines and the titles: "Quinlan a Brilliant Success," "Quinlan Gives Splendid Performance at the Opera House," "The Prince of Interlocutors." "The Chesterfield of Modern Minstrelsy." "America's Premier Interlocutor."

I'm the only person besides you who's spent hours looking at your scrapbook.

*O*F COURSE," an old Elmira friend of my mother's told me recently, "your grandfather forbade his daughters to marry." *Forbade his daughters to marry?* Who was this, some wicked king in an old fairy tale who wanted to keep his six virginal daughters imprisoned in the castle? Was this some curse he wanted to place on them? Or a strange unintended blessing, freeing them to pursue lives outside the marriage plot?

Three daughters would marry, three would not. My mother married my father in New York City, not Elmira—Handsome Dan was opposed to the match, and so the whole family decamped to the city for a wedding at St. Patrick's Cathedral, leaving him alone and uninvited. My aunt Margaret, the original defier, eventually divorced her husband and spent her middle and aging years in what Henry James would have discreetly called a "Boston marriage" with another woman. My aunt Ruth divorced her first husband after a short marriage and later found a happy, unconventional lifelong marriage with Norman Sun, who had emigrated from China in the late 1940s.

Of the three who never married, I think only my beautiful aunt Marion, who always wore matching gloves and hose and sailed to France every summer on the Cunard line, would have wanted to. She fell in love once, family rumor goes, with a charming confidence man who promised to marry her and then absconded with all her savings—a performer like her father. My aunt Dorothy, awkward and shy, seemed content working for the government and living alone in her Washington residential hotel. And my aunt Geraldine enjoyed a lifelong relationship with her colleague, Geraldine Morrow. Together they ran the drama department at Elmira College from the 1920s until the 1950s. The two women—known on the Elmira campus as "the two Gerries"—lived discreetly in their separate apartments, but they shared a farm house in the Pennsylvania hills where they spent summers gardening, cooking, and reading. I imagine the Gerries thumbing their noses at Handsome Dan's prohibition. "Fine with us," they'd say.

My mother always portrayed herself as afraid of her father's anger, but she neglected to tell her children the story of her defiance. Dot Cummings, one of her original "chums" from elementary school, told me that "Quin" would defy her father whenever she got the chance. "Quin would do anything she could get away with," Dot said. "Steal out her bedroom window at night, go off with a boy, she was a devil. I always thought it was strange that she was so rigid with you kids. At reunions she'd say 'I don't let them do this, I don't let them read that,' and I'd say 'Now Quin, what the hell's gotten into you? You're sounding just like your father,' but she didn't want to talk about it." Family patterns have a way of getting passed down, despite our best intentions. They change shape, they mutate, they persist.

𝓜Y GREAT-GRANDFATHER, John Cullinan—Handsome Dan's father—was part of the original wave of famine immigration. He arrived in Elmira in the late 1840s and worked in the rolling mills before he became a

Marion Quinlan, late 1920s

saloon-keeper. Perhaps that was when he bought a gold-tipped cane with his name inscribed, a name he would have been unable to read: he remained illiterate in his new country, signing his will with a shaky X that was followed by the clerk of court's translation: "John Cullinan, his mark." He had no desire for his son to rise higher than he, but Dan—who became known as a "Shakespearian scholar," according to some of his clippings—would not remain mired in illiteracy and manual labor.

Dan's leap from laborer to performer is part of the larger story of Irish upward mobility and assimilation in this country. Upward mobility for the Irish meant breaking the symbolic link native-born Americans made between Irish Americans and African Americans (Irishness then being thought of as a racial identity—"Celtic") and gradually defining themselves as Caucasian—an invented category that expanded during the late nineteenth century to include, little by little, the new immigrant groups: first the Irish, later the Poles, Slovaks, and Croatians.

Minstrelsy was the major cultural form that allowed the Irish to leave behind their own linkage with blacks. By "blacking up" and adopting an exaggerated "darkie" stereotype Irish performers could, paradoxically, accentuate and reinforce their group's association with whiteness. If they could perform a racist stereotype, then the burnt cork they left on the washrag in the dressing room when they removed their black stage makeup to reveal the light skin underneath marked them as distinct from the identities they dramatized on stage.

My grandfather's scrapbook shows that the racist stereotypes common in antebellum minstrelsy persisted. The performers he worked with and hired sang songs and did comedy routines with titles like "Ethiopian Eccentricities," "Everybody Has a Flag but the Coon," "Hottentot Dance," "Our Colored Sweethearts," "Slavery Days," "Sweet Colored Lady," "Down Where the Cotton Blossoms Grow," and "The Water Melon Patch."

In 1907, with minstrelsy in decline, Handsome Dan created a vaudeville act with the comedian John Mack that continued to exploit racist humor. His routine was called "The Traveling Dentist." The act referred to the itinerant and often untrained "dentists" who moved into small towns for a few days, sometimes equipped only with pliers, ready to extract ulcerated teeth, often without anesthesia. The one existing photo shows Dan as the white dentist, looming over his blackfaced partner in the dentist's chair, smiling diabolically, inserting some instrument of torture into his patient's hugely opened mouth, made even larger by white paint.

Handsome Dan's scrapbook contains two intentionally juxtaposed cartoons from *Judge* magazine that dramatize the racial history of African Americans and Irish Americans, showing both the connections made between the blacks and the Irish and the ways in which minstrelsy helped the Irish ascend the racial ladder, and my family to assimilate and rise. In the first one, a black man and woman are portrayed in grotesque racist exaggeration, as they would have been in minstrelsy, with ape-like features and wide white lips (they could be whites in blackface).

Positioned directly below is the cartoon that makes the whole story of Irish minstrelsy, and my grandfather's role, a little more complicated— showing the identification between Irish and blacks. It shows two Paddys meeting on a rough urban street in a poor part of town.

The dialect-speaking Irishmen are given ape-like features too, showing the link native-born white Americans made between Irish and blacks. But

Black stereotypes, *Judge* magazine, 1890s

HE WAS DEAD RIGHT.

CASSIDY—"It makes me cry to think th' b'ys wouldn't shtrike fer longer hours an' less pay."
CASEY—'Yer crazy, mon! Phwat would they do thot fer?"
CASSIDY—"Bekase we niver git phwat we shtrike fer, anyhow."

Irish stereotypes, *Judge* magazine, 1890s

in the back we see another sign of Irishness—a dilapidated fence with a poster for "Quinlan and Wall's Mastodon Minstrels" in the background with a blackface performer billed as *Ben, the Trombone Prodigy*. As the leader of "Quinlan and Wall's" minstrels, my grandfather could distance himself and his fellow Irishmen from the ape-like Paddies by reinforcing racist stereotypes for black Americans. In doing so he was distancing himself from his illiterate laborer father and moving much further up the race and class ladder than most second-generation Irish Americans did, becoming white and middle-class at the same time.

*H*ORATIO ALGER would never have cast Dan as a hero. The upwardly mobile bootblacks and newsboys in his novels are always Anglo-Saxon; the lazy or vicious foil characters are Irish.

But Dan found a way to succeed in the theater—the realm of cheap entertainment that Alger's priggish heroes always leave behind on their journey toward respectability—and he did so through the Algerian values of hard work, diligence, and self-education. He ran away from the rolling mills to join a minstrel troupe when he was sixteen, having prepared for his future by staging minstrel shows in his back yard, casting neighborhood boys in the requisite parts. "While working at the rolling mills," wrote a reporter in 1899, "Mr. Quinlan became possessed of the idea that he would like to seek his fame and fortune on the American stage as a minstrel."

The "rags to riches" formula appears in several clippings, narrated by the reporters and by Dan himself.

> The many friends of Mr. Dan Quinlan, of this city, will be pleased to learn of this gentleman's rapid progress in minstrelsy. Dan started out with Barlow, Wilson, Primrose & West's minstrels as a musician. . . . Step by step Dan has worked himself up from a bashful, giddy musician to property man and then at last to great and flowery interlocutor, large button hole bouquet in his coat, large diamond in his shirt bosom, propounding interrogations for the funny end-men. He will be a manager one of these days. No wonder he is envied by his Elmira chums.

Then he moves up a notch:

> Dan has been engaged as interlocutor and stage manager and is to receive a very fine salary. He started in the minstrel line four years ago and has steadily forged to the front until he is now recognized as one of the best interlocutors and most successful stage managers in the business. Money as well as fame is now coming his way. Dan is one of the brightest young men that ever went out from Elmira. . . . There is an evident air of refinement and culture about Quinlan which popularizes him everywhere.

BACK IN ELMIRA, Handsome Dan was the Victorian father keeping his daughters chaste. On the road, he was "the ladies' idol," according to one newspaper. "A modern Adonis," says another. "Handsome and debonair." No wonder he didn't want any of his daughters to marry. He lived a sexually free life on the road, then returned to police them: he wasn't going to allow them to lead the life he did. As I read through his clippings, I wonder how many lovely women of the road mentioned in his clippings were his companions over the years. Who did "the ladies' idol" prefer? Did he choose "the charming comedienne," Miss Lizzie Derious? Or the "pretty, vivacious, imperious and petulant" Miss Rose Whipfer, who played Ernestine to his Captain Amesfort in *The Loan of a Lover*? What about Myrtle McLoughland, who might have stirred his patriotism as "The Goddess of Liberty?" Or perhaps he felt the need to protect Maybelle Adams, "The Waif Violinist."

Dan could keep his different identities and roles separated, living his wandering actor's life for ten months of the year, living the role of father and Elmira citizen for the remaining two. During his road life, he could be sure that my grandmother and her mother and sisters were raising his six daughters. Perhaps that is one reason why the one song he includes in his scrapbook is titled "A Little Wife Waiting at Home." "Go where you will, you'll find no place that's like your own fireside / With wife to greet you at the door, to smooth your cares away." "My sentiments exactly!" Dan wrote in the margins.

I KNEW my mother was afraid of Handsome Dan but I don't think I understood quite how destructive a presence he was for his daughters until I came across a letter my aunt Geraldine wrote to her sister Margaret in 1947. Geraldine was the daughter who stayed home, teaching at Elmira College, taking financial responsibility for her younger sisters during the Depression when her father was living at home, by then unemployed. Her meager salary from the college ($2,200 throughout the 1930s) would have had to support both parents and provide for household expenses. Margaret was the one who'd escaped, leaving Elmira for medical school, marriage, and eventually residence in Los Angeles—about as far away as you could get.

Margaret had accused Geraldine of being bossy, taking on her father's imperiousness, and Geraldine gave her an eloquent (and painful) answer:

> As to my "compulsion to play my father's role," I feel that was true only when I did it against him, himself, to free the younger three so far as I could, from the tyranny we had known. How else do you suppose they had as normal lives as they did? If ever I took on a self-assumed Voice of the Family, I had to so they could have any lives at all and if then, it spread to other situations, that was the price I paid for getting myself in such a spot. It is hard for you to understand what has really gone on at 531 all these years because as you say you've been out of it.

I think it's likely that even with Geraldine's protection, Handsome Dan's "tyranny" increased throughout the 1920s and 1930s, when my mother would have been a teenager. He was home almost all the time then. His acting career, in decline since the late teens, had ended completely by the mid-1920s. While he was losing power in the outside world he would have been spending more and more time at home, ultimately dependent on Geraldine's income, and according to my mother insistent upon "ruling the roost."

WHEN I first began recovering my grandfather's story, I was fascinated by his public, performing self. After discovering Geraldine's letter, I wanted to know more about the aging Dan; I wondered if his tyranny might be connected with his loss of power in the outside world. His scrapbook couldn't tell me this story: it ends with scores of blank pages, his last clipping dating from 1916.

To find out more about the story of Handsome Dan in decline I decided to call up the Elmira court house, hoping that his will might tell me something. The clerk sent me the contents of his file—no will, but a copy of a complicated court case from 1911 involving life insurance. In 1903, the year he formed "Quinlan and Wall" and thought he was headed for brilliance, Dan had taken out an insurance policy naming his wife and six daughters as beneficiaries. His 1911 petition to the court was to remove his daughters as beneficiaries and to name his wife, Margaret, the sole beneficiary.

In order to have the insurance policy unencumbered, dispensing with his children as beneficiaries and so making it more easily convertible to cash, he and my grandmother both had to attest to his dubious earning power as an aging actor. They both read, and signed, the following document:

> Daniel Quinlan is an actor by profession, and his income is derived solely from what he is able to earn in his profession, and the amount is so fluctuating and uncertain as to cause this Petitioner [Margaret Quinlan, his wife] to entertain grave fears that it may prove insufficient for the comfortable support of herself and her children. Moreover Daniel Quinlan is of the age of 50 years and is beyond the age of his greatest earning capacity and is fast approaching the time when he will be obliged to retire his acting profession. Moreover, all of his six children are wholly dependent on their father for their support, education, and maintenance. . . .

This is a different man from the Handsome Dan of the scrapbook—the young man on the rise to fame, the famous interlocutor with the diamond pin, the nationally renowned minstrel man, here a husband and father admitting that he could not be counted on to support his six daughters and his wife, an actor admitting that his career was over. It must have

77

Profile of Handsome Dan, late 1920s

been humiliating. This is the father that my mother, then four years old, would grow up with; this is the father from whose "tyranny" her sister Geraldine tried to protect her, as she gradually took over the role of family breadwinner.

My detective work complete, I realize how far he had slid back down in his later life, reduced, finally, to a dependent. He continued to play the role of the elegant retired actor, living off his former fame at the Elks Club, his "haunt," according to my mother, where he'd adjourn every afternoon to "hoist a few." Known as an accomplished orator—he had a reputation for wit and eloquence—Dan's latter-day theatrical moments included Flag Day orations in upstate New York small towns and leading the Fourth of July parade in Elmira.

But these were small potatoes. He wanted a job as an announcer with the local radio station, and he always held it against my father—the advertising manager—that he was never given so much as an audition, even though my father had nothing to do with it. The up-and-coming new station wanted nothing to do with an aging vaudeville actor, his voice filled with the rotund tones and flowery speech of the last century. He must have felt the loss of his power and freedom keenly, but he could never have told anyone this—certainly not his wife or daughters, and maybe not even himself.

During the Depression he seemed, remarkably, to have found employment again—a mysterious job with a local business which never seemed to give him any money. "I give it away," he would tell his wife and daughters. "We should be helping the poor and disadvantaged of our community." Every morning he would dress up to the nines, pick up his gold-handled walking stick from the umbrella rack in the hall, and stroll grandly out of this house. "Off to the office," he would say, but he never let the family know exactly where the office was.

One day my aunt Ruth and my cousin Bob—Margaret's twelve-year-old son, visiting from California—decided to follow him. "We trailed him for a few blocks," Bob told me a few years ago, "hiding behind parked cars, watching him stop to chat with old-timers. He bought a copy of the *Star-Gazette* and settled on a park bench to read. He stayed there for hours."

They never spoke about their discovery, letting the old man think his last performance had succeeded, once more, in keeping his family in the dark.

Danny Boy

As the last glance of Ireland faded into the mist
Each one fought back tears and felt strangely alone.
  —"The Emigrant's Daughter," traditional Irish air

SOME PEOPLE BELIEVE that the untold stories of your ancestors get passed down in your blood and bones, generation after generation, without your even knowing it. You can feel your great-great-grandfather's sorrow, you can dream your great-grandmother's dreams. In her study of children of Holocaust survivors, *No Voice Is Ever Wholly Lost,* Louise Berkinow finds that the silenced stories of the parents and grandparents show up in the children's dreams, as well as shape their waking lives. In his beautiful memoir of the Armenian holocaust, *The Black Dog of Fate,* Peter Balakian writes that when he was twelve years old he had a nightmare which—years later—he realized was the record of his grandmother's pain.

I am one of these believers: I think that we inherit our ancestors' emotional histories, particularly their unexpressed stories of suffering, exile, and yearning. It's only recently that the Irish and Irish Americans have begun to name the Famine as a holocaust-like devastation, to construct memorials, and to begin to remember. As a result of the Famine, the population of Ireland dropped from eight million to five million within a few years; everywhere was death, starvation, and forced emigration. From what we know of trauma now, it's clear that both those who stayed in Ireland and those who left, never to return to their homeland, were marked emotionally and psychologically, and that inheritance has to have marked their children and grandchildren. Jews and Poles and other groups that came from eastern Europe thought of themselves as immigrants, but the Irish, as historian Matthew Frye Jacobsen tells us, considered themselves "exiles," cut off from a homeland they did not want to leave and to which they longed to return. I'm a great-grandchild of famine immigrants, so the sources of loss and exile seem very far away. How could any of this far-off Irish suffering or yearning for home ever have been passed on to my generation? And yet I think it has been. That is why I keep being drawn back to Ireland, wanting to uncover more of the story of the past. And maybe that's why, when I was twelve years old, I did something very out of character: I chose to play "Danny Boy" on the flute in the Belmont Kiwanis Club talent show in 1957.

⟡HIS DECISION seemed to come out of nowhere. I was just completing the seventh grade, and I'd been playing the flute since fourth grade. I was not a musical star. I didn't even particularly like the flute. But one day I saw an advertisement in the *Belmont Herald*—"Tryouts for Kiwanis Club Talent Show, ages 11–15, Saturday morning 9–12"—and I knew I was going to go. My parents had nothing to do with this strange decision. In fact, they were perplexed.

It wasn't like me to want to perform on stage. I was shy. I didn't like musical recitals before large groups of people. I wasn't that good at flute. I was fourth chair in the Junior High band, and there were only five flutes. The fifth flute was Martha Kremsky, and she had a cleft palate that made it hard for her to get a clean tone.

My mother had arranged for me to have flute lessons with Mr. Knight, a courtly, white-haired gentleman who arrived at my house every Thursday at 5:00. I'd have practiced frantically for the half hour before he arrived, and viewed his appearance with dread. He was patient and kind and disappointed, and I knew he should be doing better things with his life than teaching flute to untalented seventh graders. He was surprised—maybe shocked—when I told him the news. "I'm going to try out for the Kiwanis Club talent show."

"On the flute?"

"Yes."

"What are you going to play for your tryout?" he asked, rifling mentally through all the music I had butchered.

"Danny Boy," I said. I had discovered the song in the book of flute music we were using, which said it was a "traditional Irish air." "Danny Boy"—the most famous Irish ballad—felt like my own personal discovery. Mr. Knight had not assigned it. My parents, neither of whom could carry a tune, had never sung it or even mentioned it. I didn't know the song's history, or its evoking the Famine and emigration. All I knew was that the phrase "Irish air" had popped out of the flute book at me.

81

My mother was the parent who maintained the thread of connection to the Irish past, slender as it was. I'd only heard the word "Famine" in connection with my great-grandparents' emigration: "All your great-grandparents came over during the Famine," my mother had told me, and I just assumed this was a time when people were hungry. I knew we were Irish, and that my mother was proud of that. She gave me a biography of St. Patrick for my tenth birthday, and always had us dress in green on St. Patrick's Day; sometimes she bought us green-tinged carnations for our lapels. Sometimes she'd refer to "the ould sod" in an affectionately comic way, and every spring she'd go off to the annual banquet of the Daughters of the Potato Famine, where I assumed everyone just ate potatoes.

Otherwise there weren't many signs of Irish culture in our family. No cuisine, no language, no folklore, no reminiscences. No one in the family had ever been to Ireland, and my parents—who rarely ventured out of New England—had no plans to go there. My grandparents, the children of immigrants, might well have had stories of Ireland to pass on, but they were all long dead.

So we didn't have much in the way of history. Just a few scraps of the Irish past that my mother kept alive, often through corny stage Irish business, like waking us up on St. Patrick's Day with her fake Irish brogue "Top o' the mornin' to ye" or referring to how the Irish loved their "wee drop." And there was her misty-eyed longing when she heard an Irish tenor singing on the Lawrence Welk Show. "Listen to that voice," she would say, "the soul of Ireland in it."

On the surface, it might seem that my mother's love for things Irish was superficial and sentimental—the kind of Irish American infatuation with leprechauns, green beer, and tourist-trade visions of an enchanted "Emerald Isle" that native Irish people can't stand. The year I lived in Dublin, it was always embarrassing to see the Irish American tourists through Irish eyes, men clad in bright green sweaters and cloth caps, women wearing "Kiss Me I'm Irish" buttons, all speaking in loud American accents and asking directions to the book of Kells, which they would gaze at for a few seconds. The Americans wanted to claim Ireland as their own, and the Irish would be annoyed by this presumption—the tourists wanted the stage Irish version of Ireland they'd brought with them from the States, a landscape at once mythic and kitschy.

And yes, my mother's Irish affinity was partly that—because those forms and stereotypes were what American culture gave her, absent the family connections that had been severed by emigration, to connect back to her Irish past.

But I think there was something deeper and more powerful in my mother's yearning for Ireland, below the surface of shillelaghs and Irish blessings. She would tell, many times, the one story that gives us the link to emigration and the Famine: the story of my great-grandmother Moira Castles's trip across the Atlantic, all by herself, when she was only eight years old, landing in New York to go in search of cousins in Albany. Moira became "Grandma Doherty" in my mother's narrative, her mother's mother, who lived with the family until she died in 1910. So my mother had *known* the woman who came over on the boat by herself; that woman had told her the story, and my mother had passed it on to us. So when she sent us those St. Patrick's Day cards in the green envelopes or smiled dreamily to Bing Crosby's rendition of "When Irish Eyes Are Smiling," she was traveling back to a homeland left behind, at once imaginary and real.

When I chose "Danny Boy" I didn't know that although the music was Irish, the words had been composed by an Englishman long after my great-grandparents had left Ireland. I didn't know that the speaker is a mother addressing her emigrant son. He is leaving Ireland, probably to emigrate to America:

> Oh Danny boy, the pipes, the pipes are calling
> From glen to glen, and down the mountain side
> The summer's gone, and all the flowers are dying
> 'Tis you, 'tis you must go and I must bide.

When I read the lyrics now it's clear that the speaker is longing for the son's return to Ireland.

> But come ye back when summer's in the meadow
> Or when the valley's hushed and white with snow
> 'Tis I'll be here in sunshine or in shadow
> Oh Danny boy, oh Danny boy, I love you so.

When I was twelve I thought the speaker was the one who was in America, looking back at Ireland, the one who had left, not the one who had stayed. I thought the yearning in the song came from the Irish American exile, yearning to go back to the land of glens and pipes and valleys hushed

Flute performance, 1957

and white with snow. And this is how the song was often interpreted in America, while in Ireland it could be used to express the grieving for the emigrants.

The imagined land of pipes and glens was the Ireland my mother wanted to find. Hers was not the Ireland of the Famine; it was a mystic far-off place that was full of wonder. A place my mother always talked about, but had never seen, and knew she never would see. It seemed a kind of paradise to her, and through her, to me.

My father drove me to Daniel Butler Elementary School for the try-out. I went by myself; my friends were not interested in the talent show, so this was a solo venture. I tried out in front of three judges, playing "Danny Boy," making all the notes even though my tone wasn't that good, particularly on the high B flat. Five days later I received a letter: I was a finalist, and I'd go on stage in the Belmont High assembly hall along with nine other acts.

While I waited backstage for my turn, I saw the other kids were going to be lip-synching to rock 'n' roll, playing the drums, twirling batons, doing all this *cool* stuff. I felt like a fuddy-duddy, my hair all curled by my mother, wearing my purple cotton dress with the starchy petticoat: why couldn't I look like Sally, about to dance to "Jailhouse Rock," dressed in turquoise leotards and wearing lots of glittery eye makeup? Or Carol, the head drum majorette, in her white boots with tassels and skirted white uniform with gold epaulettes and pancake makeup that gave her skin a healthy bronze glow? Here I was with my pale Irish skin and freckles, no lipstick, holding a flute, standing off by myself while the other contestants twirled and jumped and pranced. Why on earth was I doing this?

I remember little about my performance, except that it wasn't very good. Breathy, and probably flat on the high notes. But I got through it, and people applauded. I came in eighth. It didn't really matter. My ego wasn't involved. I knew my stock in coolness at Belmont Junior High was not going to rise as a result of this evening. I'd been given a mission and I'd carried it out. I didn't have to excel, I just had to play "Danny Boy" on the flute, in front of a lot of people.

Those were the rules.

A Nice Irish Catholic Girl

Q. Besides depriving the sinner of everlasting grace, what else does mortal sin do to the soul?

A. Mortal sin deprives the soul of the right to everlasting happiness in heaven, and makes it deserving of everlasting punishment in hell.

—*The Baltimore Catechism* (1953)

Sharon's First Communion, 1952

I TOOK CATHOLICISM SERIOUSLY. I wasn't pious and I didn't love God, but I believed everything the Church taught. Motivated by guilt, fear, and the need to please, I went to Mass every Sunday with my parents and to confession twice a month, where I fabricated sins for convenience (*Forgive me Father, for I have sinned. I disobeyed my parents twice and I lied once*). I memorized the Baltimore Catechism, which consisted of questions asked by some anonymous source and answers you were supposed to give the nuns. I became a Catholic Youth Organization leader and received a dictionary, first prize for the First Communion Catechism test. I collected Catechism prizes the way I collected merit badges and A's. I wanted to do well.

The kids who went to Catholic school were always wilder than the Catholics who went to public school—so much exposure to authority sparked rebellion. The Catholic school kids partied and drank and made out in the back of the bus on CYO ski trips when the lights were out, priest sitting right up front, and then they'd say "Good night, Father," nice as pie, and show up at Mass the next day.

I was in awe of those kids, but I couldn't emulate them. I got my doses of Catholicism at Sunday Mass and Monday afternoon Catechism, which may not seem like much, but it really took hold of me: the authority that comes and goes can be harder to defy than the authority that's around you all the time.

The first question in the Baltimore Catechism is "Who made us?" and the answer is "God made us." The second question: "Why did God make us?" The answer: "God made us to know, love, and serve him in this world and to be happy with him in the next." I hid from everyone the fact that although I could memorize the words in the Catechism, I could not feel them at all.

I did not, in fact, love God. I didn't even know him. And how could I be happy with him in heaven? With this invisible stranger?

$\mathcal{K}$IDS IN MY catechism class used to plague the nuns with hypothetical problems. If you died in a state of mortal sin, you were supposed to go straight to hell. Clear enough. Then somebody like Tommy Murphy would complicate things with a real stumper. "But sister, suppose a man who'd committed a mortal sin was on his way to confession, and was hit by a car, and when he recovered he had amnesia, and didn't even *remember* that he'd committed a mortal sin in his past life. And then he lived a holy life until he died. Would he still go to hell, sister?" Or, in connection with the obligation to receive the sacrament of confession at least once a year: "Sister, what if someone was on a cruise to Australia, and on the 365th day they went to the priest to make a confession, but they'd just crossed the international date line and it was really the 366th day, would that be a sin, sister?"

The one time I plagued the nuns I was really troubled, not trying to trip them up. I was really troubled about heaven. Not only did I not really love God, but I didn't feel attracted to heaven. Of course it was better than purgatory, which I imagined as a long line of people on an endless tread-mill, walking and walking but never getting anywhere, and of course better than hell, which was a lot of people living inside flames being tormented by devils, who would pierce them with pitchforks whenever they tried to escape.

But heaven seemed so *vague*. I couldn't picture it. What I really wanted to know was: how was I going to find my parents if we didn't have bodies anymore? "Sister, if we're just spirits, how can we ever recognize anyone?" I imagined myself a wandering spirit, endlessly roaming through heaven, looking for my parents, lonely and lost in the huge crowds of dead people— if everybody who'd died since Adam and Eve was milling around, heaven more crowded than Filene's Basement on Saturday morning, how could I possibly find my family, particularly now that they were invisible?

"God takes care of everything," the nun said, a most unsatisfying answer.

The one lesson in the Baltimore Catechism that really wormed its way into my soul was the one on sin. The different levels of sin were illustrated by milk bottles. I can still see them today: a pure white milk bottle on the left, illustrating the cleansed soul after baptism or confession; a gray-ing milk bottle in the middle filled with spotty, disgusting milk, the soul stained with venial sin; and on the right, a midnight black milk bottle, the soul after mortal sin, headed straight to hell. Venial sins were the misde-meanors of Catholicism—lying, cheating on a test, eating before Commu-nion, talking back to your parents. Mortal sins were the felonies. Many things were mortal sins: adultery, murder, stealing a lot of money, having sex before marriage. I would probably be one of the few young women who went off to Radcliffe in the sixties convinced that sex was a mortal sin and knowing that dating was what the Church called an "occasion of sin" because you could be tempted to go "all the way," which was definitely a mortal sin and would turn your soul into the solid black milk bottle and mean that you'd go straight to hell if you died before you could get to confession.

It never occurred to me to question the authority of the Church. I'd been programmed by all those Q's and A's. The Baltimore Catechism asked *me* questions; I didn't get to ask any back. There was no option, then, of the kind of "cafeteria" Catholicism that evolved after Vatican II, with Catholics rejecting some beliefs of the Church and still considering themselves Cath-olics. Vatican II changed everything: if the Church decided that eating meat on Friday was no longer a sin, then people began to wonder . . . so who gets to say what's a sin? Fifties Irish Catholics—more deferential to church authority than Italian Catholics—did not ask that question.

I worked hard at being a nice Catholic girl. "Nice" was the adjective my mother seemed to apply only to Catholics, as when she'd praise some "nice Catholic girl" who obeyed her mother instead of sneaking around the way I did, or wonder why I didn't find some "nice Catholic boy" to date, instead of the outsiders I turned up with. I knew what a nice Catholic girl was: someone like Katherine Monahan, who lived across the street and went to the 6:45 A.M. Mass *every day* during Lent, said the rosary every night, and never missed the novenas for St. Francis. One Lent I almost made it through those 6:45 A.M. Masses, sure I was impressing my parents with my piety, not telling them I was praying to make cheerleader at the April tryouts. I consoled myself with the vision of a visit to Henry's Bakery right after church, the windows all steamy in the early morning light, the smell of fresh bread and doughnuts enveloping you in a warm cloud as you opened the door. I'd kneel while the priest was going through the Credo, telling the ritual story of Christ's suffering and death, and I'd be wondering if I'd choose the honey-dipped doughnuts or the iced raisin rolls. No one could read my thoughts: niceness was a performance, niceness was what other people could see.

Now I wonder whether niceness is one of the sources of women's higher rates of depression.

When I ask my women's studies students to define "nice," most will say it means "bland," or "not rocking the boat," or "just being on the surface," or "conforming." "You can be a nice girl," one student wrote, "or maybe a nice woman, but you'd never say 'She's a really nice feminist.' I just don't think you can couple that adjective with anything that challenges authority."

I think she's right. It used to be said that one cause of depression was anger turned inward. I would add that depression can stem from *any* deep emotion that gets suppressed—any feeling that isn't "nice," like anger or grief or sorrow or desire.

When I think back, the word "nice" never turned up in the Baltimore Catechism. Jesus never said "Only the nice shall enter the Kingdom of Heaven," or "faith, hope, love, and niceness, but the greatest of these is niceness." I memorized the corporal acts of mercy: *to feed the hungry, to give drink to the thirsty, to shelter the homeless, to clothe the naked, to visit the sick, to visit those in prison, to bury the dead.* Those are good things to do. *To be a nice girl* wasn't on the list.

Catholicism as I experienced it wasn't about the corporal acts of mercy. It wasn't about social justice or spirituality. It was about accepting dogma. And you either accepted everything, or you weren't a Catholic at all. Being a Catholic was an either/or proposition, just like being a member of my family. You either toed the line and belonged, as Kevin and I did, or you rebelled and got thrown out, like Maureen. You want to have your own opinions? Follow your own inclinations? Experience *the other thing?* Fine, stay out in the cold.

I used to envy my older sister. I wanted to have been a defiant one. What bravery, what independence, for Maureen to have followed her own path, ignored the Church and stood up to my parents! She took niceness, rolled it up into a ball, and threw it out the window. Why couldn't I have done that too?

Now I'm not so hard on my younger self. Given the choices church and family offered her—conforming or exile—being a nice girl was a rational choice. Protective coloration, keeping her safe until she found the courage to change.

A Town of Homes

It has been no idle boast over the years that our beautiful town is so truly called a Town of Homes. This description of the Town has attracted thousands of fine property owners and tax payers who come here to escape the evils of loose zoning in other cities and towns. . . .

—Belmont *Citizen*, March 9, 1951

THE WALLPAPER IN MY PARENTS' BEDROOM had the same pattern as in my room—apple blossoms on the verge of decline. Hundreds of browning apple blossoms marched up and down the light green wallpaper in my bedroom, up and down the deep blue wallpaper in my parents' room, more overwhelming there because the dark background seemed to push them right into your face. You were choked by apple blossoms. Looking closer, you could see that the wallpaper was growing stained and spotted, and beginning to buckle and peel near the seams. In the living room, dining room, sun room, the story was the same—dark, patterned wallpaper growing dingier and shabbier over the years.

When I ask my friends if they remember the house I grew up in, they always say the same thing. "It was so *dark*. And that wallpaper . . ."

"I know," I'd say. "Made you feel like a prisoner."

MY MOTHER had been proud of this wallpaper when it was new. In 1950 the landlords decided to redecorate and told my mother she could choose the paper for every room from a set of patterns they had sanctioned, all of which seemed to have featured dark backgrounds. In addition to the apple blossom patterns, my mother chose a grey color with yellow flowers for the dining room, green for the living room, and a patterned beige for the sunroom. Kevin got a white, maroon, yellow, and black plaid for his bedroom.

This luxurious moment of leafing through books of samples allowed my mother to become the woman she wanted to be, a woman who had the power to choose new wallpaper. A woman who did not have to think about money and scarcity and where the children's new clothes would come from. A woman who could make her house beautiful, matching the houses in women's magazines like *House Beautiful* and *Good Housekeeping.*

EXCEPT THAT 28 Lewis Road wasn't my mother's house. My parents were tenants in 1950, and they would stay tenants throughout the 1950s and 1960s and 1970s, while everyone around them was buying houses, too afraid or too poor to take the risk of a mortgage. My mother did not leave 28 Lewis until 1980, five years after my father died, when she moved to an apartment in the less prestigious Waverley Square area.

WHEN MY mother first moved to Belmont in 1945, she would naturally have expected that one day, perhaps quite soon—since my father had such a good job—they would leave their Lewis Road apartment in a two-family home and buy one of the single-family homes that dominated the local landscape, securing their place in the Town of Homes. The area in which we lived—called Payson Park—had several streets of two-family homes, dating back to the early twentieth century, when Belmont was still allowing multifamily housing to be built close to the streetcar lines. The usual pattern on Lewis Road when my parents moved there was for the homeowner to rent out the other apartment to a young family who would stay for two or three years and then buy a house. Staying on for decades as a renter in Belmont—so close to those who had succeeded!—kept my mother's disappointments keen. It's hard to be on the threshold of a better life and not be able to cross over, particularly when many of the upwardly mobile Belmont homeowners in the 1950s and 1960s were Irish (as well as Italian, Greek, Jewish, and Polish). The town fathers were for the most part descended from Yankee stock, but the new homeowners of the postwar period did not have to hearken back to the Mayflower: they just had to be able to afford to buy a house in Belmont.

OVER TIME, my father's inability to buy my mother a house became the unspoken sign of his economic failure. When they attended a Harvard reunion, my mother would always return talking about the men who made "big bucks" as lawyers or businessmen, men who gave their wives "carte blanche to redecorate" their homes, every word an implicit reproach to my father, who only made enough money to keep her in a rented apartment with darkening wallpaper.

"They live in one of those big houses on Belmont Hill," she might tell us after one reunion, referring to another Harvard '27 couple, "on *Rutledge Road.*" Belmont Hill was the priciest part of town, and Rutledge Road the priciest part of Belmont Hill. "Mrs. Baxter was very nice, really, she invited me over to see their house and garden."

"You should go, Jeannie," my father said.

"Of course I won't go."

"Why not?" he asked, innocent.

"Oh Norb, really. I could never have her back. How on earth could I invite her over *here?*"

IT WAS INDEED impossible to imagine the wife of a successful Harvard graduate, living in an elegant house on Belmont Hill, walking up the steps to our modest apartment. I used to be angry when my mother made such statements—they were sharp rebukes to my father, the inadequate breadwinner, and I always silently took his side. Now I have more sympathy for my mother, who was also brought down by my father's economic fall, and was even more helpless than he to control the family's economic fate. It wasn't the money she wanted, it was the home, the beautiful home American advertising was promising every middle-class fifties housewife. She had grown up in a house her parents owned: now, throughout her married life, she was living in a rented space. This wasn't what was supposed to happen in the fifties, when not only middle-class but also working-class families made the leap from renting to owning.

BUYING A SINGLE-FAMILY home in the suburbs during this period was practically a patriotic act, a way of celebrating individualism and capitalism and denouncing Communism. In his famous "kitchen debate" with Nikita Khrushchev in 1959, Richard Nixon pointed out the superiority of capitalism by giving the example of the suburban home—which, with all its conveniences and appliances, was "designed to make things easier for our women." Khrushchev cited military and space technology as evidence of his country's prominence, but Nixon trumped him with color televisions and washing machines and houses like the one on display before them, a model of the kind of home any working American could buy.

Given how anomalous her experience must have seemed my mother would not have had the words to describe her disappointment and loss. She would have experienced our family story as isolated, perhaps even as deviant. In *Falling from Grace,* Katherine Newman observes that our culture has no stories for middle-class people who descend the economic ladder, since upward mobility is the required narrative. So those middle-class Americans who, like my parents, "fall from grace" into unemployment, lesser jobs, and diminished income "often mourn in isolation," she writes. If you fall from grace as a middle-class person, ending up renting an apartment your whole life with aging wallpaper instead of buying a house in a town of homes, you lose not only your former income and expectations, but also what Katherine Newman calls "your place in the social landscape." And if this loss occurs during a period when the economy is expanding, not shrinking, it can be all the harder to bear.

The wallpaper tells the story of my mother's lost social landscape. "Remember that awful wallpaper?" my siblings and I would ask each other years later. "Why didn't they ever get rid of it?" I think I know why. The landlord did not offer to replace it and my parents would not spend money to improve a rented house. And so they stayed in a house where the walls emanated depression and gloom. For a while my mother dreamed of a house with a modern kitchen and gleaming walls and shiny floors. And then she stopped dreaming. It was too late.

FROM THE VANTAGE point of Irish upward mobility, my parents had chosen well when they originally selected an apartment in a two-family house in Belmont, a gentry-class suburb where the triple-deckers you now find all over Charleston or South Boston were outlawed in the early twentieth century—too likely to bring in working-class ethnic renters to what the town fathers wanted to maintain as an upper-middle-class "town of homes" and homeowners. My mother hated the town fathers, the men who controlled the Board of Selectmen, the School Board, and the Zoning Board, railing at them when we were growing up, calling them "stingy, greedy bastards," as when they refused to allot money for a new high school band room. "Where do they come off," she'd say, "making you kids rehearse in that *hovel* of a place while they go home to count their money." I was always surprised by her anger, since I didn't mind rehearsing in the basement room with the clanking pipes, but now it makes sense: her anger about inferior housing coursed through her life, bubbling up at any opportunity. Later she would rage about Belmont's inferior and scanty housing developments for the elderly. My mother always refused to live in them. "Rat holes," she said. "They didn't put *two cents* into those buildings. They have the nerve to put up those little boxes and call them *housing?* Typical of Belmont."

*T*HE APARTMENT she was supposed to pass through on her way to somewhere else became a place to live, but it never felt like a home. I always used to wonder what she did during the day when I was in junior high and high school—no more kids at home, no job. She didn't garden or take on house projects, like the other Belmont housewives. She didn't frame any family pictures and place them on top of the piano, or write her favorite recipes on index cards, or sew her own clothes, or knit sweaters, or spend hours making gingerbread houses, as *Family Circle* advised her to do. She didn't really enjoy the domestic life that was supposed to absorb the fifties housewife, and it wasn't until she got her job at the Belmont Library, when I was in college, that she found her means of expression was in matching books with readers, not in matching fabrics.

I ASSUMED THAT over the years she had grown attached to 28 Lewis; after all, she had stayed there until she was forced to move.

"Do you think you'll miss the old apartment?" I asked my mother right before she moved to Thayer Road.

"I *hated* that place," she said, shockingly.

I SOMETIMES WONDER what my mother's life would have been like if my parents had stayed in Elmira and we'd grown up with our aunts and grandmother and cousins a few blocks away. My father would have had his job as marketing manager of the Elmira radio station—he wouldn't have made as much as if he'd been working in New York or Boston, but his salary would have gone a long way in Elmira, and we would have been able to buy a house. If depression had visited him anyway, both my parents would have been in familiar surroundings with friends and relatives close by, and it might not have been so terrifying. I think my father would have enjoyed this quiet, small-city life too. The pace would have been slower than in the big city, and that would have suited his temperament.

But that could not happen, because my father was succeeding. The job he was offered at a Hartford radio station in 1936 could not be turned down: it was a promotion, and Hartford was what the trade would call a "bigger market." Then New York could not be turned down, or Boston—more promotions, more money, bigger markets. My father was following the path of professional mobility. It would have been unthinkable for a man of his education and professional ability to turn down a promotion and a raise, just so he and his family could stay in a place where they had roots.

I am quite sure that it never occurred to my mother to say, when my father received his promotion to Hartford, "but Norb, what about staying in Elmira?" Just as they did on the Overland Trail, wives were supposed to follow their husbands through job changes in postwar America, moving geographically as they moved upward economically, leaving behind relatives and community, headed for modern kitchens and new appliances, headed for the suburbs, headed for happiness in a town of single-family homes.

My mother would have followed my father willingly: she had so much to look forward to.

A FEW years ago when I was up in Boston visiting my sister, I drove down Lewis Road for memory's sake, and saw—to my shock—that the front door had been painted blue. Didn't they realize it was supposed to be cream-colored forever? The new owner, I'd been told, had decided to live downstairs, in our former apartment, and rent out the upstairs. I'd also heard that she had renovated the place.

I had to see for myself, so I stopped and knocked on the door, rehearsing my apologetic "I'm sorry to bother you, but I grew up here. . . ."

"Do you want a tour?" she asked.

"Yes, thank you."

"Come in, I'll show you around."

The house was beautiful. The basic structures were the same, but everything was different. The woman had transformed our sad, dark apartment into a place I could imagine myself living in—white walls, bare wood floors, sky lights, plants. It was filled with sun. Everything shone.

My parents' bedroom had become an office with light pine floors, creamy walls, a teak desk, a red couch and matching chair, bright Navajo rugs, and a blue enamel woodstove where the vanity used to be. The mirror and the closet were gone, replaced by wood bookshelves filled with psychology books, spiritual reading, baskets, and pottery.

"I'm a therapist," the woman explained. "I see my clients here."

96

Somehow, in a weird way, it all made sense.

*Y*OU'LL NEVER guess," I told my sister later that day. "The house is *gorgeous* and she is doing therapy in their *bedroom*."

"Too late," Maureen said. "She should have been there when we were growing up."

The Bedroom

The heart that has truly loved
Never forgets
But as truly loves
On to the close.
—THOMAS MOORE, "Believe Me if All Those Endearing Young Charms"

I LOVED IT WHEN MY PARENTS DROPPED HINTS about their lives in New York City in the late thirties and early forties, when my brother and sister were little, my father a hotshot radio man, my mother a black-haired beauty. They'd talk about people dropping over for dinner, about going to Broadway plays, about the fun they had with their "crowd," the other young marrieds in the same Bronx apartment building. "This was before you were born, Sharon," they'd say, and I'd be so jealous. I'd missed out on my parents' golden years. In Belmont no one ever dropped over for dinner; in fact, no one came to dinner at all, except when relatives visited. My parents rarely went out. There was no "crowd." I was jealous of Maureen and Kevin for having had these younger parents.

Every family is a mystery; every child is a detective. When I was ten I decided that my parents' bedroom held the secret of their vanished and glorious past, and I'd sneak in when they were out and investigate.

The bedroom closet belonged to my mother (my father had been assigned the hall closet for his suits and coats). When I opened the mirrored door I'd breathe in the smell of old wood, lavender sachets, and perfumed talcum powder. (My mother and all the Quinlan aunts used talcum powder in hot weather, sometimes emitting little white puffs when they raised their arms or leaned back to laugh.) The housedresses my mother wore every day were right in front, but these were cotton and what my mother called "ratty," so I plunged into the back, where her "dressy" dresses hung, the ones dating back to her New York life. I remember two: a navy blue silk dress with white buttons and a white belt, and a silvery-pink brocade. I would finger the sleeve of her one and only suit, a grey wool that had belonged to her sister Marion. This was her "going-out" outfit.

On the floor were the hat boxes. I'd pull them out and unwrap the white tissue paper. Inside were small, jaunty hats with black veils, the ones my mother wore to church: black velvet for winter, grey straw for summer. I'd try them both on before the mirror. I liked the way the veil cut across my face, leaving my eyes half-covered and my nose—which I thought a huge disfigurement—nicely hidden by the spidery veil.

Then it was on to the vanity, my favorite place. This held the secrets of my mother's young womanhood and early married years. The vanity told the story of the mysterious eras before I was born: the time when she was the belle of Elmira; then a new bride, living in Manhattan and drinking Manhattans, going to shows, going dancing, going out; and then a new mother, cooking on a shoestring, welcoming friends for dinner, the pot roast would go around.

A huge round mirror bloomed from the back, a circle in which my mother's younger selves perhaps still lingered, caught somewhere in the quicksilver. In the drawers were costume jewelry, delicate gold watches, crumpled kid gloves, programs from long-ago Broadway plays, tickets to forgotten musicals. I'd try on the jewelry and the gloves and look at myself in the mirror, ears stinging from the clip-on earrings, draped with necklaces and pendants, imagining myself sinking into a red velvet seat while the orchestra tuned up.

The top was littered with rouge, lipsticks, and perfume bottles in different colors—straw yellow, amber, honey, peach, rose, bronze. Some bottles were frosted, others clear glass. Some were round, some heart- or flower-shaped, some rectangular, some graceful ovals. Some had spongy circles you had to press to release the scent; others had gilded gold or silver spray caps. The most elegant bottles had little glass stoppers, shaped like fans and turbans and mosques and globes. I'd unscrew the cap or pull out the stopper, mixing perfumes indiscriminately, rubbing my wet fingers on my face and neck, not quite sure what to do.

"Perfume goes on your pulse points," Patty, my most sophisticated sixth-grade friend, told me. I loved the idea that you administered perfume to the places where the throb of your heart came closest to the surface—your temples, your wrists, the hollow in your neck. I imagine the tiny, regular surge of blood in my veins sending out pulses of scent. Patty also told me

99

that perfumes smelled different on different people, and every woman had one special perfume that was her "signature."

What perfume had been my mother's signature? What one would be mine? I wanted to know.

$\mathcal{B}$Y THE TIME I was in high school my parents' bedroom held less magic, but I'd go in there when they were out so I could primp in front of the full-length mirror, the only one in the house. I did not want them to witness my private encounter with—not vanity, since I did not prize the reflection I saw, but my unacknowledged desire to be beautiful.

It seemed then that my mother's perfume bottles were growing dimmer, dustier. Perhaps I was seeing more clearly what had always been there, or perhaps the bottles were aging. Several now had caps missing and the perfume had evaporated, leaving a gummy residue. Other perfumes had darkened with age and the scent had gone off, like bad wine. The only up-to-date scent was Jean Naté, the mass-produced "pour le bain" toilet water of the sixties—piney, innocuous, inexpensive. It came in a huge apple-green plastic dispenser with a black cap, and looked for all the world like an over-size bottle of Phisohex, my miserable anti-acne soap. For my mother to use this bargain-sized toilet water seemed a diminishment: I wanted to have known her when she was playing with her medley of scents, sitting in front of the vanity in her New York apartment, daubing perfume on her pulse points, wearing silk stockings and a brocade dress, about to go out dancing with my father, who was still, then, a handsome Irishman on the rise.

Instead of forbidding me to use lipstick until I was sixteen, that mother would have beckoned me over to the bench. "Sit here," she would have said, patting the space next to her, and then she'd have given me her priceless makeup hints. "Always get toilet water or perfume," she would have said, "the scent of cologne doesn't last, and put little daubs on your pulse points, your wrists, your ankles, your inner elbows, behind your ears, and the hollow of your neck." That mother would have given me my very first bottle of perfume for my fourteenth birthday, and I would have placed it on the dresser top and looked in the mirror to see a girl who might actually be pretty.

When I was in my twenties and thirties, at last freed to collect perfume bottles and boyfriends, I came to connect the darkening perfumes with the untimely ebbing of my parents' sexual life. The vanity had been part of the bedroom suite my parents bought after they were married; its partners were a double bed and a bureau. When I was twelve my mother committed the unforgivable fifties sin of breaking up a bedroom suite: she bought new twin beds for me and my sister, took our hand-me-downs, and gave the double bed away to Goodwill.

I suspect that my mother initiated the change; she made household purchasing decisions. I enjoyed thinking of my mother as repressed (unlike myself, I thought flatteringly).

She must have wanted herself and my father safely ensconced in their twin beds, as chaste and sexless as Lucy and Ricky and Ozzie and Harriet. *Poor Dad, married to a woman who didn't want sex.*

I no longer hold to this self-serving story. But I still believe that the disappearance of the double bed and the entrance of hand-me-down twin beds marked a change in my parents' marriage. Something was ending, and nothing was, as yet, beginning to take its place. Their bedroom—and the life they lived in it—was no longer a place to invest in.

I am sure my parents never discussed the change of furniture, or its significance. One day my mother would have said, "I'm taking the girls shopping today, Norb, for new beds, and I think we should take theirs—after all, they're newer than ours."

"Oh," he would have said, maybe hesitating a little. "Well, this is your department, Jeannie."

And that would have been it.

A few months after they moved to their twin beds, my parents celebrated their twenty-fifth anniversary. My father proudly gave my mother a new stove, and my sister remembers her going into the bedroom, shutting the door, and weeping. I can see her now, throwing herself down on her single bed, perhaps not even knowing where the tears were coming from. My father must have been baffled: my mother loved new appliances, she hated the old stove, and here was a shiny white replacement, all four burners working, two ovens, and even a griddle. He would have been proud of his purchase and waiting for her to clap her hands, her sign of delight, but evidently he had made a terrible mistake.

Now I think I understand my mother's tears. Perhaps she hoped the departure of the double bed would provoke a response; perhaps my father would court her again. For her twenty-fifth anniversary, perhaps he would give her a weekend in the country, or diamond earrings, or an elegant bottle of perfume—some gift to her beauty. But the stove, practical as it was, was a gift for her as mother and housewife, not a gift for her as wife, as woman.

And maybe she also thought *is this all I'm going to get, a new stove? Never to have a house of my own, a beautiful kitchen? All this is going to do is make everything else in the kitchen look worse.*

My mother dried her tears, came out of the bedroom, and put on a brave face. We were all supposed to go out to dinner at the Ritz-Carlton, and go out we did. I remember my father asking my mother to dance, and her accepting. My sister, brother, and I sat at the table, watching our parents dance, the disaster of the stove now forgotten. Perhaps as they moved across the dance floor, holding each other, as they had in many ways through a twenty-five-year marriage, they knew that this marriage and these watching children had been created by the young dancers they had been in their twenties, and they were glad.

WHEN I look back at my parents' marriage from the vantage point of my fifties, I see another story again. Perhaps they didn't have sex as much after those twin beds arrived, but that's not an uncommon pattern for couples married twenty-five years. And—could I possibly be saying this—what's the big deal? Sex isn't everything, and by the time my mother was in her mid-fifties, her own autonomous life was at last taking off. She had started working, reveling in the praise she received at the library; she enjoyed contributing to my father's income, and the two of them tootled all over the New England countryside on their vacations—Vermont for the leaves in the fall, the Maine coast in the summer. They were having fun, as they moved from their fifties into their sixties, probably more fun than they'd had in years, with their routines and their rituals, going back every summer to Thompson's Cottages in New Harbor, then, later, to the Rock Gardens Inn, seeing the same people, developing summer friends, coming home with photographs and stories.

And they had their own quiet love story, which I think resurfaced after we'd all grown up and left and finances were a little better. For their thirty-fifth anniversary in 1971 my father gave my mother an engagement ring, accompanied by a poem.

> So if with me, in later years
> You'd like to stay and linger,
> Please take this ring, a sign of love
> To sparkle on your finger.

Regina and Norbert in Elmira, 1935

My mother would tell the story of the ring over and over after he died, to us and to her friends and, later, confined to her last bedroom, to her final audience for family stories, the hospice nurses. She'd be lying in bed and the nurse would be checking her pulse and temperature, and I'd be watching from the doorway.

"We were so poor when we got married," she would say, "we could only afford the wedding ring, and then for our thirty-fifth anniversary Norb surprised me with *this!*" and she'd wave her left hand, showing off the engagement ring, small diamond sparkling in the light. "I went into the library right after we got back from Maine and said 'Look, everybody, Norb and I are engaged!'"

"How *romantic*," the Irish hospice nurses would say, and my mother would nod and look at the ring and tear up a little, because they hadn't made it to their fortieth, and I'd be listening and feeling proud of parents who got engaged in their sixties.

The Book of Ruth

I've flown from my West
Like a desolate bird from a broken nest,
To learn thy secret of joy and rest.

—ERNEST FENOLLOSA (the epigraph to
The Asian Animal Zodiac, by Ruth Quinlan Sun)

MY AUNT RUTH ALWAYS SEEMED THE OPPOSITE of my housebound mother. World traveler, journalist, writer, teacher, bestower of gifts from far-off lands, she became my mentor and model. Maybe that's why I became so frightened and judgmental when she became depressed: if she was vulnerable, what hope could there ever be for me?

After her husband Norman died, my aunt Ruth—then in her mid-seventies—spun off into a kind of inconsolable grief that after a while seemed indistinguishable from soul-stopping depression. Freud called this "melancholia" and distinguished it from mourning, the natural response to loss that can allow the mourner to return, eventually, to the ongoingness of life and even, at times, to contentment. Melancholia is different: it consumes the self. After Norman's death, all the threads binding Ruth to this world seemed to have snapped.

She wept constantly for weeks after the funeral, for months, for what seemed like years. She visited the grave every day, sometimes twice a day, a time-consuming venture since the cemetery was a half-hour drive over crowded New Jersey roads. I accompanied her a few times. Ruth would throw herself on the ground, her fingers plucking the grass, caressing the stone, tracing the letters NORMAN SUN, keening. "Oh God Norman where are you Norman O God I can't live without you why didyouhavetodieOGodO GodNormanNorman." The keening would go on for several minutes. It was like a force of nature, the grief and abandonment so powerful and archaic that I felt awestruck. The losses of centuries seemed to course through my aunt's frail body. I would wait, silently, off to the side, a witness to this theater of mourning. Coming from a family where grief was stifled, I found it frightening.

Ruth would slowly rise from the grave, and I would take her arm and lead her back to the car. As we drove home, she would sit silently beside me, lost in memory. I would keep silent as well.

Once home, Ruth remained possessed by grief. She didn't sob—that would have been more bearable because you could hope for catharsis. Tears leaked slowly down her cheeks, an endless stream of sorrow. She had no interest in going out. She could only talk about Norman, her speech slurred by sobbing and the effects of a long-ago stroke. When we spoke on the phone I often could not understand what she was saying, but I stopped asking her to repeat herself: her rephrasings were equally incomprehensible. She was speaking a language of her own.

I did not say this to anyone at the time—how could I admit that I couldn't be more compassionate to a bereaved woman in her seventies?— but I found Ruth's presence almost unbearable. I could only stand being around her for limited amounts of time. Once I bolted from a weekend visit after twenty-four hours, speeding down the Pennsylvania Turnpike toward Carlisle through a cloud of excuses, guilt, and relief.

Looking back, I think now that I was also feeling the unacceptable emotion of anger: depressed people can make others furious. *Snap out of it!* I probably wanted to say to Ruth, as others must have wanted to say to me during periods of chronic depression. *Stop wallowing! Everybody has problems! Get a life!* But I didn't say any of these things; I didn't even know I wanted to say them. Instead I offered suggestions: *Find a grief support group: I'll call around for you. Meet a friend for coffee twice a week. Go to lunch at the senior center—I'll take you.* Ruth would look at me, eyes glazed with tears and numbness, uncomprehending. I wasn't speaking her language.

Once I made her come to the Woodbury Senior Center for their daily lunch—"Come on, Ruth, let's go, it'll be good for you to get out." She sat obediently at the table, shoulders hunched, as if warding off invisible blows, while I chirpily introduced us to the elderly ladies around us—all regulars. "And this is my aunt Ruth, who lives in Woodbury. . . ." Ruth nodded silently and took minuscule bites of her egg salad sandwich while I chatted with the ladies. We never went back. Another time I took her to a movie at the Ritz in Philadelphia: again she accompanied me compliantly. "How did you like the movie, Ruth?" I asked her on the way home. "What movie?" she asked. This wasn't memory loss. She had sat beside me, but she hadn't been there. We didn't go to the movies again.

*R*UTH'S CRUMPLING into melancholia surprised me. She had been my most independent and flamboyant aunt. When I was a child, Ruth was my Auntie Mame: her red hair signified her exoticism, as did her acerbic wit and her fondness for expensive cigarette holders. Ruth detested small-town Elmira ("I had to get out," she told me once, "if I'd stayed it would have killed me"), and in the 1940s she divorced her alcoholic Irish husband, left her reporting job at the *Elmira Star-Gazette*, signed up for a master's in Asian studies at the University of Southern California, moved to Los Angeles, and never looked back. There she met Norman Sun, who had left China to study economics at USC before the war broke out and then could not return. They married and moved to Parkville, Missouri, where Norman chaired the economics department at Park College and Ruth taught journalism and creative writing. They traveled in Asia, took Fulbrights together in Thailand in 1957, and in 1959 moved to Tokyo where Norman taught economics at International Christian University and Ruth worked as an editor and journalist. They were best friends, traveling companions, and partners. In later years they each had their own bedroom. "We have assignations," Ruth whispered to me once. "Makes it more fun."

When the offer came from International Christian University, Ruth knew she would miss the home they had just designed and built in Parkville, but it was time to go.

"We'd only been in the house six months," Ruth once told me, "we loved it, but we couldn't turn this down." Then, leaning closer, she gave me the wisdom she wanted to pass on: "Never hesitate to leave the things you love behind at a moment's notice, Sharon," she said, "if you're called to another life. Don't get trapped. Remember, you can just pack up and *go.*"

When I was growing up in the 1950s, the era when women were supposed to stay put in the home, it seemed that Ruth was always packing up and going somewhere. She and Norman would "go abroad," as we then called it, at least twice a year, and after their Fulbright year in Thailand they circled the globe, coming back to Kansas via Australia and Africa.

Throughout the 1950s Ruth sent me dolls from every country in the world, it seemed—from Japan, Thailand, and Burma; from Ireland, France, Italy, Spain, Scotland, Portugal, Morocco. As they sat on my bedroom radiator covers, the dolls spoke to me of the places I might travel; they were the voices of my aunt's wandering soul, urging me to leave home, to go beyond familiar shores. I knew that my mother would never bring me dolls from foreign countries: she hardly left New England, and would never, until the day she died, need a passport.

Ruth also traveled easily in the country my mother held in awe, but never entered—the land of writing and publication. Ruth had earned her master's in journalism and taught "at the *graduate* level," my mother would point out; later she would be an editor at Temple University Press. A freelance journalist, Ruth kept files of her clippings, many representing Asian culture to an isolationist 1950s America. She wrote articles with titles like "Beauty of Ancient Lore Seen in Visit to China," "Hong Kong, the Jade of the Orient," "New World Meets the Old in Ancient Bangkok," "India Observed, Russia Remembered," and "Tokyo—Giant with Growing Pains" that appeared in the *Kansas City Star.*

After her Fulbright year in Vietnam, Ruth turned more to book-length publication. In 1966 she edited a collection of Vietnamese folk tales (*Land of Seagull and Fox*), dedicating it to her Vietnamese students and telling her American readers that she hoped the stories would introduce them to "an incredibly lovely, incredibly beset land." In 1974 she published *The Asian Animal Zodiac,* drawing on folk tales from China, Japan, Korea, Tibet, and Vietnam to illustrate astrological wisdom and dedicating the book to "my family Sun," Norman's parents and, in particular, to "Sun Nien-min (Norman), a scholar, a gentle man, an artist, and a judge of fine wives."

*R*UTH BECAME my literary mentor, writing me encouraging letters when I was in graduate school filled with references to books she'd read and wanted to recommend to me. She read my dissertation all the way through—probably the only person besides my adviser to have done so— and sent me off to talk to a friend of hers, the director of a university press. When I took a part-time teaching job at a local Catholic women's college, Newton College of the Sacred Heart, she cheered me on, thrilled that I was going to be teaching them a course on women writers (a new academic idea in 1970). I was considering *The Second Sex, The Awakening*, and *The Golden Notebook* for my reading list. "Sharon dear, " Ruth wrote, "I approve of all your subversive plans for young Catholic womanhood. Have you read Mary McCarthy's *A Catholic Girlhood?* Do so. I think you've got a really good thing going in that course on women and literature. Gore Vidal has a great thing on women's lib (sympathetic) in the *New York Review of Books*—I'll Xerox and send it to you."

We seemed to be kindred spirits, and when I looked up my sign—year of the Rooster—in Ruth's *Asian Animal Zodiac*, I decided my aunt was passing on more, telling me I would need to be brave.

> People born in the Year of the Rooster are considered to be profound thinkers, although they want to be left alone to do things in their own way. They seem on the surface to be rather adventurous spirits, but there is always a certain insecurity deep within themselves. But when the occasion calls for it, they can reveal real bravery.

I was sure that Ruth must have been born in the year of the Rooster as well, but hers turned out to be the year of the Ram.

> Ram-year people are elegant, well-bred, and endowed with innate good taste. They are also talented and accomplished in the arts. Indeed, these wise and gentle people can live well on the fruits of their own talents. But they are passionate, pessimistic, often puzzled about life. Their passions are not only emotional, but are concerned with everything about which they feel keenly.

It was startling to discover that the only Quinlan sister who shared my sign was my mother, born in 1909—surely Ruth and I had more in common! And besides, my mother's insecurities weren't buried "deep within," they were all over the surface. Maybe Ruth had gotten the rooster's qualities wrong. My mother? Brave? I couldn't see it.

Always Ruth was connected to a larger world—larger than Elmira, larger than the United States. My aunt and uncle took up residence in Woodbury, New Jersey, shortly after I began teaching at Dickinson in 1976. A five-bedroom house in a secluded, woody grove became their retirement home. College professors, scholars, and writers would be frequent guests, and visiting Asian poets and scholars were often in residence. I would sometimes stop off in Woodbury on my way back to Boston for Christmas, and I'd be amazed by the number of Christmas cards they received, cards from all over the world, hundreds of cards with strange foreign stamps, stamps in unusual colors—amber, plum, peacock blue, stamps of temples and shrines, of wildebeests and koalas, of remote waterfalls and strange vegetation, stamps of mustachioed, unfamiliar statesmen.

$\mathcal{A}$CCORDING TO O'Brien family mythology, largely created by my mother, I resembled Ruth physically. (This comparison rankled because—also according to family mythology—Ruth was one of the less attractive Quinlan sisters, while my mother was a beauty.) I was also viewed as Ruth's kindred spirit because, like my traveling aunt, I was the exotic in the family, the one who left home and returned with non–Irish Catholic tastes. I'd lived for a year in England and another in Ireland, I traveled to Europe in the summers and came back with tags of foreign airlines on my luggage, offbeat presents, and new recipes to which I stayed committed for several months.

Eventually my enthusiasms would fade, to be replaced by others, and my mother would say, with mixed pride and criticism, "I can never keep up with you, Sharon, what will you be into next?" I insisted on fresh garlic for cooking, not my mother's garlic powder, and I favored dangly earrings, jeans with silk shirts, wines with names like "fumé blanc," red leaf lettuce instead of iceberg, runny blue cheeses instead of the orthodox cheddars the O'Briens favored, half and half instead of milk.

While my exotic habits were developing, my mother must have felt judged every time I came home for a visit and opened the refrigerator. "Mom, is this Chablis the only wine you have? What happened to that Italian wine I left here last time? Do you have any seltzer? Any limes? Any butter, or is there only margarine? Any half and half?" I never criticized her openly for lacking these luxuries, but I'm sure she could read my "Oh, never mind, that's okay" without much trouble. As time went on, I became more gracious and never asked about what might not be available, and she learned which of my preoccupations were the most enduring. So in the last years I would open the refrigerator and say "Mom, you remembered the half and half!" and she would say "Of course I did."

$\mathcal{R}$UTH AND Norman always "entertained beautifully," my mother used to say. "And they have the house for it," she would sometimes add in a tone that was admiring on the surface, but with envy and anger seeping out through the cracks. Then she'd change the subject: she didn't want to criticize Ruth in front of me, she wanted me to have a relationship with my aunt that wasn't tainted with Quinlan history, a gesture I now see as deeply generous. When my mother and I would visit Ruth and Norman in their "gargantuan" house—"Why they need five bedrooms I'll never know"—and sit sipping our gin and tonics on the flagstone patio, looking out at the landscaped yard, I thought I knew what my mother was thinking. Why should her sister live like this, and she have next to nothing? Ruth had decorated the house with furniture, paintings, and knickknacks she had brought back from Asia. You walked into the house on the hush of creamy wall-to-wall carpeting and entered a tasteful museum, room after room graced with burnished cherry-wood tables, raw silk pillows in peach and lime and burnt orange, bronze candlesticks, Chinese porcelain vases filled with iris and peonies that scented the air. Original oil and watercolor paintings were everywhere, even in the bathrooms and the stairwells. The house was crowded with precious things.

My mother's anger at Ruth's plenitude—acquisitiveness?—broke out more often after Norman died and she saw Ruth showing no signs of cleaning out the house and so preparing for her own death.

"My God, the *stuff* in that house," my mother would say, spitting out "stuff" as if she were expelling all Ruth's things into the outside world. "I hope to God she doesn't think I'm going to be the one to clean out that house, if she does she's got another thing coming. Buy, buy, buy, that's what they did, and now she'd better get rid of it."

Ruth's melancholia left her with no interest in cleaning out the house, and as each month passed and the sobbing phone calls continued, it became less and less likely that Ruth would dispense with any of her things. She had become, it seemed, an orphaned child. She did not know how to cook, we discovered: Norman had been the chef. Ruth had the benefit of all those endless sets of plates and glasses, a kitchen crammed with a utensil for every purpose, from apple corers to whipped cream whisks, pots and pans for every purpose, and cupboards stocked with food. But there was nothing to eat, she told my mother, no way to prepare dinner, it was all too complicated.

My mother became Ruth's mentor in widowhood.

"You could buy a nice chicken," I heard my mother say patiently on the phone one night. "Just put it in a broiling pan, put some butter, salt and pepper on it, put the oven at 350°, and in an hour or so you'll have yourself a roast chicken; and if you put a potato in about fifteen minutes later, you'll have baked potato with it. Put some broccoli in a pot with water, boil for about ten minutes, and there you'll have your green vegetable. And then there can be leftover chicken, for a nice sandwich the next day."

It was hard to believe. Here was my mother, who never thought of herself as much of a cook, giving good advice to Ruth, whom I'd always thought of as a gourmet. When you went to dinner at Ruth and Norman's, you'd be eating fried dumplings for an appetizer (my mother never had appetizers), and for a main course maybe chicken Kiev, a salad with homemade soy dressing, and for dessert, a brandy Alexander pie Ruth had made (she could do desserts). My mother's dinners were basic—pan-fried pork chops, baked potato, broccoli, store-bought rolls, salad with bottled dressing, and maybe a Mrs. Smith's apple pie for dessert. But my mother knew how to cook by herself, and for herself. Ruth, it seemed, could not cook without Norman.

It was as if Norman's death had released a hidden weakness in Ruth, just as my father's death had released some hidden strength in my mother. Those recipe-giving phone conversations in which my mother urged Ruth to cook and eat ("You have to keep your strength up!") gave me an insight into my mother I hadn't seen before. Ruth had lived in an expanded world, my mother in a narrow one; Ruth, I had thought, had expressed her gifts, while my mother, like so many wives and mothers of her generation, had not brought all of hers to life, had not found a big enough stage for her energies. And yet when my mother was left alone, she, unlike her sister, continued to cook. She would go into her tiny, dimly lit kitchen to bake her potato, brew her tea, and broil her occasional treat, a small chunk of halibut from Greer's, Belmont's pricey fishmongers.

Ruth and Norman, 1960s

TWO YEARS after Norman died, we were burying Ruth under the head-stone she had prepared, her name and birth date already inscribed next to her husband's. On her death certificate the doctor wrote "heart failure," but she had really died of starvation. "She just wouldn't eat," the nurse said. "She just refused."

After Norman died Ruth wanted to die. I'm no longer angry with Ruth for her desire: she was ten years older than my mother was when she was widowed, and it would have been hard to start life over in her seventies. She loved her house and belongings; this was the world she'd created and shared with Norman, and after he died her beauteous possessions must have felt as empty as Gatsby's did after he lost Daisy—"material without being real." Sometimes you just have to pack up and leave a life you've loved when you're called to something else, by someone else.

Catalogues

As stylish as a summer day is long, our Summer Solstice watch ushers in the season with a shimmering mother-of-pearl dial on a light green, pink, or blue suede band; please specify color.
                                                     —Sundance catalogue

SOMETIMES WHEN I'M DEPRESSED I can't concentrate enough to read or even watch a video. That's when I look at catalogues, numbly entranced by all the things you can buy.

Sometimes I'm drawn to the Hold Everything catalogue, which seductively promises "Organized Living." I yearn for the peace, quiet, and order offered by vanity cosmetic trays, cedar shoe stackers, Swedish shelf baskets, and—most mysteriously transformative of all—modular desktop systems.

Other times I want to enter the slicker world of glossy surfaces, redemptive objects, and beautiful people. Whether they're modeling Eddie Bauer wool sweaters or Victoria's Secret teddies, the people in catalogues have shiny hair, healthy skin, and the smug knowledge that they're envied. None of them are depressed. How could they be? They have each other, a whole family of people with good bone structure.

I stare at pictures of things I might want to buy, things that might make me happy, things that might make me feel I've lived well. A shirt with Native American beadwork from the Sundance catalogue. Egyptian earrings (replicas) from the Smithsonian. A silk shirt from J. Crew. During one long, low-grade depression I went on a credit-card rampage, ordering garden furniture from Smith & Hawken, wicker chairs from Pottery Barn, cotton shirts from J. Crew, a CD rack from Hold Everything, a leather backpack from Sundance, a black Chinese silk dress from J. Peterman (slinkily cut, with a slit up the back), a birdbath from Gardener's Eden, candle holders from Williams Sonoma.

I was on sabbatical, structure-deprived and lonely. Coming home to find a brown UPS package on my doorstep made me believe that somebody out there cared about me, even if that somebody was me, a few weeks ago. I had ordered so many things that I was never sure what was inside the brown box, so opening it was like a birthday surprise.

Then the inevitable letdown. The birdbath was smaller than it looked in the catalogue, the Chinese dress several sizes too big, the CD rack instructions incomprehensible. I'd feel even lonelier. But loneliness leads right back to catalogues. I'd sit down with a bunch in my lap, gazing at women showing off their silver and turquoise jewelry while the Rockies surged in the background, telling me that all my desires for accessories were really spiritual.

Sometimes I'd ponder the colors of the shirts. The colors of depression are muted: Grey. Brown. Black. Dingy beige. The colors of silk shirts in the J. Jill catalogue are luscious and sensual. *Cassis. Currant. Persimmon. Periwinkle. Teal. Plum. Nectarine.* This catalogue, filled with beautiful, thin women wearing silk shirts with colors you want to taste, tells me that depression is not a tellable American story. No one is wearing a grungy sweatshirt turned inside out, available in *Slough of Despond* or *Damp Mushroom* or *Endless Night.*

*C*ATALOGUES APPEAL to my American desire to have a fresh start. If I can't spend a year in a one-room cabin at Walden Pond, maybe I'll be reborn as an un-depressed Sharon if I just buy that silk shirt in elderberry, sandstone, or iris—maybe in all three?—or that cotton sweater in heather rye or petal (*Petal?* What kind of color is that?). As I stare at the glossy pages I experience an odd mix of hope and hopelessness. Hope, because it's possible that one act of consumption will change everything. Hopelessness, because I know it won't. Emotional or spiritual deprivation cannot be satisfied by material things, no matter how many colors they come in. There's a famous scene in *The Great Gatsby* where Gatsby throws all his shirts—"piled like bricks in stacks a dozen high"—in front of Daisy as a love offering, a sign of abundance, and a declaration of his upper-class status. "I've got a man in England who buys me clothes," he tells Daisy and Nick, and then

> began throwing them, one by one, before us, shirts of sheer linen and thick silk and fine flannel, which lost their folds as they fell and covered the table in many-colored disarray. While we admired he brought more and the soft rich heap mounted higher—shirts with stripes and scrolls and plaids in coral

and apple-green and lavender and faint orange, with monograms of Indian blue. Suddenly, with a strained sound, Daisy bent her head into the shirts and began to cry stormily.

"They're such beautiful shirts," she sobbed, her voice muffled in the thick folds.

"It makes me sad because I've never seen—such beautiful shirts before."

Catalogues always seem to promise spiritual meaning, incarnated in those material things. Products can even give meaning to the passage of time and the cycle of the seasons, replacing worship and ritual. *Wear our Solstice Watch on the longest day of the year! Visit the unconscious in our beautiful basket-weave cotton! Connect to inner and outer divinity in our gauze tunic, available in coral, citrine, bark, and amber!* These words beckon me on a journey I'm desperate to take when I'm depressed, a journey into happiness and beauty and beautiful shirts, a journey that starts with shopping and has no ending.

Departed Acts

Remorse—is Memory—awake—
Her Parties all astir—
A Presence of Departed Acts—
At window—and at Door—
        —EMILY DICKINSON

SHORTLY AFTER MY AUNT RUTH'S DEATH I had a dream in which my father gave me a mysterious warning: *Ruth is your dark side.*

I don't think he was referring to Ruth's melancholia, or to her love of beautiful things, but to a troubling excess in her purchases—the opposite of my family's scarcity.

If you opened a kitchen drawer in Ruth's house, you might find twenty crisply ironed damask tablecloths, or fifteen pristine potholders. In the dining room sideboards (she had two) would be three sets of dishes, a dozen sets of place mats, a whole drawer of trivets, five or six corkscrews of different sorts (one with a gold elephant handle). On a shelf in the hall closet were twenty or thirty vases—shiny black round vases, small earthen vases, tall oblong indigo vases, crystal and glass vases, Italian vases decorated with orange birds and blue roosters, purple-red Chinese vases wound around with ebony cranes and storks. There were vases for buds, vases for tulips, vases for roses, vases for everything.

Upstairs in the guest room, the closets and bureaus were crammed full of treasures. Every time I stayed there I would open the drawers and look at kimonos in every color of the rainbow, pillowcases embroidered with dragons, raw silk scarves. On the windowsills and bureau tops were dozens of little items—jade elephants, porcelain vases, colorful ceramic animals from Mexico, Italian candlesticks, straw baskets filled with tissues, Lifesavers, or matches.

The overflow was in the basement. Ruth and Norman had put up shelves and tables that held row after row of dishware, utensils, glasses, pots and pans, blenders, more trivets, electric frying pans, ice crushers, mixers, electric can openers, hot plates, soup tureens, and candelabra. (She had clearly trumped Handsome Dan.) All these things were new or barely used, spread out for viewing as if in readiness for a yard sale that never arrived.

I UNDERSTAND RUTH's cravings for material things. Although I'm not affluent—or deprived?—enough for duplications, I follow the "I deserve it" theory of shopping, particularly when I'm depressed, using my credit card to give myself elusive solace.

I felt such cravings after Ruth's funeral: was her dark side speaking to mine? We returned to her house for a reading of the will, and her executor told us that we could take a few things from the house, if we wanted. I felt overcome by greed. There were so many *things*, and they were all for the taking. Did I want that raw silk scarf, or did I want all ten? And what of jewelry, and dinnerware, and silver, and vases? What about that china elephant I'd always admired: was I going to compete with my cousin for it? I made a selection, curbing my appetite for the sake of decency. I drove home with the portable items—a set of dishes and silverware, four vases, six scarves, three tablecloths, a set of placemats, three paintings, and a tea pot. I would return later with a VW bus to pick up the furniture I wanted—a couch and a cabinet—along with Ruth's photograph albums and letters.

My mother had spent the afternoon searching for the elusive Repoussé. She scorned taking anything of Ruth's, except for a black suede suit to which she grudgingly gave her highest clothing accolade, "stunning." But she would almost never wear it. She had never forgiven Ruth for being the older sister who always cajoled her mother into buying her new clothes while my mother got rejects from Marion and Dorothy. To my mother, the black suede suit and all the other items in Ruth's overstuffed closet, including more than a hundred pairs of shoes, were nothing but the hand-me-downs of childhood, and she did not want them. She wanted only the family silver.

W HEN MY uncle Norman died my mother knew she was expected to be compassionate, but talking with her weeping sister on the telephone was as far as she was prepared to go. She did not visit, and she did not invite Ruth for the holidays. "She has plenty of friends," my mother said. "Let her go to one of them." Ruth whittled down my mother's portion in her will, and my mother retaliated by not staying on to clear out Ruth's "stuff" after the funeral. *Let someone else do it.*

Except no one else did.

At the time, handling Ruth's estate had seemed simple enough. We all left after the funeral, taking our portable pieces of Ruth's stuff, knowing that the executor would hire someone to prepare everything for an auction, and would box up private papers, which I would pick up when I returned for the furniture. My mother was off the hook.

One sticky, hot June day I pulled into the familiar driveway after a hellish drive from Carlisle—construction, accidents, reroutings—on my way to a weekend with friends at the shore, with three hours allotted to handle the packing. I was prepared for a couch, a cabinet, and maybe fifteen boxes. When the garage door opened it was like entering a box warehouse—there must have been more than three hundred boxes. Boxes of photograph albums containing pictures of people I did not know, landscapes I had never seen, houses I had never visited. Boxes of manuscripts, both Ruth's and Norman's. Boxes of address books and telephone books. Boxes of bank statements. Boxes of checkbooks, cookbooks, family photographs, diplomas, notebooks, magazines, newspapers, yearbooks, Christmas cards, catalogues, all the written and visual remembrances of two private lives, plus everything Ruth had inherited from her sisters.

It would take two or three days, maybe a week, to go through all the boxes carefully, and I had allotted an afternoon for the task.

Why had my mother not dealt with this? Why was I the one? I went through boxes like a furious whirlwind, saving only Quinlan family letters and photographs, consigning to oblivion—ruthlessly!—records of my aunt's shared life with Norman. Photographs of Chinese people I had never met? Japanese landscapes? Tokyo gardens? Correspondence with unknown people? Who cared! Into the trash! On to the next box.

Melinda, the estate organizer and Ruth's companion during her illness and dying, watched me with what I now think must have been shock, and maybe disgust. How could I be so callous, she must have thought, coolly consigning my relatives' history to the dump? I had no mercy. Driven by anger at my mother and at Ruth, I let most of the records of her life slip away.

But I wasn't acting alone: I now see a family conspiracy. I was propelled by all the lost words, all the hidden hurts and hungers of the Quinlans:

Ruth's attack on my mother after Geraldine died, my mother's unsaid words of pain and anger to Ruth, Ruth's unsaid apology to my mother, my unsaid questions to Ruth ("How could you ever think my mother was greedy? How could you accuse my father of being devious? Why didn't you ever say you were sorry?"). And then there was my own unacknowledged anger at the weeping Ruth, the melancholic Ruth, the Ruth who fell apart when she was left alone, the Ruth I didn't want to resemble, the Ruth I feared I did resemble. These feelings I had never put into words, and so more words were lost as Ruth's letters and papers waited on the side of the road for the trash collectors.

I regret the hours and days I did not spend in the garage during that hot June after my aunt died. Ruth and Norman's "stuff" had been sold at auction; what was left were documents and records. I saved a few boxes, but what was in the ones I let go? As a biographer, I know there are always gaps in the record, texts that do not survive, but I had never been responsible for discarding memories before. In the letters we do not find, the photograph albums we do not see, the boxes we do not open, what stories are buried? Now I understand these questions more deeply than before.

Ruth playing the photographer, mid-1930s

I FRAMED a photograph of Ruth I found in one of the boxes I kept. It was taken in the late 1930s, when she was a reporter and photographer for the *Elmira Star-Gazette.* She looks like Margaret Bourke-White—dressed in a khaki jacket and baseball cap, bulky flash camera draped around her neck, smoking a cigarette, her eyes narrowed knowingly. The photo is stagy, and maybe a little tongue-in-cheek. But one thing's for sure: this is my outrageous Auntie Mame, the aunt I need when I have to take some risks, pack up fast, put on some lipstick, grab my checkbook, buckle my seatbelt, and *go.*

No Shrinking Violet

When the occasion calls for it, people born in the Year of the Rooster can reveal real bravery.
—RUTH QUINLAN SUN, *The Asian Animal Zodiac*

YOU LEARN A LOT FROM EACH PERSON'S DYING you go through: you learn how you want to do it different, and better, next time. When my father died I was thirty, and I did a terrible job. My whole family, except for my father, did a terrible job.

Terrible was the best we could do.

Afterward I pledged that when my mother's dying came about, I'd do a much better job. But of course I never thought my mother was going to die.

My father died in 1976, when I was thirty-one; my mother died the year I turned forty-six, 1991. You'd think it might get easier, as you get older, to lose a parent, and I guess in a sense it does. But in another way it doesn't. People expect you not to grieve so much when you're older, but they're wrong. Even if you're sixty-five and your parent is ninety, you're still losing the only mother or father you'll ever have, and if you're losing the second parent you can still feel like an orphan.

MY MOTHER's illness came on quickly. She was diagnosed with terminal lung cancer in February, and she died in June. It was a good death, as deaths go: she didn't suffer much, and we had time to spend together and to say good-bye, and to say how much we loved each other. We were lucky in that.

That spring I was split into two pieces and places—the teacher in Carlisle, the daughter in Boston. I'd leave school every Thursday afternoon and drive to the Harrisburg airport, where I'd take the nonstop, but slow, USAir flight to Boston. For the first weekends I'd go straight to the hospital, where she was having chemo. Then, when she went home, I'd go straight to her apartment and spell one of the hospice nurses; throughout the weekend I'd take the evening and night shifts. Then, when the Sunday morning nurse arrived, I'd take a taxi to Logan and start my journey back, grading papers and preparing classes on the plane. I did this for three months, and I still wonder why I didn't do more.

My mother was thrilled that I was coming up every weekend, even though she worried about me flying. "Be careful on those planes," she would say when I left, and I promised only to take the safe ones.

*M*Y MOTHER agreed to take an experimental form of chemo to combat what her oncologist called an "aggressive" form of lung cancer, the fastest-growing, most deadly variety. She wanted to live to be with us, even for only six months, all the doctor thought possible.

"She's really pissed that she's dying," I said to Maureen.

"Rip-shit," she agreed.

Eighty-five years (her birthday came in May) were far too few on this earth. "Lots of people live *well* into their nineties," she said. "Why couldn't I be one of them? You see them everywhere, ninety, ninety-five," my mother went on, her eyes tearing up. "I always thought I would be one of them."

In the hospital we'd surround her bed, my brother, sister, and I, sometimes joined by her grandchildren—Maureen, David, Beth, Ted, John. The larger the crowd, the more she'd rise to the occasion, Handsome Dan's daughter taking center stage. She'd tell our archetypal family stories, passing them on to the next generation.

She told the one about Maureen's high school graduation, about how the teacher in charge, Miss Anderson, was going to have Maureen march in last and all by herself because she was the tallest and everyone else was paired up. Maureen came home crying from school, so Mom called up Miss Anderson. "You have two choices, and I do not care which one you choose, but you will choose one, since my daughter is not going to march in by herself. You can change your *idiotic* system of arranging the class by height and arrange it by academic achievement, and have the National Honor Society students, like my daughter, march in first. Or you can simply have the last three girls march together. The choice is yours." Miss Anderson took the latter choice.

She also told the catheter story, my favorite because it was about when I was born. She'd been catheterized after Maureen and Kevin were born and "it wasn't pleasant." So after I'm born she thinks to herself, "You've got me once, you've got me twice, you're not going to get me three times. So I asked for a pitcher of water right after Sharon was born. I must have drunk three pitchers, but I was determined they weren't going to bring that damn catheter near me again. And they didn't."

We all loved all these stories about Mom's power, confronting authorities and winning. "I'm no shrinking violet anymore," she said. "Look at me here with all these tubes in me," waving her IV-wreathed arms.

Sometimes she still had to play the nice girl role, even in the hospital, particularly with the one male nurse. Pretend seductive, John liked to make powerless old women flirt with him. "We'll get out the bourbon after your family's gone, right, Jean?" he'd wink at my mother when visiting hours were ending. "Pretty soon we'll be pumping Wild Turkey through this IV, won't we?"

"Right," she'd say, seeming to go along, waving her IV-trussed arm like a promise, or a dismissal. She had to be careful. "If you annoy the nursing staff they can retaliate," said my sister, wise in hospital power relations. "They'll leave you in the bathroom, not remove the bedpan, delay your pain meds. You have to watch it."

Sometimes my mother would have it both ways, managing to placate John and trump him at the same time. Once, removing her chemo IV, he said, "There, honey, we're getting rid of this nasty IV," infantilizing her and waiting for gratitude. *"Deo gratias,"* she said, and John went off puzzled, not sure if he'd been flattered or rebuked.

One time when I was alone with her in the hospital room the phone rang and I answered it; Mom was sleeping. The caller was Anne McHenry, a church-leader type. Anne tried to figure out who I was.

"Are you the one who went to Ireland?"

"Yes, I am."

"You went to school, that's right."

"No. I taught at Trinity, on a Fulbright."

"Oh," she said, light dawning. "you're the veterinarian."

There were no veterinarians in my family.

"No, I teach American studies."

"Oh, so *that* was what you were doing in Ireland. I remember now, that was the year when your mother couldn't get up the gumption to get on the plane to come visit you."

Get up the gumption? Right then my mother was flying off into the unknown with a new kind of chemotherapy because she wanted to live a little longer. Strange medicines were dripping into her veins as she took on what terrifies all of us—doctors, hospitals, cancer, and death. *She is on the fucking airplane and I want to kill Anne McHenry.*

"I have to go now," I said abruptly, and put down the phone. My mother was annoyed with me for being rude, but I never told her why I hung up.

W
HEN SHE came home from the hospital she played the queen bee in the ambulance, flirting with the young male attendants. She wept when she entered her apartment, which now seemed beautiful to her. "This is a palace," she said, settling into the hospital bed we'd placed in the living room. "I'm living in a palace."

Maureen, Kevin, and I all thought the same thing, that in her last months, she was expressing her best self—life-loving, gritty, funny, relishing the small things, like drinking tea, arranging for my birthday present, watching *Jeopardy!* She even liked praising the unknown inventors of the commode. "What a good idea," she would say. "Makes it so much easier."

The hospice agency was staffed mostly by nurses from Ireland, and I liked thinking that in her last days she'd be surrounded by those soft Irish accents, reminding her, perhaps, of her grandmother's. Bernadine was her chief nurse, and she was both a caring person and a tough cookie. She made my mother get up to walk every day, all the way from the bedroom to the living room so she could sit in the pink chair by the window, her former throne. One day my mother's legs gave way. Bernadine caught her before she fell, but she was too terrified to try the walk again. *Jean afraid of the pink chair,* Bernadine wrote in the nurses' log. I wanted to correct it and write *Jean is getting ready to die,* but left it alone, it was a historical record. When, later, I reread the nurses' log, I discovered they all thought she was putting up a front for us, making it easier when we visited, not letting us see the fear or depression she let them see.

Yes, she was probably putting on an act: elderly parents often do that, when they're dying, to protect their middle-aged children. What the nurses couldn't see was how much power my mother was also exerting. Once she woke up to find the nurse gone—she'd gone outside for a smoke—and called 911. "I'm an old, dying woman,' she said, "alone in my apartment, and I need someone to get here right away." Five minutes later the police drove up.

"Good for Mom," Maureen said. "That'll show the nurse to sneak out for a smoke."

SOMETIMES I'D have this nagging voice inside my head saying *Why aren't you doing more? Why weren't you a better daughter?* Other times the voice would quiet. I remember one such time: I was asleep in the living room when I heard my mother's voice call from the bedroom.

"Sharon? Are you awake?" She was almost whispering, she didn't want to disturb me.

I got up. Looking in through the bedroom door, I saw my mother sitting up in bed, her newly thinned hair wispy and white in the lamp light.

"Are you okay?"

"I can't sleep. I'm sorry to bother you."

"No bother. How about a nice cup of tea?"

"Tea? We can't have tea, can we? It's three o'clock in the morning."

"Mom," I said, sitting on the bed and holding her hand, "there are no rules. We can do whatever we want."

"Oh. Then I'd like some tea."

So I put the kettle on to boil, rinsing out the teapot with boiling water the way my Irish friends had taught me, and picked out the loose Darjeeling tea my mother must have bought with me in mind. I found a tray and brought it in with two mugs and some Pepperidge Farm cookies. I made myself comfortable on the bed next to my mother and we stayed awake for quite a while, sipping our tea, nibbling our cookies, sometimes talking, sometimes being quiet, together in a lighted bedroom on a dark street in the middle of the night.

I think we were as content as it's possible for two people to be.

THE DAY my mother died the three of us met at her apartment in the morning. She was in a coma so we held her hand and talked to her and said we were going off to the priest and the funeral director, and we'd be back in a few hours. "Don't worry about a thing," we said when we got back. "We called the caterer and the funeral Mass is all organized, and the priest is going to let Sharon talk about you and read the Seamus Heaney poem, the one you like about the soul as a homing daughter, and Maureen and Kevin are going to be reading from the gospel, and we picked out a good coffin, nice but not too expensive, a honey-colored wood, and we've arranged for the tenor to sing 'Amazing Grace' and 'Ave Maria' and 'Panis Angelicus,' just like at Dad's funeral."

She must have been waiting for the report, because half an hour later her blood pressure started dropping and Bernadine told us her vital systems were shutting down. "Her breath will move up her body as she dies," Bernadine said, and she was right. First her stomach stopped moving, then her chest, as the breath started higher and higher. Finally she was breathing just from her throat, fluttering like a bird's heart. Her throat was hollowed out like a cave and I could see the breath there, a tiny bellows. Then the beating stopped. "You can kiss her good-bye now," Bernadine said, and we did, in order of age—Maureen first, and then Kevin, and then me.

THE DAY of her funeral dawned warm and rainy. She'd have been rip-shit, we all agreed.

Rain wasn't predicted. Damn weathermen, she'd say.

My Mother's Willa Cather

May we, borne onward by our daughters, ride
in the Envelope of Almost-Infinity,
that chain letter good for the next twenty-five
thousand days of their lives.

— MAXINE KUMIN, "The Envelope"

WHEN MY BIOGRAPHY of Willa Cather was published, my mother was probably more excited than I was. "I'm dining out on your book, Sharon," she would say, and I knew she was basking in the attention of her friends and coworkers at the Belmont Public Library, showing them her autographed copy, opening to the dedication page first—*To my family, especially to my mother and in memory of my father.*

None of her fellow librarians had a child who had actually *published a book*, and the day my biography arrived at the Belmont Library to be catalogued resembled, in my mother's version, the opening of an exhibit at the Louvre. My book lay in state in the cataloguing room, temporarily swathed in cellophane to protect the white cover, and staff members on break paid reverential visits to see it. "Jean, you must be so proud of your daughter," they'd say, and she'd give that little gasping inhaled breath the Irish do when they want to agree or emphasize. When I gave a talk on biography at the library later that year and a reporter for the *Belmont Herald* asked to take our picture together, she could barely contain herself.

My mother cut out every review she could find and read them to me over the phone, exalting at the praise, attacking my critics vituperatively (in our family parlance, this was known as Mom's "blasting"). "Who is this Earl Rovit person?" she demanded, mid-blast, reading the *Library Journal* review to me. " 'Richly documented and passionately argued,' well that's right, but where does he come off saying you 'use the novelist as a cardboard

Sharon and Regina at the Belmont Public Library, 1989

exemplum?' I'll make him an *exemplum* of full-blown ignoramus, I'll *exemplum* him, I'll tell him a thing or two, just let him talk to me!'"

"He'll never talk to you, Mom, he'd be too scared."

"And he should be, the lily-livered so-and-so!"

My mother was always wanting to tell anyone who had the slightest whisper of a reservation about my biography "a thing or two." Sometimes she wanted to give them "what for," which struck me as an even graver threat. I'd be delighted by her anger, unreasonable as it was, it felt so good to be on the same side. "Look at how this man ends his review, 'Still, there is more material and more illuminating reading here than in any previous Cather biography.' Well, could he spare us a dime? *Still.* That's what I call damning with faint praise. Why on earth would they give your book to a man to review anyway?"

My mother was always more incensed if the offending reviewer was male. It was as if all her silenced anger at the men who had power over her, like the "joke" who ran the Belmont Library—keeping his door closed because he was afraid of the staff—was released by any male who dared to criticize her daughter's book. By contrast, positive reviews by women were proof of our gender's greater acumen. "I like this Carolyn Heilbrun," she said. "Now *that's* someone who knows what she's talking about, not like this . . . this *thing* of an Earl Rovit."

"Mom," I'd say, "leave the poor guy alone," trying to quiet her, hoping to egg her on.

She'd snort into the phone, her way of saying that her contempt for the benighted reviewer was now spinning into outer space, well beyond words.

This mother of my adult years was very different from my childhood mother. Of course she reveled in my academic successes, but that wasn't the point. I had come to see that she loved me, simply as her daughter. She was on my side. When I'd drive up to Belmont she'd be waiting at the door when I got there, arms outstretched to hug me, thrilled and happy just to see my face.

When the three of us children were growing up, we were way out there in the ocean, swimming toward land, and my mother kept thinking we could drown. Once we reached shore, safely into our adult lives, she relaxed. There wasn't anything she could do to shape or save us any more, and that helped her to let go.

But the biggest reason for the change in my mother was her job at the library.

She loved her work and received praise for her skills. She found a community outside of us: her new friends, the library staff, became another family. They were a sociable bunch and my mother soon became, with her life-of-the-party spirit, the energizing spark for people much younger than she. "Let's go to dinner," she'd say on a Friday afternoon, organizing a crew to go to an Italian restaurant. "Let's take in a movie. Let's take a drive to see the Christmas lights." She got to know a wide range of people while working at the library, and her former concern with class distinctions lessened. Her best friend, for the last years of her life, was Frank, twenty years younger than she, the library's custodian. She talked him through his divorce, he drove her to get groceries. They were the lucky holders of a friendship that spanned many differences.

I HAD ALWAYS wondered if my mother had even read my Cather book, knowing it was possible for her to defend me fiercely without having read a word. After she died, I took her copy of my book home with me. I can't tell how much my mother read; perhaps she read the acknowledgments, perhaps she read it all. What's clear is that the white cover, smudged and wrinkled and slightly torn, shows the signs of many handlings. I can imagine my mother sitting in her living room on a winter night, just cradling the book in her lap, dipping into it, feasting her eyes, content just to hold its solid weight against her—the achievement and family vindication she had long hoped for at last given tangible form. Inside the back cover are dozens of reviews and advertisements and listings, all crinkly from her touch.

I leaf through the clippings and riffle the pages, hoping for a penciled note, wondering if I will find any traces of my mother's reading, her presence. Perhaps I want a message. I do not find any of her words, but tucked away in an envelope I find something else: the index card from the Belmont Library catalog for my book. It's a copy, and I remember, now, that she told me the staff had made up two cards, one for them, one for her. Here is my work, once a string of ideas in my head, then handwritten notes, then typewritten pages, then computer files, then a published book, here translated into her library's language and tucked back into my book for safekeeping.

The Aptitude to Fly

My Cocoon tightens—Colors tease—
I'm feeling for the Air—
A dim capacity for Wings
Demeans the Dress I wear—

A power of Butterfly must be—
The Aptitude to fly
Meadows of Majesty implies
And easy Sweeps of Sky—

So I must baffle at the Hint
And cipher at the Sign
And make much blunder, if at last
I take the clue divine—

—EMILY DICKINSON

My sister and I once made a list of my mother's fears. It was impressive.

dogs
insects
loud noises
thunderstorms
travel
flying
escalators
elevators
cars and driving
heights
stairs (going up)

enclosed places
theater balconies
dentists

We made this list a few months after my mother's death, sitting on the beach at the Cape, reflecting on her paradoxical nature like soldiers reminiscing about an old general. We remembered how she could terrify us, particularly when we were children, with her sharp tongue and Irish ability to "turn the cold shoulder"; how, later, as we came to enjoy her vitality and wit and party-girl spark, we could also, more and more, see the depth of her fears and phobias. The all-powerful mother of our earlier years was supplanted by other images. Our mother at the bottom of the clunky, cumbersome escalator at the Park Street subway station, looking up helplessly, wanting to rise but afraid to move; our mother refusing a trip West with her dear old chum Dot (*Mom, Dot will drive you to Arizona!*) because she could not take the train home alone; our mother trudging up six flights of stairs at Massachusetts General Hospital to see my dying father, able to confront the ICU but afraid of the elevator.

Sometimes my mother's fears were contagious. Once I postponed a trip to New Hampshire because my mother, glued to the TV weather, said "Sharon, there's a *tornado watch*. I wouldn't go outside that door if I were you." Ninety-nine times out of a hundred I could dismiss her anxiety—one of my earliest statements was "*Mom*, don't *worry*, I'll be all right"—but this time I got infected. I could just see that little funnel-shaped cloud heading straight for my Honda, so I called up my friend Mary to tell her I'd be driving up the next day.

"There's a tornado watch," I explained.

"Oh," she said politely.

My mother loved—or maybe hated—weather and weather reports. Certainly she was obsessed. If my parents were planning a trip, she'd start tracking the weather a day or two ahead, comparing reports in the *Boston Globe* to all three TV channels, watching the news and waiting for the weather, impatient with the little teasers the news people would give at 11:05 just to make sure you waited for the full report at 11:25.

"So, Don, are we going to get that storm that's brewing down in the Carolinas?"

"Well, Bob, it depends on what happens with a hot-air mass that's stalled over the Great Plains. Stay tuned for the complete forecast!"

My mother would glare at the screen and switch to another channel. "You'd think," she'd say, "a city the size of Boston would have decent weather reports at a decent hour." Belmont never did get cable during my mother's lifetime. Quite a shame, my siblings and I agreed: our mother was made for the Weather Channel.

If the weekend weather report was "iffy," my parents would be unable to decide whether to take off to the Cape or Maine. Thursday night would go by, Friday morning, Friday afternoon, and there they were, bright sunshine outside, still comparing forecasts. "Why don't they just *go?*" the three of us would ask each other, knowing they couldn't. My mother needed to know what was going to happen. Ambiguous weather reports were no help at all.

Weather represented everything that was uncontrollable in life; weather was life itself, life in all its changeable, mercurial disorder. Weather reports were stories that promised reliability and order, and when they proved wrong, my mother was left with the unacceptable truth that we cannot control what happens to us. No wonder Boston's hapless weathermen were targets for her rage.

"Idiots! Imbeciles! They're getting paid an arm and a leg for this incompetence! I could do a better job just by sticking my nose out the door!"

Flying in particular terrified her. It comprised so many fears: enclosed spaces, heights, travel, *weather.* No "easy sweeps" of sky for her: in that blue dome lurked thunderclouds, tornadoes, tempests of all kinds. A little silver tube filled with people, eight miles above the earth, promised disaster.

Late in her life my mother decided to confront her fear of flying, and so, in a sense, to confront all her fears at once. The lure was powerful: Ireland. In the late eighties I lived in Dublin for a year, teaching at Trinity College on a Fulbright. Desperate to visit me and to see the home of her ancestors, my mother enrolled in a course at Boston's Logan Airport with a famous fear-of-flying expert, a behavioral psychologist named Dr. Forgione who enjoyed a stunning success record. Founder of the Institute for Psychology of Air Travel and developer of "The Fearless Flying Program," Dr. Forgione had used the principles of behavior therapy to develop a seven-week course to get phobics in the air. Even though his promotional materials claimed that "the treatment is so effective that the course is guaranteed," my siblings and

I felt that Forgione had met his match in my mother, and we were right. She was his Armageddon.

Kevin and Maureen took turns driving her to the airport for classes, and for several weeks things seemed to be going well. In fact, my mother seemed to be one of the star pupils—at seventy-nine she was the oldest member of the class, which was perhaps why she was chosen for an interview when a local TV crew showed up. She sent an excited letter to me in Dublin:

Dear Sharon

First of all, I must tell you about my exciting experience! Last Monday, at my flying class—who appeared at the outset but a crew from Channel 4— headed by Dan Rea. He started chatting with a few of us—asking why we were there, etc.—And then told us he would interview us on camera! So Julie (my little friend who gave me a ride home), another gal, a man, and *I* were interviewed! He also shot film of the class with Forgione talking—It was on that night on the 11:00 news! and repeated the next day at 6:30 and noon—I called Maureen—tried to get Kevin but he wasn't in—But loads of people have called me—What a riot!

Hope the ould sod will be good to you—and that all will go smoothly with your classes, etc.—Good luck—Take care

Love, Your old mither

Some of my Boston friends caught my mother's (quite confident) appearance on the 11:00 news, declaring that she was "looking forward" to her flight to Ireland, and Jonathan was so startled that he called me in Ireland the next day. "Looks like your mother's going to make it," he said. "I know," I said. "Hard to believe, but she really wants to get over here."

My mother wrote me again two weeks later, and she sounded more measured than she had to her TV audience, where she'd gamely acted the part of the excited future flyer, Handsome Dan's daughter on stage.

I still keep hearing from people about my TV debut—We're more than half done now—only four more classes—It's hard to assess how I'm doing— Everyone says it works—so I hope it will for me. Since I'm yet to be confronted with a flight it's hard to know. Maybe the classes on the stationary plane will tell me something—Don't like your getting a cold so soon—don't wonder tho' with that awful Dublin weather—I see it's always cloudy in the 50's—do take care and be careful driving on the wrong side—sounds horrendous!—more later

Much love Mother

When she wrote me again two weeks later, as the course neared its end, her anxiety was rising. By then she was entering the territory of Cassette #3, "Portland Flight," which required her to listen at night to Side 1, "An individual guided relaxation flight with cueing at every step from takeoff to landing," and later Side 2, "Former phobics talk about their fears and successes." How my mother must have wanted to become a former phobic! But she was not feeling confident, and she was beginning to establish Boston's "iffy" weather as her escape route.

There are just two meetings left, tonight and next Mon—both in a plane—and then Nov. 22 *the flight* to Portland—Hope I can do it—needless to say, if it's bad weather, I won't—and of course this time of year, that's a real possibility— . . . Take care—Keep away from Belfast and The Troubles—More soon—Love Mother

My brother and sister teamed up to drive her to Logan for her momentous graduation flight, the short hop from Boston to Portland that must have struck my mother as equivalent to an Apollo launch. As soon as she got to the airport, my mother must have been attacked by all the fears she'd ever had. She became hysterical, refusing to go on the plane. The other phobics, who'd been sitting quietly in the departure lounge, began to get restless. A few began to defect. Trying to calm my mother and placate the other frightened flyers tripped off by her terror, Dr. Forgione lost track of time.

The entire class missed the flight.

As agitated as his students, Dr. Forgione ran off to the Delta Airlines desk, only to run back a few minutes later, phobics trailing in his wake, once a great leader, now a fallen Messiah. It was all over. Delta wouldn't have another flight until morning. He was apoplectic. This had never happened before, he told everyone.

"Your mother," he said to my brother and sister, arms waving like useless propellers, "your mother has a lot more wrong with her than just *fear of flying!*"

Tell us about it, they thought.

Meanwhile my mother trembled quietly in a chair, hands clutched in her lap, her head lowered in shame. She had saved herself from the terror of annihilation, and she must have felt some relief, but now she had to confront what seemed only her personal failure of nerve. She would never make it to Ireland.

I've only heard the fear-of-flying story from Maureen and Kevin, but I feel as if I was there at Logan when my mother's bottled-up fears exploded into something almost magnificent. What power fear can have! My mother did not feel powerful, though: she felt ashamed. She felt that her inability to get on the plane came from weakness, just the way some people with depression can feel they have a character flaw. "I just couldn't do it, Sharon," she wept to me on the phone. "I'm so sorry, I just couldn't do it."

"That's okay, Mom," I reassured her, "it's not your fault." But I don't think she believed it, and I don't think I meant it.

$\mathcal{M}$AUREEN, KEVIN, AND I often talk about that disastrous day at Logan airport. It's one of those unforgettable family moments that you never understand fully at the time. You keep going back, trying to understand what happened, and the meanings change over time as you change. In this case I think we've come to appreciate my mother more deeply, the reasons for her fear as well as the fact of her bravery.

"There was no way she could have gotten on that plane, I know that now," Maureen said a few years ago when the three of us were congregating for Kevin's birthday. "Not without medication. But I gave her the silent treatment all the way home in the car, I was so pissed."

"Me too," Kevin said.

By then—after a decade of breakthroughs in our culture's understanding of the neurochemistry of mood disorders as well as our own struggles with anxiety and depression—we could all see that my mother's fears had a strong biochemical component. Like us, she could have been substantially helped by medication. She suffered from what *Mental Health: A Report of the Surgeon General* (2000) calls "generalized anxiety"—a low-level, chronic form of anxiety that is difficult or impossible for the individual to control, often disrupts normal functioning, causes worry and brooding (my mother's preoccupation with the weather!), and can erupt into panic under stress.

The web site for the Institute for Psychology of Air Travel reveals this new understanding of the biochemical component of fear, and the realization that panic disorder cannot be handled solely by behavior therapy. The reader who suffers from agoraphobia or other generalized fear is advised to "overcome your fears on the ground before you attempt to overcome your fears in the air" and is counseled to consider "a combination of medication and behavior therapy." But such wisdom was not available in the mid-1980s, and so my mother was left, after the great Portland flight fiasco, with nothing to confront but what seemed to be her own weakness.

Sometimes I look back at the Logan Airport incident through a psychological lens, seeing my mother battling not only her panic, but also male authority. In rating a list of fears in her *Fearless Flying* handbook, she scored "Being Under the Control of Someone Else" higher than "Death," which to me recalled her vexed relationship with her father.

My mother liked to tell two stories about her childhood struggles with her father. Her most impassioned memory of his tyranny dates back to a summer when she was twelve or thirteen. Her mother had gone off to California for a few months to be with Margaret, who was having her first child. Her older sisters were away or spending time out of the house; she was Handsome Dan's captive for a whole summer. "It was terrible," she said. "I felt like I was in jail." That was the summer my aunt Geraldine learned to drive and bought a roadster, and her father decided he would build a driveway, a new innovation for Elmira homes. All summer he labored in the sun, digging and sweating and raking and transporting crushed stone.

My mother, his youngest daughter and more malleable than Ruth, the other choice, would have to stay home all day and run to the well in Grove Park whenever he needed water. "Of course there was water in the house," she said, "but only the Grove Park water would do—it was the purest and the coldest, and that's what he wanted. I had to run up and back with the pitcher whenever he called for a drink." She couldn't go off with her friends, or ride her bike, or plan a trip: "at his beck and call, that was it, all summer. When my mother came home, I ran into her arms sobbing and clung to her for dear life, begging her never to go away again and leave me with him, and she looked straight at my father and said 'What on earth have you done to this child?'"

The other story recorded early defiance. She was five years old, and Dan had required his daughters to perform some act of obedience—she couldn't remember what—and she had refused. "I just stamped my foot and said *I won't!*" my mother said proudly. "And there was nothing he could do. My sisters just looked at me: nobody could believe I was standing up to him." My mother told and retold this story, always with relish.

My mother's fear of flying went back a long way, to the emotional atmosphere of her home and a father who tried to clip her wings. Who was Dr. Forgione but another authoritarian male trying to control her life? She both feared and defied him: perhaps it was a sweet unconscious victory to see this powerful male figure brought low by her breakdown, to be the cause of his most glaring failure.

EVERY ONE OF my mother's sisters could fly, and every one of them, she thought, had flown higher than she. "I was the smallest in the House," writes Emily Dickinson, "I took the slightest Room." Her five older sisters, my mother always told us, were all brilliant achievers, each one of them smarter and more accomplished and braver than she.

- How crucial it was that her children soar high in the world, making up for my father's unlived life and hers too, and, if all went well, equaling or surpassing her sisters. She wanted us to make our "dim Capacity for wings" bright and shining, and she knew where we would have to fly—off not just to college but to graduate school, pulling in degrees and jobs, incomes and publications, status and power, navigating those "easy Sweeps of Sky" as she had not been able to. And if she ever realized she had tried to determine our flight paths for us, she never let us know.

My mother felt empty in comparison to her sisters' seeming fullness. She never sought employment despite my father's barely adequate income, hemmed in by cultural attitudes and her own fears. Finally, when she was fifty-eight, a job found her—as a librarian in the Belmont library—and she began to explore her competence with delight and flair. When she was dying I asked her if she had any regrets, and she mentioned only one: "I wish I had gone to work earlier."

My mother was telling me she wanted to have conquered more of her fears, to have flown a little higher and longer on her own wings. I think of literary critic Ellen Moers's groundbreaking study of women writers, *Literary Women*, where she notes how often in women's writing the image of flight signifies a female character's aspiration to transcend the social rules and regulations that limit her to an earthbound, subordinate role. When Willa Cather wants to signify her artist heroine Thea Kronborg's soaring power in *The Song of the Lark*, she describes her straining after the "strong, tawny flight" of an eagle.

When Freud analyzed women's dreams of flying, he found in them evidence of women's desire to be men. Ellen Moers disagrees, as do I, as my mother would have. In women's literature flying is not "a way for a woman to become a man," she writes, "but . . . a way for the imprisoned girl-child to become a free adult."

*I*F YOU look at my mother's literal attempt to fly, from one perspective you can see all the limitations she passed on to her children—biological, emotional, cultural. But if you climb a little higher and look at the larger view, you can see another story, another legacy. Here's a seventy-nine-year-old woman, afflicted with a list of fears and phobias as long as your arm, unsupported by therapy or medication, living alone (no spouse to travel with!), retired from work (no coworkers to egg her on!), who signs up for a fear-of-flying class and gets herself to the airport every Monday for seven weeks, listening to the whine of the jets and inhaling the sharp, exotic smell of jet fuel, going to class, walking onto stationary planes, confronting a fear that harbors all her other fears inside it, like Russian dolls, all because she has the aptitude to fly.

The Book of Lists

We think back through our mothers if we are women.
—VIRGINIA WOOLF

5 layer cass. dinner
In a casserole slice one layer of onions then another layer of sliced potatoes—
season—then spread on hamburger—if you like, thin onion slices—then add
1/2 cup uncooked rice, 1 can tomatoes—you may add a little water for mois-
ture. Bake 350 till done.
—From my mother's "Memo Note Book"

IT HAS BEEN CHALLENGING for historians to tell the stories of ordinary
women from the past, because they left so few written records. Even if they
were literate, journals, diaries, and letters most often did not survive their
deaths. My grandfather Dan Quinlan left his descendants a scrapbook filled
with clippings, reviews, interviews, and speeches along with card catalogue
entries in collections of theater history; my grandmother Margaret Doherty
Quinlan left no written records at all. My father was not as prominent in the
public world as my grandfather, but still he left us many recorded words—
autobiographical accounts in Harvard alumni books, his undergraduate Harvard file, newspaper clippings about the radio stations he worked for, copies
of unpublished essays he wrote on education, and a reading journal. My
mother left only a few letters, cards, and some memo books.

It can take daughters so long to learn how to read the few records our
mothers and grandmothers have left, many of which were not written at
all. Historians have had to learn how to read the stories hidden in samplers
and quilts, houses and rooms. In "In Search of Our Mother's Gardens," Alice
Walker reads her mother's bountiful flower garden as the site of her creativity; in *A Room of One's Own*, Virginia Woolf reads the dreadful food served
at Oxford's college for women—which she contrasts to the feasts enjoyed

by male students—as the sign of female subordination. When I was writing my biography of Willa Cather, I grew to see her ability to read the creativity and meaning in ordinary women's lives, manifested in the farm wife's cooking and storytelling in her early stories, the recipes a French mother passes on to her daughter in *Shadows on the Rock*, and the soil Alexandra Bergson brings to life in *O Pioneers!* ("It is in the soil that she expresses herself best"). In her memoir *Dream House*, Charlotte Nekola sees the story of the women in her family passed down through recipes, which to her awakened gaze become revelatory. "I decided to read the recipe book, in order to look for my mother, sister, aunt, grandmother, to dwell with them for a while in the presence of cornmeal weighed in the hand, cherries pitted by the sink."

Like these women in history and literature, my mother—vibrantly alive in her children's memories and stories—left very few public marks behind. After she died I didn't think consciously *you need to preserve all her written records so her voice will not be wholly lost*, but I must have been concerned about preservation when I gathered up the hospice log book, her annotated copy of *Fearless Flying*, and all the letters and cards she'd send me over the years. Her little books of lists struck me as her most important writings—the equivalent of journals or memoirs—and I scoured the apartment for them. The one she'd been using during the weeks of her dying was on her bedside table, the others tucked away in a drawer. I gathered them up, sensing that here was my mother's book.

AFTER MY mother's funeral, I took home to Carlisle six 5-by-3-inch memo books from Woolworth's and CVS, wrinkled and worn with use, pages fraying and curling at the edges, still curving with the shape of her hand. There must have been more—dozens, hundreds—that my mother had thrown out over the years. All the books are completely filled, except for the last one, only just begun: to leave many blank pages would have been to waste space and money. Having spent her young married years during the Depression, and then living on my father's spare and fluctuating income, my mother kept her parsimonious habits until her death. She spent money on her children but not on herself: she would never have put out the fifty-nine cents for a new memo book until all the pages in the old one were filled.

I flipped through the notebooks when I got home, seeing shopping lists and Christmas lists, financial calculations and jotted notes, all in my mother's familiar handwriting. At first these lists only confirmed the reading of my mother's life I then held: she had been confined in spaces that were too small for her, she had never found her power. During the years I knew her she was hemmed in by fear—of flying, of travel, of the outside world. As she aged she spent more and more time in her small apartment, particularly in the winter. She'd sit in her pink chair by the window, doing crossword puzzles, this woman who loved words putting letters into tiny squares, responding to others' definitions. I'd see stacks of *New York Times* puzzles headed for the trash, all the squares filled in, and I'd wonder what would have happened if my mother could have released all the energy in those regulated words. She was rootbound, I thought: like so many women who raised children in the fifties, she'd needed a bigger pot and better soil in order to bloom.

In those days I even saw my mother's name as a sign of her diminishment: in Elmira she'd been called by her proper name, *Regina*, the queen, but in Belmont she was "Jean" or "Jeannie," her queenly self left behind. In her obituary we had to put Regina ("Jean") O'Brien so that people would know who she was. "Jean" seemed a weaker name to me, maybe something about those vowels hidden in between the consonants like women hiding indoors: my parents had given this to me as my middle name, and for years I wiped it out of my signature, never using it as part of my author's name. What if my mother had brought "Regina" with her from Elmira to Belmont? Would things have been different? *Regina coeli* is the famous Catholic poem-prayer to Mary, the "queen of the skies." I kept wondering what skies my mother could have flown in if she'd only been born at a later time, a time when women were allowed to soar.

Something had happened to my mother's power. Trying to find the source of diminishment, I looked up the roots of her name: it's derived from the Latin word *regere* "to rule," and further back, the Indo-European root *reg-*, meaning "to move in a straight line, lead, rule," a source of regal nouns (regent, reign, realm) and active verbs (direct, erect, surge). How did my mother lose the power of motion hidden in the source of her name and adapt to insufficient realms?

"Silence is starvation," writes poet Cherrie Moraga, and we can also say that silence is suffocation—when we do not speak our lungs learn not to expand, and we breathe shallowly within the cage of our ribs. Many women fear to take up space, and I saw my mother as one of this timid sisterhood. "Sharon?" she would say on my answering machine. "It's just me." Emily Dickinson could also speak in that choked-off voice: "I was the slightest in the House— / I took the smallest Room— / At night, my little Lamp, and

Book—and one Geranium." This could be my mother: she had her reading, her lamp, her one geranium, but like the speaker in this poem, not enough room to develop a voice. "I never spoke—unless addressed— /And then, 'twas brief and low— / I could not bear to live—aloud— / The Racket shamed me so—."

When I first looked at those little memo books, almost ten years ago now, I was looking to explain the sources of depression and constriction in my own life. All I could see was my mother trying to fit into spaces that were too small. *Couldn't she even buy bigger notebooks? Was fifty-nine cents all she could give herself?* I'd be writing in my journal, enjoying the flow of ink across the page, thinking that my mother—who had all of three inches to work with—literally had to cramp her style. "Ruled notebook," her books said. *Narrow ruled.* That was my mother, I thought, narrow ruled, not the expanding queen and ruler. She was born at the wrong time: this woman was meant to come of age at a time when possibilities for women were expanding.

*O*VER THE ten years since my mother died I've kept looking back at these memo books, and gradually the story my mother was telling there became more complex as I learned how to listen, how to read—as I no longer needed the story of my mother's constriction to explain my own. I came to see signs of her power in these lists, of her loving heart, and maybe even more important, of the heroism of everyday life.

Shopping lists—*c flakes, bananas, p butter, milk*—signs that my mother, then in her early eighties, wanted to go on living. Christmas lists, her delight in ritual and refusal to just give money. ("That's no fun!") The three of us used to dread my mother's annual pre-Christmas phone call—usually right after Thanksgiving—when she'd ask brightly, "Any hints? What do you want for Christmas?" We'd be paralyzed—no ideas at all—and fend her off with promises we'd get back to her with lots of suggestions. We'd do nothing, dreading the next phone call. "Sharon? It's just me. Wondering if you came up with any Christmas ideas yet." Her little books show her coming up with ideas herself, making our lists—(Beth—scarf, Paloma Picasso—Kevin—car cushion, VCR cleaner—Maureen, jr.—*Joy Luck Club*—Sharon—*Paris Trout, Cat's Eye*, turtleneck—Maureen, sr.—sweater—other kids, ask Maureen).

These jottings prepared her for the heroic trip to Harvard Square on the trolley to shop at Wordsworth's or the Coop. "Take a cab, Mom!" we'd say, trying to erase the image of our increasingly frail elderly mother going out in the cold to shop for us. But that would have been an extravagance.

Lists of savings accounts, certificates of deposit, calculations of interest, my mother confronting her fears of poverty and her stubborn desire to leave us an inheritance. On one page, sometime in the early 1980s, she calculates her entire savings—123,848. On another, her yearly pension from the town of Belmont for the fifteen years she'd worked the library—4,482.

Lists of books to read—*Breathing Lessons, Writing a Woman's Life, Midnight's Children, Annie John, Love in the Time of Cholera, The Music Room, Collected Stories of William Trevor*—and videos to see—*Rain Man, Empire of the Sun, Do the Right Thing, The Fabulous Baker Boys*. When she was in her late seventies she joined a reading group and started introducing me to books I should read, and I find them scattered throughout her memo books: sometimes book titles (Ernest Gaines's *A Prayer for the Dying*, John Updike's *Self Consciousness*), sometimes writers she was discovering (Anita Brookner, Robertson Davies, Larry McMurtry, Toni Cade Bambara).

Notes on the lectures she attended at the Cambridge Adult Education Center, probably on Toni Morrison's *Song of Solomon* ("Pilate—woman = earth—circularity—metaphor"), notes on a poetry reading run by the town of Belmont ("metaphor—compressed meaning"), my mother expanding her

Calculation of life savings

mind, even if she wasn't brave enough to go off on an Elderhostel expedition, as I kept bugging her to do. "Compressed meaning," that's her little memo books.

Most touching to me are the shopping lists she prepared for my visits—at Christmas, sometimes at Easter, and in the summer—filled with treats for her fussy gourmet daughter.

> R beef
> Potatoes
> Cheese (havarti w/ dill?)—crackers
> Greenery
> Candles
> Sharon: Perrier, half and half
> Dry white wine

This shopping list—for a Christmas in the late eighties—says that there was a place in my mother's life for beauty and decoration as well as meat and potatoes, and that she loved me. Bless her heart, going beyond her humble cheddar to a more exotic cheese she knew would please me, giving up Chablis for pinot grigio.

And then there are the sadder, braver entries, my mother's notes on talks on nursing home care, assisted living, home health care, insurance for the elderly, probably sponsored by Belmont's Council on Aging. ("Long term/chronic/Home Health . . . Fix amt per day, $10–50 day, 10–30 visits . . . pay 80% for ambulance.") Notes from a talk on aging, my mother confronting her death ("problems when kidneys don't work well," "when older multiple disease," "no med unless necessary"). Notes from a talk on Medicare: "If denial—appeal." Notes from a talk on hospice care, which we would later choose, eerily prophetic. There's the entry where she intuits her death. And the one where she made notes for her long-delayed visit with the doctor, moving from symptoms of what she hoped was her emphysema (*Almost no energy—Back discomfort—Not eating much*) to the bolder, frightening questions, circling around the silenced word "cancer": *Anything else contributing? What can be done if anything?*

And then, at the back of her last notebook, the lists I find it hard to look at even now, the ones in shaky handwriting when she was close to the end, the ones that tell me how to face my own death. On the back of two doctor's prescriptions for painkillers—she'd run out of pages—are lists of bills to pay and thank-you notes to send, my mother settling her accounts ("Call credit office . . . call Frank to ask him to deposit check . . . write checks for bills in basket. . . . Thank yous Floss Mary Beale Ella Barbara Ella Frank Kennedy").

Much is missing from these books of lists. I see neither the scary mother of my childhood and young adulthood nor the frightened mother I came to recognize later, the one whose fears constricted her life and annoyed her children. "Just take a *cab*, Mom," we would say, "you should get out more," and she'd shrug her shoulders and nod her head, saying no and yes at the same time, asking us, without words, to leave her alone. And in the last book I find many blank pages—surely my mother would have filled this in had she lived longer!—a sign of how many sides of my mother I will never see. "She was a private woman," the hospice nurses told me, reminding me that I would never see her fully, that no one would.

But I do see more of my mother here than I could when she was alive. I get a glimpse of the heroism of an elderly woman simply living her life while her health and strength were fading. I used to think of my mother's life as sadly incomplete—that was why she thrived so on my more public life—but these memo books are brimming with the ongoingness of daily life, which is what you lose when you are claimed by depression, the source of the blank patches in my life that I never let my mother see.

What can be done if anything?   **Last list**

Y MOTHER MADE these lists and jottings for herself, but there are a few entries that I think were intended for my siblings and me, to be read after her death. One book (purchased at CVS for forty-nine cents, on sale) begins with a genealogy:

Margaret Doherty
m
Daniel Quinlan Dec 28 (?) 1890
    Geraldine Nov 22–1891
    Margaret—Feb 12–1893
    Dorothy—Aug 13–1895
    Marion—Dec 12–1903
    Ruth—May 16–1907
    Regina—May 6–1909

and continues to list her own marriage ("m Norbert O'Brien, Sept. 5, 1936") and children ("Maureen E., July 1 1937, Kevin L., July 20 1940, Sharon J., April 20 1945") and my sister's, the family rupture now erased ("m W. Courville—Maureen, July 5 1958—David—July 4 1960—Beth—July 30 1961—Ted—July 20 1965—John—March 9 1968").

Quinlan genealogy

Then the entry stops, as if my mother were content just to have given us this lineage of four generations; the next page begins new Christmas lists, followed by calculations of the slowly growing interest on her savings. A few pages later she returns to the family past: tracing her Irish heritage was on her mind during her last years. I find what at first seems to be another list of ancestors, but on second look I see the verbs that have been missing throughout my mother's lists. She is telling a story. I have found the only instance of narrative that occurs in all my mother's memo books.

She begins by telling the immigration story of Grandma Doherty, my great-grandmother:

> Mary Castles—County Cavan town of Cavan—came to America 8 yrs—from dock to Waldorf 34th—then to Saratoga—married Frank Doherty—came from County Donegal fishing village—one of 7 brothers—shoe maker

Then the story of her father's family:

> John Cullinan—County Clare—mother Cork—Bridget Larkin—died giving birth to Tommy—died young—remarried—Mamie Lonergan—half sister

Now I know how I want to read this list: my mother begins a story, leaving blank pages for me to add to it and then pass on.

PART TWO *In the Shadow of Harvard*

———

Life began for me when I ceased to admire and began to remember.
—WILLA CATHER

You Don't Always Get What You Want

Why did I ever think this move was a good idea? And now I can't go back. I have to go forward. Yikes.

Entry in my journal, June 24, 1996

IN 1995, EXACTLY FIFTY YEARS AFTER my father had moved the family back to his beloved Boston, I decided to take an early sabbatical from my teaching job and move back to the place that had once been my home.

I WAS FIFTY-ONE, still searching to understand my family past, and how depression, family, and culture were interwoven. Looking back, I can see that I also wanted permanent relief from depression: I wanted a clear-cut recovery story, not an ongoing illness that I had to manage, mixing and matching contemporary aids and remedies.

I didn't know it then, but I had projected some magical significance onto this return: by going back to my roots, I would surely be transformed! "I have to go back to my family past," I wrote in my journal that spring, "and find out, on a deeper level than I have, what happened, what went wrong. . . . The past is hiding a story, and I have to know what it is." But inheriting depression, I would come to realize, does not mean that something *went wrong*: that's a view I had absorbed from American culture, and it would take some time for me finally to let it go.

I also, and maybe mostly, wanted to reconnect with my father, by then dead almost twenty years. His dying had been so awful, such a rent in my life and in the life of my family, that I had not, for the longest time, been able to grieve, and so to remember.

Now that I had begun this process I wanted simply to spend more time with him: you reestablish a relationship with someone who's dead just the way you do with someone who's living, just being together. I knew that I would feel closer to him in Boston; places hold memories until you are ready

151

to retrieve them. We had shared so much, this father and daughter: our love of books and school, our links with Harvard, our depressions (although he had never known about mine). Our conversation had been broken off too soon. Perhaps it could resume.

I wanted to understand how our depressions, shared and unshared, were linked up with American culture: with success and failure, education and academia, the pressure to achieve and produce, roads taken and not taken. In the last few years I had been seeking ways of living that allowed for creativity and contemplation, and so had fewer visible accomplishments to offer the world. I missed the praise and the recognition; I also knew I was on the right path, and that my father would be cheering me on.

I had questions, too, about our shared Irish past, something my father never talked about. The O'Brien great-grandparents, like the Quinlans, had come from famine Ireland; could something valuable possibly have been lost in the story of success that had led, in three generations, from an illiterate mill worker to a Harvard graduate?

I HAD ANOTHER REASON for wanting to return to Boston and my father's past—more professional, and a little self-serving, interwoven with the culture of success I had called upon myself to challenge.

For a few years I'd been moving from academic writing to what we now call "nonfiction creative writing," working on two stories that had originally seemed separate—a memoir of depression and a family memoir. This meant a departure from professional upward mobility, since I was starting all over again as a writer. The previous summer I realized I was writing one book, not two, and yet there was still a major gap in it: my father's story, and the story of my life that linked with his. My mother and her colorful family had always taken center stage, and I had written mostly about them. I would have to return to Boston and re-immerse myself in my father's landscapes—Cambridge, Harvard, Lowell—if I wanted to make his world come alive in words.

In the early spring of that year I felt excited about both the year and my writing. I'd been working in this new genre for several years without the public recognition that had greeted my academic and biographical writings—probably a good thing, since I had begun to see the link between depression and seeking external approval. Recently it seemed that my new writing might be leading toward—could it be?—commercial success. (Maybe I could have it both ways, be spiritually correct and appear on *Oprah*.) A friend's agent had expressed interest in my work, and I'd sent him everything I'd written.

*I*N EARLY February the agent, a young man whose severe blonde crew cut contrasted oddly with his flowing black silk shirt, took me to lunch at a pricey New York Italian restaurant. He wasn't ready to take me on yet, but he was encouraging.

"Of course there are problems with structure," he cautioned. *Of course there were, how had I not seen this?*

"You should start over, writing chronologically," he said, digging a garlic-laden mussel out of its shell, "just give us the story, the basic black dress."

"The basic black dress . . . ?"

"You know, the basic outline, classic, timeless. Once that's done you can accessorize."

"Accessorize?"

"The pearls, the scarves, the flashbacks and forwards, a few metaphors."

An elegantly dressed man with coiffed grayish-white hair and a tanned face walked by, guided by a deferential waiter.

"That's Ralph Lauren," the agent said. "Don't stare."

*W*HEN I got back to Carlisle I realized I had no idea how to write a memoir. I was just a college professor trying to be creative. This agent was hot, and I was lucky to get his advice. I would start over in Boston, research my father's story, and restructure my book.

I would write a chronological black dress.

*A*LMOST NOTHING would work out the way I planned. I needed more money to supplement my sabbatical income, and I got turned down by every granting agency and fellowship I applied to. I was lonely in Cambridge. My depression, which had been more or less under control with medication, intensified nightmarishly and mutated, whenever it felt like it, into anxiety. I hated writing chronologically (no surprise for the writer, no surprise for the reader, Robert Frost says, and besides, memory doesn't work that way). The agent hated the plodding chapters I sent in ("And then, when I was fourteen and a half . . .") and stopped returning my phone calls. I gradually became too depressed to write and thought about moving back to Carlisle, but I'd rented my house out to a colonel at the Army War College.

I stayed in Cambridge, where I could at least fulfill one part of my prom-ise. A colleague in the English department at Harvard had arranged for me to be a visiting scholar, which meant I had a library card. I began researching and re-imagining my father's story; and slowly, slowly, as he and his world began to return to life, so did I.

As I traveled back in time, I found that the past held two intertwined stories: the one my father would give to me, and the one I could give back to him.

Veritas

Honesty is the richest legacy.
—WILLIAM SHAKESPEARE

IN THE EARLY MONTHS OF 1945, just as the war was winding down, bringing soldiers home for postwar prosperity, my father was already riding the crest of the American dream. Too old to be drafted—in 1941 he was thirty-five, with a wife and two children—he had spent the war years rising to the top of the emerging field of radio advertising. His career in radio had been slowly advancing throughout the 1930s and early 1940s. In 1932, he had moved to Elmira, New York (where he would meet my mother), to take up the position of commercial manager of a new Elmira radio station, a member of the Gannett group of newspapers and radio stations. From there he moved to the position of commercial manager of a Hartford, Connecticut, station, and then, in 1938, quickly moved up again to the advertising firm of J. P. McKinney and Sons in New York City, where he was in charge of national radio advertising for all the stations owned by the Gannett Group. His photo appeared in the *Elmira Star-Gazette* when he received this promotion. He's staring at the camera confidently, a man in charge of his destiny.

He stayed in this position until 1945 and was finally tempted to leave because he got a more attractive offer: to be commercial manager for a Boston radio station—WCOP, a new and ambitious outfit. This was a chance to enter a growing big-city radio market. New stations were opening rapidly as the nation shifted from a wartime to a peacetime economy, and he would be ahead of the curve. Even more appealing, the job would allow him to move back to Massachusetts, his home state.

My father turned forty in July 1945. When my parents moved to Belmont they would have expected my father's career in radio to thrive, and them-

Norbert, 1940

selves to achieve the middle-class American dream. All our lives would be shaped by the loss of that expectation, that story, perhaps the lives of the children even more than those of the parents.

In 1945 my father did not know many things. He did not know that within a short time he would be fired from his new job. He did not know that he carried with him to Boston a genetic inheritance of depression, and that his sister Gertrude, like him, would fall into depression's darkness. (Her case would be worse: she would be in and out of hospitals for shock treatments throughout the 1950s.) He did not know—and in fact would never know— that all three of his children would inherit depression. He did not know that within a few months, instead of going out for lunches with new clients, or enjoying office camaraderie, or devising advertising campaigns, he would be sitting on the bed in his room, staring out a strange window at a new street.

The reasons for my father's firing, which occurred after less than a year at the new job, were never clearly explained to us. In his Harvard reunion report, written in 1952, he says that he found his new employers "uncongenial," and I imagine that they found him not as aggressive a salesman as they would have liked. The reasons for the bad match are lost in the personnel history of the radio station, but I have one speculation.

During radio's early years, when my father was learning his trade, pressures for economic expansion were not that intense: many radio stations were small operations, not yet concerned with the bottom line. "Profit" and "radio" were not closely connected terms; radio stations were more closely aligned with newspapers than with any other form of American enterprise, considered more a form of public service than a new kind of business. By the mid-1940s, however, things were changing—new radio stations were opening and competing with each other for advertising dollars and for survival. My father would have entered a high-pressure sales atmosphere at WCOP. He would have been expected to produce measurable profits, and to do so quickly: several new stations were competing for Boston's emerging radio market.

My father's temperament was more that of the reflective teacher than that of the fast-talking salesman. He could be successful in sales, as he had been before and would be again, but his approach would have been more quiet, conversational, and perhaps leisurely than the new station wanted. Until WCOP my father had always worked within the Gannett "family" of radio stations. The Boston station was a business, not a family; the station managers wouldn't have thought twice about firing a commercial manager who wasn't boosting advertising revenues as fast as they wanted.

$\mathcal{I}$T WAS NOT really the firing that changed our family history. It was the resulting depression that kept my father from partaking in the upward mobility story of his generation, and it was that that changed everything. He did not "bounce back" from his job loss; he would be out of work for more than two years, spending most of his time, my sister and brother remember, in the bedroom, alone. No unemployment insurance. No income. The family living on loans and gifts from relatives. Living in a new neighborhood, surrounded by strangers, at a time when the word "depression" was even more shameful than "unemployed man," a time when "masculinity" was synonymous with "breadwinner."

And there was my mother, prevented by culture and temperament from finding a job herself, depending on a man who was no longer there. It must have seemed as though the solid world had disappeared.

Had they still been living in Elmira when this tragedy happened, or even in New York, where they had a group of young married friends, they would have been known; people would have dropped over, relatives would have visited after work, they would have been part of a community. Suffering the stigma of unemployment and depression would have been much harder in upper-middle-class Belmont. To be jobless and downwardly mobile in this milieu was to be marked as different and set apart as inferior. I used to wonder why my parents never made close friends in Belmont, as they had during their early married years; now it makes sense. "I had a story / I could tell to No one, " writes Emily Dickinson. Or, as my mother would later say, "We got off to a bad start."

I AM SURE MY PARENTS worried, among other things, about how they would ever pay the rent. When I was growing up, "ending up in the poorhouse" was to my mother still a powerful icon of a frightening destiny, perhaps a primal fear passed on by her Irish grandmother, who had left a starving country. I knew that the poorhouse was not too far away from our rented door. I could see it in my mind's eye, a long grey building with cell-like rooms and a yard where no flowers grew. We would sit on benches at long tables, holding our bowls out for gruel, like in *Oliver Twist*.

Living on money borrowed from relatives, shameful as that was, my parents managed to pay the rent and keep the apartment. By 1948 my father would secure a part-time job as a lingerie salesman, and by the early 1950s he had fashioned a self-employed life as a manufacturer's representative, a choice I now understand in my bones. When you're prone to depression, high-pressure jobs are a risk. The Catholic church taught us to avoid "occasions of sin," circumstances that could lead us astray. There are also "occasions of depression" which the vulnerable among us need to avoid or manage carefully. I think my father realized that America's competitive corporate culture was, for him, an occasion of depression. He made the choice of self-employment because he could more easily control the rhythms of his own work and avoid having to meet others' expectations for his performance as employee. A thoughtful, intellectual man—I always associated him with Adlai Stevenson—my father was not really suited for the high-pressure world of business, although he made his separate peace with it. He should have been a college professor, family wisdom agreed, and occasionally my father would tell the story of the road not taken during his senior year in college, when he decided not to get his master's degree in English literature, and to go into advertising instead.

My father's modest income as a manufacturer's rep—a ten-percent commission on sales to companies like Corning Glass and, to my joy, Dunkin' Donuts (we'd get free donuts from our local)—fluctuated yearly, depending on sales. Sometimes it was hard to make ends meet. In later years, when their children were all launched and my mother working in the Belmont library, my parents could have made the leap to home ownership—they sometimes talked of this—but they had become fearful of taking risks.

𝒟URING HIS period of unemployment and depression my father made the unusual decision to see a psychiatrist, perhaps a measure of how ill and desperate he was, or how brave. Men are still much less likely to seek psychiatric help than women, and Irish Catholic men might be the least likely of all, particularly in the 1940s—the religious and cultural ethic of Irish Catholicism stresses silent suffering. "Offer it up," people used to say about some tragedy or setback, which might, if endured well, grant you "a higher place in Heaven," as if the hereafter were organized by the reverse of earthly values. If you're Irish, suffering is supposed to make you a better person: you're supposed to endure it, not seek help to deal with it. The shock treatments my aunt Gert received for her depression in the 1950s seemed appropriately punishing Catholic treatment for flawed behavior, but my father's visits to the psychiatrist—which only involved talking—struck me as civilized and mysterious. I've always wondered what the two men talked about.

"Did Daddy ever tell you what he talked about with the psychiatrist?" I once asked my mother.

"No," she said.

"You never asked him?"

"No," she said, looking away, as if to say "this conversation is now over."

So this was a time of silence for my parents. My mother only knew that her husband's depression had to do with his work. Fearful and anxious, she would not have been a reassuring confidante for my father, even if he could have expressed his feelings to her. I think he saw a psychiatrist in part because he simply needed someone to whom he could tell the truth. The doctor would have been able to listen to my father say *I can't get out of*

*bed in the morning. I feel worthless. I'm scared. Everyone's depending on me.
I don't think I can bear this anymore* and not be destroyed by these words.
In fact, he would have nodded and said "Go on."

The therapy helped; eventually the depression wore itself out. My father
did not have the help of medication: antidepressants would not be available until the early 1950s, and as far as I know, electroshock therapy was
never considered. By 1952, the year of his twenty-fifth Harvard reunion, he
had patched himself back together and was beginning to take some modest
pleasure in his changed life.

We NEVER TALKED with my father about his depression, but the fact of it
was never hidden in the family. My father would routinely use phrases
like "during my depression" and my mother, to date events, might say "when
Daddy was depressed." We children absorbed the story without ever remembering when it was told or even what it meant. (We were also told, later,
about my aunt Gertrude's shock treatments.) I am grateful for that naming:
other parents might have covered up that dark time, or referred to Daddy's
"fatigue" or "exhaustion."

As a result, I must have been one of the few American children growing
up in the fifties who heard about her father's depression long before she
learned about the Great Depression. On the day my eighth grade history
teacher began to speak about the Great Depression, I was shocked—how
could this stranger know about my father? It didn't occur to me until much
later that there might be a reason why my country's economic collapse and
my father's personal collapse had the same name. Both were affronts to
capitalism—in the national case, the economy fell apart and there was no
work; in my father's case, he was unable to work. (Sometimes I wonder if
depression is, in part, an unconscious form of resistance to the work ethic—
in my father's case, to the speed-up and pressure he encountered at WCOP.)
Because my father, unlike the millions who lost jobs during the 1930s, was
an isolated individual—like the depressive Bartleby, who resists work in
Melville's story—he would have believed that he was at fault, out of step
with the bustling times.

In other ways this period of my father's life, and of our family life, was
oddly blank and silent. We never talked about what actually happened during those years, and I have no memories of my father for the first five years
of my life, despite the fact that I spent much time in his presence. My crib
was in my parents' bedroom, and I would stay incarcerated there, still in the

crib, until I was five and was allowed to share a room with my older sister. I sometimes wonder if this early exposure, even more than our shared genetic history, predisposed me toward later depression—and perhaps, although I don't want to go too far with this, toward relationships with thoughtfully troubled, emotionally remote men whom I kept trying to charm and save, a pattern now blessedly far enough in my past to have become a story.

I have only two photographs of myself with my father from this time. In one, I am going on a pony ride, and my father is holding my hand. Perhaps I am reading too much into this photo, but this father seems to be forcing himself to hold on—to his daughter, to his life.

In the second photograph we are on the way to church, my father in Sunday suit and tie pushing me in a baby buggy. You can tell that this father is doing the best he can—see how nicely he is dressed!—but his depression is palpable, and the troubled little girl seems to be mirroring his mood, even as she looks away from him toward the camera.

I learned most of what I would ever know about this painful time in my father's life by reading the personal statement he wrote for his twenty-fifth

Norbert with Sharon on pony, late 1940s

Norbert and Sharon going to church, late 1940s

Harvard reunion in 1952, just as he was getting on his feet again. There it sat, three whole pages in the huge maroon book published by the Class of 1927, the story of Norbert Lawrence O'Brien sandwiched in between those of Frederic Oatman and Henry Vining Seton Ogden. (There were no other O-apostrophes in the class, and only a handful of Irish Catholics. Brahmin, Protestant Harvard hadn't opened its doors too generously yet to Jews and Catholics.) When my parents were out of the house I would go into their bedroom and take the reunion book down from the bookcase and read and reread my father's statement. Then I was primarily looking for any references to myself, and so I savored the headnote:

CHILDREN: Maureen Ellen, July 1, 1937; Kevin Lawrence, July 20, 1940; Sharon Jean, April 20, 1945.

I would skim through the rest of the categories Harvard considered essential to self-definition:

PREPARED AT: Lowell High School, Lowell, Mass.
YEARS IN COLLEGE: 1924–27
DEGREE: A.B. *magna cum laude*, 1927
MARRIED: Regina Quinlan, September 5, 1936, New York, N.Y.
OCCUPATION: Manufacturer's Representative

I had no idea what a manufacturer's representative was, but I imagined it had to do with smokestacks. Later I would find out that he was a kind of salesman who represented companies that sold products that helped *other* companies sell products they manufactured—he represented printers and aluminum frame makers and slide chart makers. But the words "Manufacturer's Representative" as a description of my father never made much sense to me—my father wore glasses and loved novels and history books and popular music and read obscure nineteenth-century Catholic theologians; when he was home he talked about literature and history and listened to Benny Goodman and Jack Teagarden and never mentioned manufacturing at all.

The two men on either side of my father in the reunion book, whose stories I would glance at, had more normal 1950s occupations than my father, it seemed to me. Frederic Oatman was in "Advertising," my father's former profession, and Henry Vining Seton Ogden enjoyed the profession that my father would have loved, the one he missed, the one I would assume in his place—"English Professor."

I have inherited the fat maroon book with the Harvard shield and motto—*Veritas*, Truth—inscribed in gold on the front cover. Over the last few years I have read and reread my father's writing many times, and I have come to see what an extraordinary essay it is.

ACCORDING TO the directives sent out by the Reunion Committee, the writers were supposed to start their personal story with "Career." My father resisted this command to define himself primarily by his work and began by telling his classmates about a book he'd been reading.

I was reading Marquand's *Melville Goodwin, U.S.A.* over the Christmas holidays, feeling guilt at passively reading a novel rather than feverishly working at a 1927 biography, when a passage came along that was surely a reward for the idle. At once it gave promise of some kind of shape to a half-thought-out life story which an unrelenting committee solicited in every other mail. If you read the book, you will recall that it is told in the first person by Sidney

Skelton, radio news commentator, who had the following conversation one
night with wife Helen:

"Sid," Helen asked me, "what's the matter?"

"Nothing's the matter. I was just thinking, Helen."

"What were you thinking about?"

"Oh, this and that," I said. "I was just thinking that Life makes almost
everyone into something that he never exactly wanted to be, and then the
time comes when he can't very well be anything else."

"But you never knew what you wanted to be."

"That's right," I said. "I never gave it much attention."

I shouldn't be surprised if the philosophy contained in that quotation has
been better stated elsewhere, possibly by Mr. Marquand himself. But it will
serve. It applies, I am quite sure, to many graduates of the Class of 1927, and
certainly it applies to me.

As my father goes on to describe his early vocational drifting, it becomes
clear that, like most Americans, he connected "what do you want to be?"
with "what job do you want to have?"

After graduation I just simply looked around for a job, paying more attention
to newspaper work and teaching than to other fields, but willing to accept
anything interesting that came along. The job which came along, more or
less by accident, was a position in a Boston advertising agency. For five years
I was an advertising agency man, and I liked it. Then in 1932 the Depression
finally got through to my firm, and three of us were lopped off the payroll.

This first firing, described as an inevitable pruning, was sparked by the
economic Depression, which perhaps was why this unemployment did not
plunge my father into the personal depression that would grip him later. It
was clear, given the terrible times, that the job loss was not his fault. The
fact that the agency had to fire two other "ad men" as well must have made
his own fate easier to bear. Still, it was hard for him to find work again in
1932. This was not a time when you had the luxury of wondering what you
wanted to "be"; you were glad enough just to find any job.

Those members of the Class who have occasion to recall the white-collar
unemployment miseries of those days will probably remember that, after
months of failure to find work, you hardly had much choice in continuing

in your chosen fields. You took whatever came along. The job that I took was in radio broadcasting. I became sales manager of Station WESG, Elmira, New York, owned by the *Elmira Star-Gazette*, a paper of the Gannett group. I remained with the radio division of this company for thirteen years, going from Elmira to the company's Hartford station and thence to the New York office.

My father devotes only a sentence to the thirteen years of his successes and promotions: these were now far in the past. He is ready to bring his classmates into the harder story of the last seven years: "This brings me to 1945," he wrote, "the year of the Big Change"—his move to Boston and a radio job "that seemed to give promise of more interest, more responsibility, more money." Except, he told his readers,

> It was the year not only of the Big Change but also of the Bad Move, or the Wrong Guess. For the new firm and I were as uncongenial as it is possible for firm and employee to be. It all ended in a nice case of nerve exhaustion and months of unemployment while regaining health.
>
> There was a temporary job in 1947–48 doing promotion for a manufacturer friend in Lowell who made lingerie. There was another temporary job in 1948–1949 handling the sales of a new radio station in Bristol, Connecticut, though I retained residence in Belmont. And then, to permit me to be home with my family, I took the first likely job that presented itself, which turned out to be that of a representative of a Chicago manufacturer of advertising charts.
>
> Recently, when this manufacturer decided to change the status of representatives from salary to commission, I elected to retain the line, seek out additional advertising services to promote throughout New England, and try working on my own.

*A*LTHOUGH "DEPRESSION" was the word psychiatry textbooks were beginning to use in the 1940s to describe my father's state—and was the word our family used—the term "nerve exhaustion" was still commonly used to describe the symptoms we now associate with major depression—hopelessness, apathy, anxiety. The term connects back to the nineteenth century's "neurasthenia" and is retained in the phrase "nervous breakdown." The phrase "nerve exhaustion" reveals the positive associations neurasthenia held during the late nineteenth and early twentieth centuries. In his classic work *American Nervousness*, Dr. George M. Beard connects the illness with allegiance to the work ethic: if you are suffering from "exhaustion," that could only be because you have been *working hard.*

Even though my father used this older term in his essay, linking back to this less stigmatized view of depression, the cultural meanings of the condition had shifted by the 1940s, signified by the increasing use of the new term. By then his post-firing breakdown had been separated from the cultural origins George M. Beard thought gave rise to neurasthenia and firmly attached to psychological, and thus individual, causes, leaving my father much more vulnerable to shame and feelings of failure.

Had the theories in *American Nervousness* still been in vogue, my father would have been given an almost flattering explanation for depression's origins. Almost proudly, Beard had proclaimed neurasthenia the "American disease." He believed that technological progress was the major cause of neurasthenia, along with the pressures in American life for upward mobility. "Civilization itself" produced the illness, because of the increased pace of American life and the corresponding intensified worry. "We are under constant strain to get somewhere or do something at some definite moment," he thought, and Americans were particularly afflicted with a "painful striving to see who shall be highest."

Seeing the source of neurasthenia not in the biological or psychological realms, but in a culture he approved of (despite its stresses, he celebrated progress), Beard thought that only people of superior intelligence and ability could become neurasthenic. He called them "brain-workers." Far from being stigmatized, the illness was a sign of sensitivity, intellectual force, and overwork. Neurasthenic men were nineteenth-century workaholics who had run, momentarily, out of steam. After a period of rest, they would return, renewed, to the capitalist fray. (In fact, Beard thought that those who were *not* neurasthenic were lazy and unmotivated, most likely from the laboring classes. In America "contentment and repose" were only to be found "among the extremely unambitious.")

WITH NO CULTURAL theory for the source of depression, and lacking the biochemical one (this would come later, in time for me), my father was left to locate depression squarely in the self, and to deal with shame. He does speak of this in his reunion report, and—perhaps wanting to downplay the seriousness of his breakdown, or to reassure readers of his recovery—he refers to his "nice" case of nerve exhaustion, the paradoxical, ironic adjective showing his classmates they could keep reading, he wasn't going to let them any further into his soul.

Like William Styron, who in *Darkness Visible* would write the story of depression that did not exist in 1952, my father wanted to assure his readers that he had recovered from depression and was writing from that vantage point—like a sailor who recounts his terrifying adventures on the high seas once he is safely back in port.

He cannot tell his classmates what it was like to suffer through months and months of depression—he had stretched the genre of the reunion report far enough just telling the truth about his job loss and illness. Given what I know of depression, I can imagine the courage it must have taken just to keep going. He kept waking up every day to depression and he did whatever it took to survive. He would borrow my aunt's car so he could visit a psychiatrist who lived fifteen miles away. Sometimes he borrowed the car so he could look for work. He agreed that he and my mother would ask for, and accept, loans from her sisters as well as gifts of clothing. (These things he also did not tell his classmates.)

Y MOTHER did not like to talk about those early years in Belmont. Once I was cross-examining her about the fact that she and my father never had people over to our house in Belmont.

"I only saw relatives there," I said, remorseless as a lawyer who'd just seized on a contradiction in a witness's testimony. "You say you love people, but why did you never invite anybody to dinner, or even just over for a drink?"

She shifted in her chair, the way she did when she was uncomfortable and was not going to say why. "We got off to a bad start," she said.

She may not have had words for what had happened. Today depression is a household word in America, and there are dozens and dozens of books to consult if one seeks to understand its origins and treatments, as well as chatrooms, websites, newspaper articles. In the late 1940s there were no public stories that made depression, if not an acceptable, then at least an acknowledged illness; and that would have made everything much more difficult to bear for both my parents. At least my father had his visits to his psychiatrist; together they would have constructed a story to understand what had happened. But what could my mother have said about 1945? What happened was not supposed to take place in America. Middle-class husbands were supposed to be breadwinners: their wives depended on that, expected it, deserved it.

What would she have said, when a new neighbor asked "What does your husband do?" How could she have said, over the clothesline or the coffee cup, "Oh, Norb just got fired from his job, and actually he's sitting on the bed right now, just staring. Sometimes he borrows his sister's car and goes to a psychiatrist in Billerica. And what does your husband do?"

She would have lied, of course. This was no occasion for *veritas*. She would have said "Oh, he's in advertising," or maybe "he works out of the house," or maybe, with an "Aren't I silly?" laugh, she would have said "he's in business for himself, something with advertising, I never quite understand exactly what it is!" and then she would have quickly gone inside and avoided contact with the other housewives on Lewis Road. She would have told no one the truth, because of the shame, and she would have felt completely alone.

*W*HEN I was reading my father's words as a child, I never noticed that my mother's story was missing. My father's story seemed complete in itself; after all, it gave the requisite happy ending of reemployment, being his "own boss" as a manufacturer's representative.

Only when I reread the essay later did I see that my father did not, in fact, end with reemployment. To do so would have been to reduplicate the ideology of upward mobility as well as the illness recovery story, and he wasn't about to do that: these required American narratives didn't fit his experience, and he wasn't going to shape his story to fit the expected plot. Yes, he describes new employment, but not in the way the success story requires.

And so it is that, in January of 1952, I find myself, somewhat mystified, in business for myself working out of my house in Belmont, dealing with three lines of advertising services, and wondering how I ever got that way. I like it, I may do well with it, and there is the satisfaction of being my own boss. But all of this, quite obviously, is anything but the result of deeply laid plans stemming from school years, or even later years.

In many respects I envy classmates who knew what they wanted, hewed to the line from early days, and have made definite marks in a career that represented lifetime endeavor. But not too much. For I have enjoyed my work. I have actively liked advertising agency work, radio broadcasting activities, representation of advertising services, and yes, the sales promotion of lingerie. Moreover, some of the more drastic changes in my business career have enriched Life-in-General in immeasurable ways. If a depression had not rooted me out of Boston and advertising work and transplanted me to Elmira and radio broadcasting, I shouldn't have met and married an Elmira girl with whom I have been living happily ever after, together with three increasingly congenial children. And if I hadn't guessed badly in the choice of a new job in 1945, I probably shouldn't have dipped as deeply into matters spiritual as I have since, to my ever increasing inner satisfaction. So, though J. P. Marquand's quotation has reminded me that Life seems to have made me into something that I never exactly wanted to be, I have no kicks.

My father confesses to liking being his "own boss" as a manufacturer's representative, even though this job did not result from choice, plan, or desire. He follows the reemployment story with one that clearly has more meaning to him: the outcome of spiritual and "inner satisfaction" that resulted from his "Bad Move"—not part of the American success story, but part of his own.

In the concluding paragraph of his essay, my father reflected on what wisdom he might be able to pass on to his son as a result of his experiences. Although satisfied with his unplanned career and happy with "Life-in-General," my father wants my brother's work life to be different.

> I intend, though, to try to help my son, aged eleven, to think through during his 'teens to something that he would really want to do upon graduation from college. Certainly I have accumulated the experience wherewith to offer him some pretty sound counsel.

My father wants to give Kevin what he envied in others, "hewing to the line from early days" to a career. Later he would want me to do the same. He was reacting to the Depression and his own depression, wanting to pass on security to his children, but paradoxically not giving us enough room for choice and exploration. It would have been more of a gift if he had counseled us to find the "inner satisfaction" in our work, whatever that might be, that he began to find through his spiritual explorations. Even now, maybe especially now, though, very few middle-class American parents can give this kind of advice to their college-bound children, whom they would like safely settled in Ivy League institutions (perhaps prepared for since preschool) and mainstream professions.

*I*N THE FIRST years of my depression, I used to ask myself and my therapist, *What went wrong?* That was, I now realize, a very American question, assuming happiness, health, and what we now call "self-fulfillment" as the normal state of being. That question would make no sense from a Buddhist perspective, or from a contemplative Catholic one: if suffering is a normal part of life, nothing is "wrong" with inheriting depression. But by posing the question that way I concentrated on the family fault lines, and it's taken me longer to name the sources of strength and wisdom I inherited as well.

The mere existence of my father's reunion report is one of those sources. Not many men, even today, could tell such a story about public failure and private growth. Not many Harvard men, writing their twenty-fifth reunion report for all their classmates to read, would embrace *veritas* as fully as he did and tell the truth about unemployment, "nerve exhaustion," and the unplanned, sometimes sad twists life can take with his frankness. In fact, there is no other report quite like it in the Class of 1927's 1,300-page maroon book.

The Class of 1927 Reunion Committee had sent out directions for the reports classmates were to write. "The Class wants to know all about your career history, your family, your travels, hobbies, and your social, political, or religious convictions." Almost all the 743 reports conformed to this list, beginning, obediently, with "career history," most expressing modest to great satisfaction with life, a few showing awareness that the writer's achievements were not of the caliber expected of a Harvard man. ("I'm very much afraid that this 'sketch' will hardly measure up to the man of distinction asked for," wrote one; another apologized that he had "nothing spectacular, or even important, to report.")

For my father to have written about the dark side of the American dream in a class report—a genre in which men even more than women tend to list their professional accomplishments, or not to respond at all—that's gutsy. To admit to the stigmas of depression and unemployment in 1952—that is to honor the truth of one's experience more than the opinions of others. My father must have decided that if he were going to write this report at all, he would have to write something real. I also believe he knew that others in his class might share parts of his story, and so he might be able to put

ARTHUR LAURENCE NORTON

NORBERT LAWRENCE O'BRIEN

LEONARD JOSIAH NOVOGROD

HENRY VINING SETON OGDEN

FREDERIC OATMAN

JOHN BARTOW OLMSTED, 2D

Class of 1927 reunion book, 1952

into words something they could not express but would understand, and be comforted by.

I suspect that many members of the class of 1927 felt less alone after reading my father's words. Perhaps one of them was the man who simply sent in a stark chronology as his life story.

1928–1933 G. L. Ohrstom & Co., Investments—New York, Boston, Atlanta
1933–1937 A. G. Tomasello & Son, Boston Road Building Contractors
1937–1940 Koppers Coal Company, Mt. Hope, West Virginia
1940–1945 Watertown Arsenal, Watertown, Massachusetts
1945–1949 Store and office window lettering—contractor
Since 1949: Hospitalized

This seems to be a story like my father's, one of downward mobility and chronic illness. Perhaps this classmate—in a hospital for more than three years—suffered from depression or some other mental illness. I like to think that he read my father's story and received some consolation from it.

$\mathcal{I}$ LOOK THROUGH the other 742 narratives of the Class of 1927, and it's clear—I like my father's story the best. I don't want my father to be the stockbroker who wrote "As far as hobbies are concerned, other than bending my right elbow it is mostly golf, badminton, or squash in the winter, and an occasional theater or opera"; or the banker who wrote "it looks as though we are going to have to fight Russia if Truman does not ruin the country first"; or the doctor who wrote "pathologists can really name their own ticket, and they do not have to treat colds and neurotic women."

No: it's the man who began his memoir with "I was reading," and quotes from a novel he wants to share; the man who tells the truth about his Wrong Guess and Bad Move and Nerve Exhaustion, and acknowledges the quiet satisfactions he's derived from a life that did not work out according to plan; the man who says he's exploring "matters spiritual" and claims that reading offers a "reward for the idle"—if I could choose all over again, that's the man I'd pick to be my father.

Between Two Worlds

You are growing when you feel most hindered.

—SARAH ORNE JEWETT, in a letter to Willa Cather

DURING HIS LIFETIME MY FATHER and I never talked about his depression, and he never knew about mine. When I was stricken with my first diagnosed depression—in 1969, as a graduate student in English at Harvard—I didn't tell him. I knew he was counting on me to succeed, and I didn't want him to know the depths into which I had fallen. Even though he could have understood better than most people, I was too ashamed to tell him.

Once I returned to Boston, things would be different. I could talk with his ghost, just the way Dante talked with Virgil, and my father could be my mentor and guide. I would find out more about him and his story, and in return he'd guide me back to the surface. I'd conquer depression and write a triumph-over-illness book at the same time. It seemed like a good bargain, although I hadn't actually checked with him to see if he was on board. Sometimes the living can be really arrogant, expecting the dead will do their bidding, they should be so grateful to be asked.

I DROVE UP TO Boston in mid-May, right after Dickinson's graduation. I needed to find an apartment quickly; I was scheduled to move in a month. My sister and I had talked about my living with her, but I thought I needed independence, and we were both used to living alone. I wasn't sure where I would live; Cambridge would be ideal but had become too pricey. Belmont might be too weird. Somerville could be the best option—close to Cambridge, less expensive, a formerly working-class suburb with snarly traffic, pizza places, and Dunkin' Donuts, now just starting on the path to upper-middle-class greatness with a T stop on the respectable Red Line, restaurants with changing menus, and Peet's coffee.

*T*HE SOMERVILLE apartment has fuzzy orange wall-to-wall carpeting and lowered ceilings. There's a wet bar right off the kitchen with red vinyl stools and rows and rows of liqueurs, cordials, whiskies, gins, rums, and brandies lined up on glass shelves by category.

"The tenant hasn't moved everything out," the real estate agent says unnecessarily. "He's a bachelor, works for the phone company," as if that explained anything.

This apartment scares me. I think it has the power to kill. I see myself living here, just as it is, with no furniture and surrounded with booze. This apartment will make me so depressed I won't be able to go out for groceries. I won't answer the phone and friends will not find me. I look down at the fuzzy carpet, which looks springy and deep, and see myself lying on it, motionless in the afternoon sun, arms hugging my chest, waiting to die.

I have been trying to like this woman. She was supposed to be my lifeline, but now I have to let her drop.

"Barbara," I say, "I'm a little claustrophobic, and the lowered ceilings—"

"I *knew* it," she says. "Of course, not good for a writer. You need all that *space* over your head," spiraling her arm up toward the ceiling, pausing, "—for the *ideas.*"

She consults her notebook. "I have a wonderful second-floor in Winter Hill, high ceilings, great view of Boston. I'll call the landlord."

I escape Barbara. I had thought I could live in Somerville, but I cannot. It's not on my emotional map. Over here, I don't know where I am.

I DRIVE DOWN the Fresh Pond Parkway toward Belmont, where my next appointment is. I've decided to try it. My car flows easily into the short cuts, Concord Ave to Aberdeen Ave to Grove Street, and soon I'm driving past the Belmont Cemetery. I think about stopping in to visit my parents' graves but I decide to wait: I'm edgy and distracted. There will be a better moment.

*T*HE AGENT who's supposed to meet me in Belmont doesn't show up. I'm relieved. Driving through town, I realize I don't want to live here: it's both surrealistically close to the past and disturbingly different. My grade school and the high school have burned down, replaced by parks, and the familiar clump of stores in my neighborhood is gone, the spa transformed into a homemade ice cream place and the notions store into gourmet takeout. I drive past 28 Lewis Road, the gray stucco house where I grew up, but I don't stop.

$\mathcal{M}$Y NEXT APPOINTMENT is with a real estate agent in Cambridge. If I can afford it, maybe this is the right place to live? I'm going to be vaguely affiliated with Harvard, a visiting scholar in the English department, having a title and a library card. I lived in Cambridge during college and graduate school: it's familiar, maybe a new home.

The Cambridge agent is even more frightening than the Somerville one. She has a raspy smoker's voice, short, overpermed reddish hair, and a weatherbeaten face. Her washboardy skin contrasts oddly with her purple silk blouse. It's a pitiless face that's seen thousands of homeless renters like me sitting in the stiff wooden chair by her desk. She could care less whether I find a nest. She'll be happy to stuff me into a cubicle where hundreds of people have come and gone. The agent keeps me waiting while she talks to several renters on the phone, and I overhear alarming phrases ("a thousand a month *minimum*," "first and last month's rent, plus a security deposit"). Across the room one agent is complaining to another, "These people who come to Hahvahd, if they can't throw a rock into Hahvahd Squayah they think they're in outah space."

I don't like feeling so vulnerable where I used to belong. *Look,* I want to say to the agent, *I grew up around here, I went to school here, I've been a Red Sox fan since I was five, this is my hometown. I have roots here. Doesn't that count?*

"How much do you want to pay?" she asks, and then she's off on her checklist, number of rooms, location, length of lease. I suspect by the way she screws up her eyes when I say words like "airy" or "porch" or "quiet place to write" that hers is an ethic of deprivation, not desire. There will never be enough to go around so you'd better take what's right in front of you. It's a scarcity ethic, and I feel my fear of homelessness rising.

"This one'll go in a jif," the agent says of a tiny one-bedroom in a land-locked apartment building on Lancaster Street where there's a two-year waiting list for parking spaces. I tell her I don't want to live in a building. I want an apartment in a house. She's impatient and I feel guilty for taking up her time.

"Mr. Bonatelli's apahtment always rents the same day," she warns me as she drives us to an Upland Street second floor, "and I just got the call a half hour ago. It's a *gohjus* apartment," she adds, flicking ashes out the car window, "you're lucky to be able to gettalook at it first."

Mr. Bonatelli's apartment is hideous. I would be devoured by the wallpaper alone—red and black plaid in the kitchen, yellow with green and rust-colored peacocks in the living room, blue and white paisley in the bedroom. The porch overlooks a backyard filled with waist-high grass. A rusting grill squats on a small square of cracking cement. "And of course you can use the patio," the agent rasps.

"I grew up in a house in Belmont with overwhelming wallpaper," I tell her, hoping she'll understand why I can't take the place, wondering why she has to understand at all.

*O*N MY way back to my sister's house in Wellesley I decide to drive past the Belmont cemetery. It's on the border between Cambridge and Belmont, right near Fresh Pond, and just behind Huron Towers—a high-rise apartment building that used to drive my mother wild because it interfered with her TV reception. "Why they had to go and build that monstrosity there, I'll never know," she would say, and my father would reply "Now Jeannie" in a soothing voice, as he always did when he was trying to deflect her anger or quiet her fear.

It's nine o'clock and I assume the gates will be closed. But my headlights shine into an open space, and I drive in. It's late in May, so the days are lengthening, and the air is still filled with silver-grey light. Now the way to the headstone is long familiar, and I drive down all the paths named after flowers—Salvia Way, Rose Lane, Camellia Street. My parents live at the intersection of Orchard and Peony.

I keep seeing two dots of light as I drive and wonder what they are: then I realize they are my headlights, bouncing off the shiny tombstones. I glance out the side window and for an instant I can see my car, a white blur passing over the grey stones. I cannot see myself.

I can just make out their names in the fading light.

NORBERT LAWRENCE O'BRIEN 1906–1976
REGINA QUINLAN O'BRIEN 1909–1991

I run my hands over the smooth stone, tracing the engraved indentations of the names with my fingers.

"Listen," I say, crouching down close to their names, "I'm in trouble. I need you to help me." Passersby might think it odd, me speaking to a gravestone, but I don't care. "I'm having a really terrible time finding a place to live." I like hearing the sound of my voice in the quiet.

Being here is calming. The scent of honeysuckle fills the night air. I tell my parents about how unsettling it is to be looking for an apartment in a place where I used to belong. I don't hear a voice—not an actual one—but inside I suddenly know what to do, as if my father were speaking to me. Dealing with the outside world was his department.

"Use the Harvard housing list, Sharon."

I stand up and take a deep breath. My brother has planted marigolds in front of the grave, and the scent of fresh mulch fills the air. I breathe in the piney smell and snap the wilted flowers off the stems so the buds will have more energy. I take a bottle of mineral water from the car and pour it into the soil. The last of the twilight is gone now, and it's dark enough to see tiny white and red dots of light from the votive candles placed next to a few graves. They scatter across the hill behind my parents' grave, a constellation of stars telling me others have been thinking of their dead.

THE NEXT DAY I go back into the renter's world again, Harvard housing list in my hand. Within a few hours I've found an apartment I like—airy, shiny wood floors, white walls, windows full of light. It's the bottom floor of a house on Saville Street, in a small, old, mixed-race middle-class neighborhood called Huron Village, tucked in between Harvard Square and Fresh Pond. As I'm walking to my car I realize my new home is equidistant from the Radcliffe dormitories, where I lived thirty years ago, and the Belmont cemetery, where my parents live now.

A ten-minute walk in either direction, and I'll be entering a different part of the past.

MY CARLISLE RENTER wants my house unfurnished, which I decide is a good thing—I'll store some of my stuff and move the rest to Boston. It will be good to have familiar things around me, and I need the feeling of a major break with the twenty years I've lived in Carlisle.

For a long time, maybe a year, maybe two, I've been having the sense of an ending in Carlisle. I've gone away before, but this time feels different: I'm not sure I'll come back. I've been having the sense that there's something else I'm meant to do in my life, something that has to do with why I'm really on this earth, but I don't know quite what that is.

I do remember the moment when I started thinking I had to get out of Carlisle. For a while, or forever? I wasn't sure, but I knew I needed change.

I had driven to Washington to see Anna Deveare Smith in *Fire in the Mirror,* her performance piece about the L.A. riots sparked by the beating of Rodney King. To create it she interviewed hundreds of people, and all the personalities she takes on, all the words she speaks, are those of the people she spoke with. It's not just that this is a remarkable performance: it gives you the sense that Anna Deveare Smith has found her vocation, doing something that is socially and personally meaningful at the same time. I envied her.

Afterward she agreed to answer questions from the audience.

"Tell me," one woman asked, "isn't it emotionally draining and painful, what you do—you interview those people in the midst of tragedy and then every night, when you perform, you live through it all over again?"

Anna Deveare Smith didn't hesitate a second.

"Oh, but it's different—every night, I get to give it away to *you.*"

Her remark hit me almost physically, an epiphany in my gut. *That's the problem,* I thought, *I'm not giving it away to other people.* I wasn't sure what "it" was—some talents, some insights, some abilities that I couldn't pass on to other people. I hadn't possessed these abilities, they were still undiscovered, when I first came to Dickinson in 1975, thirty years old with a brand new Ph.D. from Harvard. These new parts of myself had grown with the living of the last twenty years, and I feared I'd never find them if I didn't take the risk of leaving my settled life.

*A*ND THEN SOMETHING happened that told me even more strongly that *I had to get out.* One day, shortly before I was to leave for Boston, I got a call from Cumberland Valley Memorial Gardens. I had been selected for a free burial plot. I would only have to provide money for perpetual care.

"It's a lovely site," the woman said, "with a good view of the South Mountain." *You mean I'm going to die here?*

"No thanks," I said. "I don't really live here permanently. I'm just passing through."

"Oh," she said brightly, "well, if there's anyone in your family who might be—"

"I don't have a family," I said. "You should give the plot to somebody who really lives here."

After I hung up I started to wonder: just where *do* single women get buried? My parents' grave site is full, and besides, I wouldn't want to be buried with them; it would be humiliating. People would be walking through the Belmont Cemetery, see the grave, and say "I wonder why that daughter's buried with her parents. Do you suppose she never really lived her own life?" I didn't want to be buried in Carlisle either, way off in the middle of Pennsylvania, where none of my family would ever find me, in some graveyard reserved for single women who didn't have any place better to go.

$\mathcal{T}$WO WEEKS BEFORE leaving Carlisle for Boston I realized I'd made a terrible mistake. What on earth I was doing, disrupting my whole life because of some intuition that I needed to go back to Boston? And who decided to rent her house unfurnished, a terrible idea if there ever was one? I stared at dressers and bookcases and tables for hours, not sure what should stay, what should go. All my furniture looked so *heavy*, so reluctant to leave. All the things I'd accumulated over ten years in this house seemed at the same time insubstantial and ominously solid. I cleared out the spare bedroom— "that'll give you a sense of accomplishment," my friend Bob said, "just to get one room under control"—and the room looked sad and empty when I was done. I felt erased, as if I were dying out of my own house.

And what if I couldn't pay the exorbitant Cambridge rent? Deliver a stunning black dress to the agent?

The enormity of what I was doing—by choice!—paralyzed me. Why had I thought this was a good idea?

When I was younger I could move at the drop of a hat. "Sharon, I can't keep up with you," my mother used to say. "I need a whole address book just to keep track of your whereabouts." I had a system down cold—different color stickers for the boxes, one for each room in the new place—and I'd write "2nd dish set" or "Cather books" or "cleaning supplies" in red magic marker on a big white sticker I put on top.

Now I didn't have a clue about a system. I gave myself three options— Take, Store, or Throw—and would find myself staring at a littered tabletop for half an hour, unable to decide whether to Take, Store, or Throw a teddy bear I unsuccessfully bought in an attempt to give myself, retrospectively, a happy childhood; a fake antique lamp from Montgomery Ward's; an

Eastern guide to sexual bliss, employing the energy of all seven chakras; a heap of earrings without their mates; velcro hair rollers; a hot water bottle I used in Ireland; a box containing twenty years' worth of unsorted photographs, and a stack of unopened mail that accumulated during my last period of severe depression that I'm afraid to look at and too guilty to throw out.

Finally I threw all the items in a box labeled *Store—Stuff.*

I WAS ONLY ABLE to sleep three or four hours a night; I'd wake up with the birds, my heart racing, unable to get up or go back to sleep. A few days before leaving I lay awake all night, drenched in terror: my first full-fledged panic attack. Going ahead with this move seemed impossible, and yet I could not stay where I was. I imagined breaking both leases and staying in Carlisle, but I was too fragile to handle anybody's anger, particularly not the Army colonel who was renting my house.

"Wandering between two worlds," Matthew Arnold wrote, "One dead, the other powerless to be born." That summed it up. Wandering between Carlisle and Boston, past and future, the first half of my life and the second, my father's life and my own.

I was filled with dread. How could I possibly survive in Cambridge, the most expensive place on earth? What if my writing didn't go well, what if I was lonely, what if I became even more depressed away from therapist, colleagues, friends, everything that held me in place? I could see the back doors of the U-Haul blowing open on interstate 95, all my possessions scattering over the highway, irretrievably lost. My mind kept clicking on, creating one disaster scenario after another.

I lay in bed all night, watching the blood-red numbers on the digital clock change, going over every mistake I'd made in my life, every bad decision, every regret. Why hadn't I gotten married? Had children? Saved more money? Exercised more? Left Dickinson? How could I have made such a *mess* of my life? I started to wonder if I were feeling my mother's fears as well as my own. I knew I had inherited my father's depression; had I received or absorbed my mother's anxiety as well? Was I dealing with a genetic double whammy?

"Leap and the net will appear," people say, but they don't mention *when* the net will appear.

Maybe it appears long after you've gone *splat!* on the sidewalk.

*T*HE NEXT morning I lay on my couch for two hours, hanging on until my appointment with my therapist, watching the ceiling fan rotate, clutching a pillow. She and I both knew what I had to do. I had to ask for help. I had to admit that I couldn't do this alone. "Give me a list of all the people you're going to call," she said, and I wrote it out for her.

*D*EPRESSION IS, among other things, an illness of isolation. When you get depressed you isolate yourself, and then it gets harder and harder to reach out. To do so you have to fight not only your depression, but also your shame—do you really deserve to ask for help, let alone to get it? If you were suffering from a physical illness, you wouldn't be as hesitant. If I were grappling with cancer or diabetes or heart disease, it would be easier for me to reach out; I'd feel, somehow, more *deserving*. But to ask for help because you're depressed or anxious—why would anyone want to put themselves out for you? Yes, I know that depression is an illness, and that I can't affect my brain chemistry with an effort of will. But I still have this mean little voice inside me that says that—only in my case!—depression isn't really an illness, it's a character flaw. I know that voice is wrong, that it's a product of American ideology, and still—it's hard to silence. Shouting back "You're an ideological construct! Shut up!" doesn't work at all. That hateful little voice lives inside my head, or in my soul. Sometimes I wonder: if my whole family had stayed in Ireland, if I'd grown up in a culture that isn't so obsessed with success and individualism, would I be . . . not depression-free, but more accepting of myself in these dark times?

Asking for help means you have to challenge all the American individualism with which you've been socialized, your belief that you should be able to do everything all by yourself. It's easy for me to suggest that *other* people ask for help when they're depressed or anxious—I do understand how crucial support is—but when it comes to me, I wait until it's an emergency.

Now it's an emergency so I let myself dial 911. I go home and call up my friends. I tell the truth, that I'm in bad shape with anxiety and that I need their help. I ask for help in getting movers, in packing, in making "Store" and "Throw" decisions. I ask for help in picking up the U-Haul, in dealing with the utilities, in finding boxes. It turns out everybody's not only willing to help, they're pleased to be asked. Pretty soon I have a schedule for the next ten days—Jane in the morning, Carol in the afternoon, Elizabeth in the evening. Then Grace, then Debbie, then Bob and Tom, then Mara, then

Jane and Elizabeth again. They drop off boxes, they leave notes (*Sharon—utilities are taken care of!—Jane; Sharon—I'll be over at 8:00 to go pick up the U-Haul, Bob*), they bring shiny green bubble wrap. They write "fragile" on my cartons. "It'll get better as soon as you get to Cambridge," they say. "As soon as you're unpacking. You just need to get there."

I also ask my psychiatrist for help—I've accepted antidepressants as necessary, but I've drawn the line at anything else. Now my belief that the fewer pills you take, the better a person you are is just too costly to maintain. I take the valium she prescribes. It takes the edge off, and at least I can sleep.

THUNDERSTORMS CRASH through the Cumberland Valley every afternoon the week I am packing and flash flood warnings stream across the television at night. The cat hides in the basement. It's hot for mid-June, low nineties every day, but the storms clear the air. I lie in bed at night and feel the breezes swirling around me, loving the reassuring whirr of the ceiling fan and the whoosh of the attic fan sucking the cool air through the house. How can I ever leave? This is the only home I've ever had. This is my solid house, the place I own, the place I have lived for twelve years. My identity is woven into the walls, the floor, the garden, woven into the friends who live down the street and across town.

I thought I would be leaving Carlisle confident that my long depression would be lifting and I'd be looking toward rebirth: that was my imaginary deal with my father. Instead I am leaving with my confidence shaken, not knowing if I'm headed for even deeper emotional trouble than I've known before. "The only way out is through," someone says, and I know this is true, and I hate knowing this is true. I tried repeating Jewett's lovely advice to the young Cather, "You are growing when you feel most hindered," but right now it's not working. Yesterday I was driving around Carlisle, scrounging more boxes from liquor stores, pounding the steering wheel at stop lights and screaming *I hate growth.*

My U-Haul's state is Alaska. Painted on the side are huskies with friendly doggy grins telling me it's okay. People have moved to Alaska, the huskies tell me. People have crossed rivers and deserts and oceans because they had to. All your great-grandparents came over on the coffin ships from Ireland: think of how they must have felt, knowing they'd never see their families and country again? They were surely dying out of their old lives before they knew what their new lives would be. Your great-grandmother Moira Castles couldn't even speak English; someone pinned her name to her coat so her

American cousins would recognize her. Fifty years ago your father moved to back to Boston to take up a new job and start his life over again. You can do this.

Yeah, right, I say to the huskies, but what if this is the Wrong Guess and a Bad Move?

In the Shadow of Harvard

I have grown up in the shadow of Harvard Yard.
—My letter of application to Radcliffe College

A FEW DAYS AFTER ARRIVING IN CAMBRIDGE I set out to walk to Harvard Square to get my Harvard identification card, which will allow me to use the libraries. A helpful colleague in Harvard's English department has secured my appointment as a "Visiting Scholar," a status I will share with a woman from Poland researching metaphysical poetry and a shy man from Japan who is working on Mark Twain. I am grateful for my connection to the university, tenuous as it is. I hope it will give me more than a library card—perhaps some scrap of belonging.

I walk slowly down Saville Street to Concord Avenue, trying to control my anxiety through breathing, and go past the Radcliffe Institute, a combination of retreat and think tank for women scholars. It's a hot, sunny July day, and three women in bright sleeveless summer dresses are eating lunch at a picnic table, right near the fence, talking animatedly. I watch them longingly. I want to be on their side of the fence. These women belong to a community, and they also have a status identifier at Harvard. I'm jealous of both. "Oh, I'm at the Radcliffe Institute this year," they can say when they meet people at receptions and cocktail parties, which I imagine them attending with casual regularity. I'd applied to the Institute to write my book and was rejected.

I'm having an attack of the poor me's. ("Poor me, poor me, pour me a drink," my sister and her AA buddies say.) I continue my walk.

I arrive at Holyoke Center, the glass-and-steel office building that houses the Health Center and the Infirmary—where I spent a day and a night after I skidded on wet leaves and crashed my motorcycle my senior year at Radcliffe—as well as the Financial and Business Offices and, I hope, my ID card.

"You're not in the system yet," the man in the Business Office says. *Tell me about it,* I think.

"Do you know when I'll be in the system?"

"Check back in a few days."

I walk back to Saville Street, too agitated to stay around the Square. I hurry past the Radcliffe Institute and then I'm out of Harvard's reach, into Huron Village, and my walk becomes more part of Cambridge. I go past St. Joseph's Catholic Church, a corner grocery, a branch of the Cambridge library, a stained-glass studio, dry cleaners, and my corner store, a Japanese lunch place specializing in sushi and ice cream. Then I round the corner onto Saville Street, walking past the kids on their skateboards, and go home, waiting to be in the system.

*M*Y FATHER'S Harvard diploma hung on the wall in my parents' bedroom, right over the bureau. Whenever I was snooping around their room as a kid, I'd always stop and look at it.

Right below *Universitas Harvardiana, Cantabrigiae in republica Massachusettensium* was my father's name, elevated and strange in Latin and Gothic script.

I remember noticing that "O'Brien" was the only word Harvard hadn't been able to Latinize; evidently it was just too Irish to be transformed into something grand.

After my father had recovered from depression and gone back to work, he spent most of his time sitting at the card table he positioned in front of the bedroom window, next to the rusty green file cabinet given him by his brother Ray. I remember him sitting at his card table after dinner, pecking away on his Smith-Corona, the reassuring *rat-a-tat-tat* of the typewriter echoing in the quiet house. There he typed his business letters, soliciting work and following up on his calls; filed his onion-skin carbon copies; planned his sales trips, trying to make at least one coincide with the New England foliage. That way he could take along his binoculars and go for a ramble late on a sunny autumn day down some Vermont back road, *The Field Guide to the Birds* in his back pocket—his modest idea of heaven.

His bout with depression had required my father to make a bargain: sacrificing status and a high-paying job for work he could control. He knew, I think, that he'd be at risk for another breakdown if he tried to get back into the corporate world, and he was at peace with his decision.

Universitas Harvardiana
Cantabrigiae in Republica Massachusettensium
Omnibus ad quos hae litterae pervenerint Salutem:
Praeses et Socii Collegii Harvardiani, *consentientibus honorandis ac reverendis Inspectoribus in Comitiis sollemnibus.*
Norbertum Laurentium O'Brien
in cursu academico Litterarum *studiis praestantem alumnum ad gradum* Baccalaurei in Artibus *admiserunt, eique*
magna cum laude
dederunt et concesserunt omnia, insignia iuraque ad hunc gradum spectantia. In cuius rei testimonium litteris hisce Universitatis sigillo munitis die Junii XXIII *anno* Salutis Humanae MDCCCXXVII *Collegiique Harvardiani* CCLXXXXI *auctoritate rite commissa subscripsit*

A. L. Lowell.   Praeses.

Norbert's Harvard diploma

My father's office equipment, the rickety card table, was an old hand-me-down covered with children's pencil scrawls. It was a cramped, inadequate place to work; he would have to spread his paperwork out on the bed and the floor. The card table shows my father making do with what he'd been given, learning to live with lowered expectations for his professional life, and doing so with grace. I wonder if its penciled surface also says something else: that he never found a big enough place in the world, or a way to express his gifts fully? Men need rooms of their own no less than women, and my father never had one. Even when Kevin and I moved out, leaving my parents with more disposable income and with vacant bedrooms that could have become offices, he stayed in the bedroom, working away at his card table.

WHAT COULD not be taken away was his Harvard diploma. This made him exceptional, and also gave the whole family distinction. There was a particular thrill in living as close to Harvard as we did—our Belmont house was about five miles away—and when we'd drop in at Harvard Square for a family outing, perhaps for a movie at the University Theater (the "Unie") or a Sunday lunch at St. Clair's, Dad would take us for a walk

186

through the Yard, pointing out the sights—Massachusetts Hall, Widener, John Harvard's statue—and I would be awed that he could belong to such a great university.

Unlike my mother, my father never told family stories. None of us can remember any tale told about our O'Brien grandparents, sitting around the dining room table on a Sunday afternoon. My father's stories were not about his family but about his magical days at Harvard in the 1920s when he took English courses from legendary figures like Charles Townsend Copeland and George Lyman Kittredge. My favorite was the one about the D-double-minus he got from Kittredge.

"Tell the one about the D-double-minus," one of us would say, and my father would lean back in his chair and begin.

"Well, first of all, I was a cocky son of a gun—I'd just transferred in from Holy Cross, where I'd gotten all A's, and I thought I would do well here. And I studied and studied for Kittredge's exam, I assure you, and I thought I'd done brilliantly on it. Then Kittredge called me into his office, and said, 'Mr. O'Brien, sit down. I have never been required to give a D-double-minus before, but your examination has called this out of me. What is your explanation?' I told him I didn't know what had happened. I had studied the material thoroughly. I knew it cold. 'Aha, Mr. O'Brien,' he said, 'you indeed have studied, but did you *think?*'"

At this point in the story my father would always laugh. *"Think?"* he would say, amused by his youthful ignorance. "I had no idea what the man meant. No idea at all."

I never tired of hearing it. I liked knowing that my father, who'd graduated *magna cum laude* in literature, had once gotten a D-double-minus from the great Kittredge. The story made him human and fallible. But it also gave him a heroic glow in my eyes, for it meant that my father had learned how to think, and now knew what Kittredge meant about the difference between studying and thinking, which I didn't grasp at all.

W̓HEN I was in graduate school at Harvard I would meet my father for lunch every couple of months at Ferdinand's, a long-vanished French restaurant on Mt. Auburn Street. When I got there—always a few minutes late—he'd be at his reserved table, reading—maybe a Civil War history, maybe a Dickens novel. Sometimes we'd get the table in the window, our favorite, and we'd sit there in the midwinter sun, perhaps sipping a glass of wine and ordering omelettes, glasses sparkling in the sunlight, talking about writers and books—by then I was immersed in Willa Cather, a writer my father loved for her Catholic themes.

At the end of lunch I'd hand over some of the books he'd requested from Widener—one of them, I remember, was *The Life of Archbishop Lamy*, the clerical biography that had sparked Cather to write *Death Comes for the Archbishop*—and he'd give me a couple to take back. The waitress would bring the check. By then money was not the terrifying lack in my father's life it had once been, although from long habit he would scrutinize the bill carefully. "This one's on me," he'd say, and I'd enjoy having my father treat me to lunch. Then we'd walk out into the winter light together, me off to the library, my dad off to the Coop bookstore "just for a browse."

I'M TRYING again to get my Harvard ID card. I walk into Harvard Square by my usual route down Concord Ave and Garden Street, passing the spa where I buy the *Globe* and talk about the weather and the Red Sox (in first place at the moment, tormenting us with midsummer hope), then passing the Radcliffe Institute. I try not to stare at a group of women picnicking on the grass—could it be the same ones?—and tell myself that it's really much better that I'm on my own. *After all, Thoreau didn't have a think-tank at Walden, did he? Willa Cather doesn't send her artist-heroine Thea off to an artists' colony for her spiritual and creative transformation, does she? No, she sends her off—alone—to the Southwest.*

I pass the Harvard Registrar's office where my father's college file is kept, packed away in some dusty basement with the other records of long-ago Harvard men. Then through the Cambridge Common, going past the new statue to the Irish Famine, and my favorite route through Harvard Yard, the one that lets you enter right next to Harvard Hall where I took my Master's written examination in 1970 and tried to fake my way through a translation of *Havelock the Dane*.

The anxiety that's accompanied me everywhere for my first month here nudges its way into my consciousness, penetrating my "All will be well" mantra with its usual doubting questions. This anxiety's view of the world is really deplorable: it doesn't trust anything; all it can see are promises made to be broken, commitments forgotten, stony, indifferent people. "What if the paperwork hasn't been done?" the niggling voice says. "What if nobody's ever heard of you? What if you'll never be in the system?"

"All will be well," I breathe as I walk into Holyoke Center and wait for the elevator. I get off at the fourth floor and go over to the window that says

"Harvard Identification—Faculty and Guests." It's the same man behind the counter. He asks for my social security number, taps it into the computer, then asks "Sharon O'Brien?" It feels as if the keel of the boat has just scraped the shore. Social security, I now know what that really means. He takes my picture, and I know I look bad: flyaway hair, eyes glinting a little maniacally, forced smile that shows the age lines I try to hide.

"I could take it over," the man says tactfully as we look at the computer screen together, but I say no, it's okay. In a few minutes I'm given my shiny plastic maroon and white card with this slightly dotty middle-aged woman staring out at me, but at least it has my name on it, and they've got the O-apostrophe right. I now have a Harvard ID number. My validation will last until 6/30/97.

$\mathcal{H}$OLYOKE CENTER is a familiar place. When I was in graduate school, I had a cubicle office on the fifth floor where I held tutorials. I remember guiding undergraduates through senior theses on Norman Mailer, Marianne Moore, Ezra Pound, Henry James, and Hollywood in film.

My favorite tutee was the Hollywood-in-film writer, a scrawny senior living in Dunster House known as "Mouse." Mouse was convinced he'd never finish his thesis—he was a B student, and he thought he might be overreaching by going for honors. "Plus," he said, "you have to know this about me, I always turn in papers late, so I'm worried I'll never make the deadline." The deadline for honors theses was infamous: you had to have your thesis, all bound and scrubbed, to Warren House by 5:00 on the due date—or the door would be locked and the thesis unacceptable. No extensions. "So do you want to go for it?" I asked. "I think you can do it." "Okay," he said. "I'll give it a shot."

I kept teasing him and bugging him and told him right up front that we were going to employ behavior therapy to get him through. Mouse was a beer *aficionado* and I told him that he had to write two pages a day before he could reward himself with a beer. Intrigued, he agreed to try this method. I made him sign a pledge. *I promise my tutor that I will write two pages every day and will drink not even one sip of beer until I have done so. Signed, this 2nd day of February 1973, Mouse.* After Mouse turned in his thesis at ten minutes to five (he would graduate *cum laude* in English) he and his roommate took me to Charlie's Kitchen and treated me to a cheeseburger, fries, and a pitcher of beer. It was one of the few times I remember in grad school when I thought that maybe, after all, I was in the right business.

I KEEP persuading myself that I've entered some spiritual zone where the worldly values no longer matter, but I get exposed here for the fraud I am. I feel obscure in Cambridge, unfamous, invisible. Partly it's sheer wounded narcissism, but even more it's the feeling that without a real role or identity here, I don't exist. It's being on the fringes of Harvard without a real place to be that's tough—close enough to see everyone at home in a place where I used to belong. I find myself getting that feeling of littleness I used to have as a grad student, like when I was telling a professor which of my friends had just gotten jobs—"Amy got hired at Williams, and Susan at Smith"—and he interrupted me and said "No, no, how are the *men* doing?" Now Harvard has several important feminist professors, and no one would ever say, of graduate students, "How are the men doing?"

I email a couple of famous Harvard scholars. I hope they'll be free for lunch or a drink. "Just too busy this semester." "Let's definitely get in touch in the spring." I understand. They're busy, and they don't know me personally, and they have lives. "Maybe you're not well-known enough to show up on their radar screen," the niggling voice says. "You're only a one-book person. You're not hot anymore."

I try to quash the voice, but it's hard to cope with the hierarchies at Harvard, the lists of who counts and who doesn't. I count at Dickinson but here I don't count. I have to get over letting that bother me and be a Buddhist about all this—but I'm not and it does.

*B*Y THE early fall I have found two Harvard buddies: Lynn and Bill are my friends and mentors. They're both assistant professors, on the other side of the status line, and they're sweet and generous. We have fun hanging out together.

One night they invite me to dinner with other faculty and graduate students. Bill's going to be giving a talk on Cather later, and I want to cheer him on. I join a group of ten or so people at a long table in a Chinese restaurant near the Square. I say "hi" to the grad students I know and Lynn and Bill, and I'm introduced to Z, a famous literary scholar. She's seated in the middle of the table, the center of gravity. When we're introduced she doesn't say anything in response to my greeting. I get pissed and say "So how *are* you, Z?" People hang on her answer. "Fine," she says. "Just fine."

During dinner I talk with the grad students at my end of the table. When there's a lull I hear Z saying "Boston just really isn't a city, compared to New

York. . . . I'm just not really *myself* in Boston—I'm myself in New York and L.A., and of course Paris. . . ."

"What about Italy, Z?" someone asks.

"Oh yes, how could I forget? I'm myself in Tuscany," she decides, and I'm thinking I don't *care* where you are your fucking self. (Later I wish I'd chimed in with "As for me, I'm really myself in Carlisle and Elmira and— of course—Lowell," but of course I don't say anything.) Then we all walk over to the lecture hall and Lynn introduces me to Y, a well-known scholar visiting from Yale. "And Sharon wrote that really wonderful biography of Willa Cather," Lynn says protectively, and Y says, vaguely, "Oh yes," as his eyes drift around the room to see who's there who matters.

*W*HEN I'M WALKING home I think what an uncomfortable evening this has been. Over the years Harvard has given me many good things— in different ways and at different times I have been nourished here and recognized and helped beyond measure by my teachers and mentors. But tonight is the epitome of what I dislike—and fear—about the place.

I'm vulnerable to Harvard's elitism right now because I'm on such shaky ground. I think about my father, so soon after his breakdown and unem- ployment, writing his Reunion essay and then taking his wife and children (except for me—too young) to his twenty-fifth reunion, not staying away because he'd be surrounded by men more successful than he. I don't think I could have done that.

*M*Y FATHER LOVED Harvard as a real place, but it was the icon Harvard that gave a glow to my father, a glow from the past; it also allowed him to be considered by others an intellectual, which he in fact was. He did not know anything about power tools or home repair and cared not a whit for sports, except for golf, a slow, meditative game that allowed him to walk and sniff the breeze and be in nature. He loved poking around in bookstores and libraries and going on reading crusades—deciding, for example, that he had to find out everything about some obscure Civil War battle, getting the requisite books out of Widener, and then actually reading them. He'd write me about his finds.

I went to Widener yesterday and enjoyed myself hugely. I had no trouble in locating a journal of Charlotte Forten, mentioned in Wilson's *Patriotic Gore*, the colored girl who taught in the South Carolina sea-island area during the war at the Union-occupied bases, where she came in contact with my friend Thomas Wentworth Higginson, commanding the first (I think) negro regiment recruited in the South, about which he wrote *Army Life in a Black Regiment.*

I also stumbled into a section at Widener where almost half a shelf had books devoted to Sherman's March to the Sea, which has always fascinated me, and from which I picked up a book by an unknown that I'm going to try out.

Widener is a wonderful offshoot for literary whims! Strange offshoots, and a lot of fun . . . wouldn't you say?

Yes, Dad, a lot of fun. Just pure intellectual curiosity, just following the trail wherever it leads, and then sharing your finds with others. Harvard helped me to do that too. That's the best of what the real place can do. I remember experiencing what Sherlock Holmes called "the thrill of the chase" when I was in grad school, but Widener still seemed grim and imposing; to my father, clearly, it was a giant sandbox.

$\mathcal{M}$Y FATHER had ideas, and could converse. The businessmen he saw during his road trips, starved for good conversations about books or politics or history, looked forward to his sales visits the way rural Catholics in the Southwest looked forward to the twice-yearly visit from the priest, who'd come and hear everyone's confession, baptize all the babies, and bless the crops. The guys from Sylvania and Corning Glass would take him out for three-hour lunches, and his galvanizing presence allowed them to talk about ideas. "Guess it takes a Harvard man to lift our minds up from the gutter," they'd say, "get us to talk about something besides office politics and cost-benefits." "Give your blessing for our minds, Norb, before you go," and he'd laugh and make a cross in the air.

When I was a kid I knew he was different from other dads—I just didn't have the language to describe it. No words, then, like "gender role" or "masculine identity." Sometimes it embarrassed me that he wasn't coaching Little League baseball or repairing broken sinks or making big bucks. But I was proud of him. He was a Harvard man, and he knew how to think.

The difficulty was, because Harvard was the sign of his worldly and intellectual success, there was no measure of success for me besides Harvard. Other schools, other destinies, were inferior. When I reached my senior year in high school, there wasn't any choice: Harvard was the locus of desire in our family. I applied to Radcliffe early decision because I wanted to become part of a tradition my father had started. Going there meant he'd passed on what was best about him.

I HAVE TO MAKE one thing clear: I didn't go there just for my Dad. I also went for myself. I knew Radcliffe was a great school—okay, the best— and I loved school. I've always loved school.

When I was a kid, I loved all the equipment of school—clean pads of paper, boxes of yellow pencils. I loved sharpening pencils, seeing the curly wooden squiggles that dropped from the lead, the sharp point: what was a sharpened pencil but the freshness of starting over? I loved the new school sets you would get at Woolworth's right before Labor Day, the plastic ruler and protractor, the scissors, pencil sharpener. At school I loved the supply room, the neatly stacked pads of paper, the divine smell of mimeographing fluid on the freshly minted page, the jars of paste, thick, gooey, and white, that smelled so good I'd have to taste it, the new boxes of chalk.

School was where I felt at home. I felt competent there: I knew what to do. I was always three or four grades ahead of myself and teachers would give me extra assignments to keep me busy. The principal would call my parents to say "Sharon is reading at a tenth grade level" when I was in fifth grade. As the grades rolled on I became aware that being singled-out smart wasn't good for a girl, it interfered with your popularity with the boys, and I desperately wanted to be popular, but I couldn't give up being smart. Being smart was just too much fun. If I knew the hard Latin passage no one else did, I'd raise my hand. It wasn't that the teacher's praise was sweet, although it was, it was simply that *I could do it* and I couldn't resist. Looking at a Latin phrase on the board, just crying out to be translated, was irresistible—it must be the feeling a car mechanic has, peering into an engine along with a distressed customer. "I have no idea what's wrong," the customer says, but the mechanic sees right away there's a dead sparkplug, he can't resist popping it out and replacing it and hearing the satisfying roar of the engine. Not to fix it would be against nature.

It was against nature for me to look at some mangled Latin on the black-board and not want to fix it. Somebody would have made a hopeless botch of a passage from Caesar, and Miss Steurwald would say, "is there anyone else who can translate it?" and I'd wait, because I didn't want to be a pill, but when no one raised their hand, I finally would, and Miss Steurwald would say "Then go to the board, Sharon," and I'd pick up the chalk and start erasing and writing and making the sentence work, as satisfying as plunging your hands into that greasy engine and fixing what was wrong. Then all the cases would agree, the subjunctive would be right, the engine would purr, and I'd walk back to my seat not so much with a feeling of triumph—more like the contentment and peace you feel when you've decided to go with the current instead of fighting it.

Let me make another confession: I loved homework too. Other kids complained, but when I opened a book, whether a novel or a geometry book or *The Aeneid*, I was in another world, a world that made sense to me, a world where I felt safe and skilled, like a riverboat pilot heading into a familiar port, knowing how to negotiate the currents and sandbars. I still remember the pleasure of translating Latin—my bedside lamp would shine a circle of light on the page and on my notebook, illuminating this breathing circle of words, Latin words becoming English words, words in a dead language entering a living one. But it seemed to me that all the words were alive.

I GET A COPY of my Radcliffe file. It's thin—grades, tutors' reports (they view my college self as smart and eager and capable of original work, but "unsure of herself intellectually"), and my letter of application stamped "OCT 15 1962." I had to write "a statement which you believe will be helpful to the Committee on Admissions in assessing your qualifications." I have no memory of writing this essay.

> I have grown up in the shadow of Harvard Yard and have heard much about Harvard from my father who graduated in 1927. What I have heard, I have liked. . . . I have a feeling in advance for the intangibles of the College, and for the spiritual and emotional impact it can have upon a student—an important aspect of screening, I think, over and above sheer scholastic ability, although I believe I have that as well.

I have to laugh a little at this seventeen-year-old telling the Committee on Admissions the truth: that her source of knowledge—and desire—was not their catalogue or their history or their worldwide reputation as the best university in the United States, but her father's stories. And indeed, this writer feels she can, quite competently, make a judgment about this august university, weigh its advantages and disadvantages critically, on the basis of these stories. I'm amazed at the coolness of "What I have heard, I have liked," and glad that this self-possessed young writer uses the word "shadow" so innocently.

$\mathcal{W}$HEN I finally get my father's file and read his letter of application (written from Holy Cross, asking to transfer into the sophomore class), I see that the source of his desire to attend Harvard was different from mine. He was the trailblazer who first had to answer the question, Why do you wish to come to Harvard?

> At present I am inclined towards journalism or teaching. In either case, the many and attractive English courses at Harvard afford a good foundation. Even if I should not follow either of these two professions, I am more interested in English than any other subject. I also realize what it means to a man to have won a degree at Harvard, a degree which is an Open Sesame in worth-while walks of life.

I find my father's tutors' reports and eagerly read them, feeling a little guilty, as if I'm going to be interrupted and reprimanded. "He has been a hard, faithful worker, and has combined with this a good deal of intelligence," his junior tutor says. "Widely read, especially in the classics. Has an agreeable personality. Would do well as a secondary school teacher." "He seemed to me a nice-mannered, nice-tempered youth, moderately intelligent, but not the type to become a profound scholar," his senior tutor decides. "He was thinking last year of journalism or teaching; in either field, I believe his pleasantness and interestedness will stand him in good stead."

Only "moderately" intelligent? My brilliant father? Part of me is a little pleased—could I be winning this competition between us?—and another part wants to smack this supercilious little twerp of a tutor around. "Not the type to become a profound scholar." And what makes *you* so goddam sure of yourself?

I look back at my father's letter of application, written by an eighteen-year-old boy I never knew. It makes me feel tender: how sweet, this Irish boy's faith in the power of a Harvard degree, the "Open Sesame" that would cause closed doors to open and allow him to enter the realms of gold.

Reading these words also makes me a little sad, because I know something the young writer doesn't. I know his life isn't going to work out that way.

The Stations of the Cross

Often, to lift a depression, we have to risk taking on that which we fear the most, that which is blocking our natural growth.

—JAMES HOLLIS, *Swamplands*

"IT'LL GET BETTER WHEN YOU GET TO CAMBRIDGE," my friends had said.

It doesn't get any better.

Every morning I wake up to terror. Morning jumps on my chest and sleep leaves in an instant. I don't even have the comfort of a sleepy cat wound around my head—Megan, traumatized by the move, is punishing me by sleeping on the sofa.

My sister has brought me a plant and my brother has made me jazz tapes. I've unpacked my green and blue Italian dishes, I've hung my paintings, I've bought potted flowers at the local garden store—white and purple cosmos, yellow daisies, blue cornflowers—and put them on the windowsills. We're all trying hard to make me feel at home, but it's not working. I have used the word "uprooted" loosely before. Now I know what it means: when I close my eyes I see roots, naked and exposed, dangling in midair, screaming for soil. An empty house washes around me, beyond that an empty street, beyond that an empty neighborhood, beyond that more and more circles of emptiness expanding outward and outward into space.

One morning I am awakened early by a terrifying, garbled announcement from a moving loudspeaker. *Nahpahkinondaritesidahdahstree, Nahpahkinondaritesidadastree.* I run to the front windows: is this an evacuation command? I see people running to their cars and a Cambridge Police van turning the corner. The translation emerges: *No parking on the right side of the street.* I get dressed and move my car.

Later people will remind me about the trauma of moving. "Number three on the stress list," a friend says, "right after the death of a spouse." "Moving is like dying," says another. I have no job to go to, no coworkers to distract me, no structure except what I create myself. Friends and family who care about me, yes, but everyone has a complete life of their own.

Why isn't my plan working? Thoreau felt better as soon as he arrived at Walden; at least that's what he wrote. Boston was supposed to be my Walden. Where are signs that I am in the right place?

*W*HEN I lie in bed at night I hear the traffic rushing past; its strangeness keeps me awake. In Carlisle I could hear the traffic on 81, and its steady, reliable roar lulled me to sleep. People were either driving south toward Chambersburg or north toward Harrisburg. Here the cars speed up Concord Ave headed for the Fresh Pond rotary. From there roads spin off in a million directions: they could be going *anywhere*. Boston is a land of rotaries, lawless, whirling maelstroms where only the aggressive survive. Signs say "Yield to traffic in rotary," but if you slow down to obey them you'll die, because the person behind you isn't stopping.

When I lived here in my twenties I loved spinning through rotaries, playing chicken with the cars nosing in on my right, watching them fall back as I moved confidently ahead. Now other cars scare me. A few days ago I drove around the Fresh Pond rotary five times before a large gap opened in the traffic and I found the courage to leave. In Carlisle my car was a solid shield around me; here it's as delicate and translucent as a membrane.

"This is ridiculous," I tell myself as I lie in bed in the morning, afraid to get up and engage the day. "Your sister lives in Wellesley, your brother's in Holliston, you have friends in Cambridge and Somerville and Bedford, you grew up five miles away from this apartment, you went to college and grad school a mile away, you've lived on Grant Street and Walker Street and Wendell Street, you've moved before—to Dublin, for God's sake!—and it's been fine, so what the *fuck* is wrong with you?"

I am spinning down a well that has no bottom and the voice that lists the people I know and the places I've lived gets fainter and fainter. I am alone in my bed and the floor seems very far away. If my feet touch the floor I will have to walk, one foot after another, into an empty world. If I stay in bed I will keep spinning down the well.

There is nowhere to go.

And so I get out of bed. I unpack, I call up my brother and sister, I talk to my friends, I make Starbucks coffee in the morning, I badger Harvard to give me email, I visit the cemetery, I write in my journal, I listen to NPR, I meditate, I weep, I run around Fresh Pond. I get through the day.

𝓜Y BROTHER drops over on Saturday morning to take me to Bradlees, a discount place in Watertown. I can't go to the pricey neighborhood hardware store, but being in a huge department store, full of noise and confusion, scares me, so Kevin's agreed to be my escort.

"Here are some coupons," he says, handing me a stack he's cut out from last week's Sunday paper. Kevin is a careful shopper, scanning the Sunday papers for bargains while his sisters generally buy on impulse. I've always scorned coupons, but my reduced salary means I have to be careful. I'm grateful for his expertise. "You'll find them in the color supplements," he explains. "You should never pay full price. Wait for the discounts." Kevin patiently follows me around while I compare prices on stacking storage bins and plastic shelves, drives me back to Cambridge, handling the Fresh Pond rotary slowly—he's a cautious driver like my Dad—but with an ease I admire.

"Have you seen *What about Bob?*" he asks as he's leaving.

"Yes, why?"

"Baby steps. That's what Richard Dreyfuss says to Bill Murray. Baby steps. That's all you have to do."

"Baby steps," I repeat obediently. "Right."

The only blessing I can see in the fact that Kevin, Maureen, and I have dealt with anxiety and depression is that we understand how the other one feels. Kevin doesn't think it's strange that his formerly adventurous younger sister can't go shopping by herself.

𝓘 TELL MY FRIEND Lisa about my trouble with the Fresh Pond rotary, and she says, "Don't worry, I'll take you in hand. You just need a refresher course."

Lisa is the daughter of my friends Henry and Chris, who joined me and our friends John and Maggy in forming a commune during my grad school days. We were an earnest, square commune; we talked about sharing income and saving the environment and moving to the backwoods of Maine, where we'd grow our own organic vegetables. When we advertised for a new person in the Boston *Phoenix*, we decided to add "no drugs, no sex" (even though we smoked pot) just to be sure we'd get people as square as we were. I used to take care of Lisa one afternoon a week when she was two and three; we'd go to the playground where I'd push her on the swings. Then to Brigham's for ice cream. Chris died of breast cancer when Lisa was eleven, and she read a letter to her mother at the funeral. Now Lisa's twenty-six, finishing her M.A. at Leslie in early education. She's been mentoring me through my first weeks in Cambridge. She appeared on my first night in my new apartment, an angel bearing a six-pack.

"I hope you like beer," she said.

"I do now."

The day after my Bradlee's expedition Lisa calls me.

"Sharon, it's time for you to become a Boston driver again. I'll be right over."

She pulls up in her Subaru and I get in—passenger's seat to start—and we take off for the rotary.

"Talk out loud to yourself," she says as she guns the engine into the rotary, "that's what I always do," cruising into the traffic. "You need to get mad at the other cars. Hey, buddy," she yells at a red Volvo trying to nose its way in, "*I'm in the rotary, you're not, you yield to me. . . . You think you're a driver? . . . Outta my way, I'm coming through!*" and then we shoot out, unscathed, onto Concord Ave. "See?" she says triumphantly.

"You're good," I say. "You're very good."

"I'll take you around one more time, and then it's your turn." We weave through again—"You have no balls, Mustang, stay right where you are!"—and she pulls over. I take the wheel and she eggs me on. "You can do it, Sharon, you're the *driver*, the others are *trash*."

"Right," I say dubiously. "I'm the . . . driver." I enter the rotary. There's an aggressive stream of cars, trying to cut in from Alewife Brook Parkway. "Not in your *dreams*, buddy," I say to the lead car, one of those really scary beat-up Boston cars with a cracked windshield and taped-up doors, squinting my eyes and looking straight ahead and I don't let up on the gas. We shoot off down Concord Ave toward Belmont. Lisa's whooping and cheering and I begin to think that maybe, just maybe, I can make it through the year.

 $\mathcal{T}$ HE DAY AFTER my driving lesson my sister coaches me through buying a week's groceries at Star Market. "Soup is good," she says. "Tuna fish. You're not going to be doing gourmet cooking right away." I can see I'm in capable hands. I stand transfixed in front of the cheeses, for the first time noticing how much my favorite—cambazola—costs. If I were by myself, I'd probably stand here all day, trying to decide if I can afford $5.69 a pound.

Maureen nudges me out of Dairy into Produce. "Baked potatoes. Broccoli. Keep it simple." When she drives me home I feel triumphant. Groceries in the trunk, I'm a warrior returning from the hunt.

"Remember to breathe," my sister says.

Baby steps.

I AM becoming acquainted with a truly frightening part of myself, a frightened part, a voice I never listened to before because I've been moving too fast. Staying in one place, tolerating panic and loss, takes all my strength. I have to fight against my desire for progress. Some days are better, some worse.

Today is worse. When I wake up panic surrounds my bed like a dark sea. Actually, it's even worse than panic: it's *dread*. The present is frightening; the future is even worse, but worse in a vague way. When dread hits, the threat to safety is everywhere, but it's nameless. I call up Maggy. She understands depression and anxiety—she's been there—and my guess is she understands dread. Plus, she gets up early, so I can call at 6:45.

"I *hate* dread," I tell her.

"Dread is the worst," she agrees. "Now tell me what you're going to do today." I tell Maggy my plan—meditation, make coffee, write in my journal, go for a walk to Harvard Square, have dinner with my friend Jeannie.

"Okay," she says. "I'll check back later."

Sometimes you just need reassurance that someone else exists in the world, someone you can tell about your day. Sometimes I wonder how much my depression is aggravated by the difficulties of living alone in America, having no one to tell my daily story to. I speak with close friends every few days, but then you only have time to hit the highlights, give the quick plot summary. I imagine people who live with partners find themselves invisibly nourished by saying little things to each other like "I think I'll stop off at the post office on the way home from the cleaners," or "Remember to pick up the half-and-half," or "How about a movie?" Knowing I can tell Maggy the trivial accomplishments of the day—which right now looms ahead like a hero's journey—helps me to keep going.

I meditate for twenty minutes, struggling just to stay with my breath, the way the books tell you. I've tried meditation before, usually giving up after five minutes, but I've been pretty faithful since I got to Cambridge. I make up my own mantra, derived from Dame Julian of Norwich, whom I remember a little from the *Norton Anthology of English Literature*—"All will be well, and all manner of thing will be well." I do "All will be" on the in breath, "well" on the out breath.

All of a sudden grief hits. It's a tidal wave that's been waiting; slowing down in meditation has allowed it to surface. I slide to the floor, curl up in a corner by the door, and weep for a long time. I weep because I have never felt so alone. I miss my parents. It's not just the love, it's the silenced wisdom I need. I want my mother to tell me how she faced death, I want my father to tell me about his depression, and how he survived. They don't have to tell me it will be all right: nobody can know that for sure, and I won't believe it anyway. I just want them to tell me what it was like for them, those times when the ropes and bridges broke and they were falling down and down into the dark. I call for them but they do not answer, and I cannot even imagine what they would say.

When I stop crying I lie on the floor until Megan comes in and demands to be fed.

I CHANGE the plan I've told Maggy. Now there's something I want to do, a brief flicker of desire or need, something to nourish. I drive out to Belmont, to my mother's old apartment, the last visible trace of a parent I can find.

I park in my familiar spot, right in front of the picture window where she had lined up the family photographs like sentinels. Next to this window my mother parked her pink chair, giving herself a good view of the street while she whipped through the *Times* crossword puzzle and waited for visiting children. When I'd be driving up from Carlisle I knew she'd begin to fantasize deathly car crashes five minutes after my expected arrival time. Heartless, I refused to call unless I was going to be *really* late: that was one way to punish her for giving me guilt, and by then I knew I could rely on her love. When I pulled up she'd be standing in the open door, arms outstretched: she placed her chair at the right angle to see cars coming down the street, scouting for her traveling child.

Walking around back, I see the new tenant has put a shiny blue Weber grill on the back porch and planted clumps of white and pink impatiens by the back door. I peek in the kitchen window. The last time I looked in, a few weeks after we'd moved everything out, the place was empty and anonymous, and its barrenness matched my mood. Now it's crammed with somebody else's stuff—packed to the gills with fake colonial chachkas, high-backed chairs and pine boxes and pewter mugs and wooden high chairs used as plant stands. Ignoring the emotional history of this place, these self-sufficient replacements push me away. "No place for your memories here," they say. "We're doing just fine without you."

MY IMAGINATION is so shaped by stories it's hard when my life does not match the narrative I've expected: there's the sadness or the loss itself, and then there's the gap between experience and desire. I know the Buddhists advise us to live without expectation, but tell that to somebody who's been raised on "Tintern Abbey" and "Four Quartets" and *My Ántonia*. These writers have told me what it's like to return to a landscape fraught with memory: it's supposed to be rich and layered and complete, literally teeming with epiphanies, and I'm supposed to walk through it and emerge an integrated person.

This journey was supposed to make me *wise*.

Cambridge and Belmont are layered, that's true; being in this landscape is a kind of emotional archeology. I drive past Lewis Road, and there's the grey stucco house I left and entered every day of my life until I went off to college, with its new bright blue door, except I can see the cream-colored paint right below the surface. I see the fortress-like Masonic Temple in Cushing Square and for a second it becomes Chandler's department store, which I loved as a kid because of its magical ladies' room, decorated in red, rose, and pink, smelling of perfume and powder and sweat, featuring enormous mirrors where the Belmont ladies primped. I drive past the groovy new bike shop near my mother's house in Waverley Square (one of those places that has a punning name like *Spoke For*). I'm still annoyed that it gobbled up the little coffee and donut place she used to visit on her morning rounds.

When Jim goes back to visit Ántonia at the end of *My Ántonia*, Willa Cather gives him a renewed bond to his memories. "Whatever we had missed, we possessed together the precious, the incommunicable past." Going back home isn't restoring my past: it seems to be taking it away. The precious past has slipped over the edge of the known world. Someone else lives at 28 Lewis Road, Chandler's is long gone, Linda's Donuts has disappeared. My parents are dead. Incommunicable.

THE BACK door begins to open and a man pokes his head out. The new tenant must have spied me.

"Excuse me," I say. "I must be in the wrong place."

The door closes and I scurry off to my car.

*J*T'S A HOT August day, the kind of day when Boston humidity slips over you like a dirty glove. The *Globe* says it's going to be in the high nineties by mid-afternoon and won't cool off much at night. I'm okay in my air-conditioned car but I'm afraid of the heat building up in my apartment. The discomfort will rob me of even the minor solace of a nap. I'm driving down Belmont Street toward Cambridge, about to pass Our Lady of Mercy, my childhood church, and the cool interior beckons.

I bless myself with holy water, an instinctive gesture even though I haven't been inside a church since last summer when I met Maureen and Kevin for my parents' memorial Mass, arranged, as always, by my brother. The church is empty—it's a weekday morning—and I sit for a while and watch the votive candles flickering before the altar.

I find myself drawn to the Stations of the Cross, the fourteen carvings illustrating Christ's suffering and death. I walk around the church, trying to piece together the story. It's a little hard, because there are no titles, and my memory is vague, but I do my best. *Jesus takes up his cross. . . . Jesus falls the first time. . . . Some woman wipes His brow. . . .* Every Good Friday when I was a kid I'd be here from twelve to three for the Stations; the priest, followed by two altar boys bearing candles, would stand in front of each station and pray. The church would be bare, statues covered with purple shrouds and the priest wearing black vestments. I liked the stripped-down church. That way the glory of Holy Saturday evening, altar banked in Easter lilies, statues uncovered, the priest in white and gold, was even more intense. Good Friday was always a way station on the road to Easter, not a destination in itself. *Jesus falls the second time. . . . Jesus speaks to some women, I'm not sure who. . . . The soldiers spit on Jesus. . . .*

On those long-ago Good Fridays I would daydream or pass notes to Barbara Coughlan in Pig Latin (Ommy-tay Rennan-bay is an erk-jay, Ister-say Argaret-may has ad-bay reath-bay), never thinking the story of Christ's suffering had anything to do with me. *Jesus falls the third time. . . .* I'm really glad that he falls three times. Right now I don't want to think that any journey is easy, and I notice that they pace the falls really well: not a bad narrative structure. . . . You know what? This is really a good story. I *like* this story. It's consoling. It seems the path through suffering can be a long one, and when you fall, the only thing you can do is get up again. Some people will torment you, a few will wipe your brow. Others want you to tell them what's happened—maybe they think you have wisdom, or maybe they just want to know what you've gone through. And you're supposed to talk with them.

As I walk around the church I realize I have no idea how the story ends. I know that Good Friday leads to Easter Sunday, but I don't want the last chapter to be the Resurrection, I'm not ready for a happy ending. I've come to Boston wanting rebirth, but if I have to face an image of renewal right now it'll feel like a reproach. (What's wrong with you, Sharon, you were supposed to be reborn *weeks* ago.)

Jesus dies on the cross. . . . Jesus is taken down from the cross. . . . Is the last one going to be the discovery of the empty tomb? The proof that Jesus has escaped death? *Please don't end with the Resurrection,* I beg the un-known author. *I can't handle it right now.*

And then the last one: *They lay Jesus in the tomb.*

Wow. That's impressive. They didn't go for the Hollywood ending.

I stand there for several minutes, watching Christ's disciples, shoulders bowed in grief, place the lifeless body in the tomb. I am so grateful I could weep.

No one knew about the Resurrection when Christ died. All people knew about was the dying. I leave the church momentarily exhilarated because there's a match between my story and a greater one.

A FEW NIGHTS later my father finds me in a dream.

My father has been dead now for twenty-three years. For many years I did not dream about him at all, I had repressed the pain of his dying that much. About ten years ago, shortly after my long depression began, he started to enter my dreams. Every two or three months he would visit. In each dream my father, who I know is dead, has returned to the family. My mother, brother, and sister act as if he's never died, as if everything is the same. I'm the only one who knows the truth besides him and it makes me feel really alone to see everybody acting like everything's okay. He *died*, I want to say to everyone. Don't you remember? This is really creepy.

I can't say anything. To mention his death would upset everyone else's reality, and even more, in this strange dream world, it would be *rude*. I look at my family and wonder *Am I the only one who knows that he died?* Then

I start to wonder: maybe they're right and I'm wrong? Maybe he never did die at all?

I know there's fear in these dreams, the fear that if anyone mentions my father's previous death, the one we all witnessed at Massachusetts General Hospital and could not speak of later, then this odd reprieve will be over and he will die again. Part of me wants to tell the truth, part of me fears that the truth will kill him.

In my new dream, I'm back at 28 Lewis Road. My Dad is there, the one who acts like he isn't dead. This time he seems younger and healthier, his hair blacker. We walk out of the house together. Once we're on the front porch, alone together, I squeeze out the question I've been afraid to ask.

"Dad, didn't you die?"

"Yes, I did," he says calmly, as if this isn't such a strange or impolite thing to ask, or a hard thing to answer. "But I come back when you need me."

Losing It

Midway on our life's journey, I found myself
In dark wood, the right road lost. To tell
About those woods is hard.
— DANTE, *The Inferno* (translation by Robert Pinsky)

A collapse of the conscious attitude is no small matter. It always feels like the
end of the world, as though everything had tumbled back into original chaos.
One feels delivered up, disoriented, like a rudderless ship that is abandoned
to the moods of the elements. So at least it seems.
— JUNG

MY FATHER'S MIDLIFE DEPRESSION began after a professional failure;
mine, after a professional success. He had been fired from his job, ending
a fifteen-year career in radio; I, a college professor with tenure—lifetime
employment!—had published a book in 1986, a biography of Willa Cather,
bringing to fruition fifteen years of work.

Despite our differences, we had a lot in common. We were both forty
years old when our depressions began, on the threshold of the second half
of life, and we both found the work and meaning of the first half of our lives
crumbling. We stood there, he with his failure, I with my success, looking
into the abyss, all structures dissolved. Both of us had spent much of our
lives pursuing academic and professional goals—I perhaps more urgently
than my father, propelled on by my parents' expectations and needs. In
midlife, like him I confronted loss, and the depression that often accompanies loss. He had been able to reinvent his life and find contentment outside
of American definitions of success. This seemed to be what was required of
me; the success story had run its course. Later I would find Jung's description of the life course helpful. The first half of life is about achievement, he

206

observes, the second half about meaning. My father had accomplished this transition—would I?

Both of us would experience what popular psychology calls a "midlife crisis," familiar to us because of the many books that have been published on the stages of life, from *Childhood and Society* to *Passages*. Such views of human development disagree with Freud, believing that the human personality is not set in stone by the trauma and drama of childhood. The transitions called for in midlife—perhaps only a luxury for the middle and upper class, not preoccupied with sheer survival—can be particularly rocky. That is when people have to face up to limitations—all the things that didn't work out the way we might have hoped—all the while just beginning to get the truth many of us have been able to avoid, that our time on earth is limited. Death pushes its cold nose past our front door.

I IMAGINE MY FATHER's depression as immediate and catastrophic, descending as he packed up the papers from his desk and took the trolley car back to Belmont, wondering how he could ever tell the news to my mother. Because I had not suffered the traumatic loss of a job and income, the onset of my depression was far more gradual. At first, after I finished my biography of Cather, I felt only relief and satisfaction. There had been many times when I distrusted my abilities as a biographer. Once or twice I came close to abandoning the project entirely. But I'd stuck with it, and that meant something to me.

I was intending to go off to Ireland in August to spend a year teaching at Trinity College, and it was exciting to have something to look forward to throughout the summer—I had wanted for years to live in Ireland. Even so, I remember that during May and June I started to feel adrift and purposeless and a little sad. I knew that my book project was over, but I hadn't realized how much else was ending. A depression that I didn't name was beginning to take root, growing out of losses I didn't, at that point, understand. As June moved into July, my vague feelings of purposelessness deepened. I found myself unable to take pleasure in things I used to enjoy, unable to make use of the long summer days and glowing evenings to garden, read, or be with friends.

When I was working on my book—evenings after school, weekends, vacations—time was always filled, there was never enough time. Now all kinds of strange, vacant times in the day and week started to open up like underground fissures. Times like Sunday night—what *did* people do on

Sunday night?—and three-thirty in the afternoon, too early for dinner, "All Things Considered," or long-distance phone calls, but too late for a nap. These times started to scare me. I couldn't fill them up anymore with work or pleasure, and so I'd find ways just to pass the time. "It passes the time," my mother would say about some activity she did without pleasure, like the senior citizen bus trips to Plymouth Rock or luncheons with the Daughters of the Potato Famine. Now I knew what she meant. I'd get up around seven-thirty, have coffee and read the paper, do errands, work on book orders for Ireland, and then look at my watch and be disconcerted to see it was only ten-fifteen.

When my father suffered from his long depression, at least he had family around him, other energies, other needs. I don't think that single people are more prone to fall into depression, but once you're stuck there it can be harder to get out of the pit. You don't have the energy to initiate contact with people, and so you get isolated, and then you get more depressed.

Willa Cather used to get depressed—briefly—after she finished a book. She had a particularly hard time after *The Song of the Lark* was published, perhaps because she put so much of her artistic self into her heroine. Her friend Elizabeth Sergeant thought that Cather was, for a time, grieving and depressed. "She depended on Thea to such an extent that when the book came out and the close inner tie was severed, she felt the pang and emptiness of one deserted." Something similar had happened to me: I'd not only finished a book, I'd lost a relationship. When you write a biography, you are involved, intimately, with another self for many years. And then, no more. People can get depressed once the goals are realized: after moving into longed-for retirement, after getting tenure, after the party is over and the guests have left. The gain is also a loss—not just of the completed project, but also of the identity and purpose invested in it.

*A*S THE RHYTHMS OF summer moved into August, my spirits improved. I began to get ready to leave for Ireland.

Going to Ireland had been my first attempt to find a new story for my life. I had two good choices for how to spend the year after my book came out. One was a fellowship to the National Humanities Center in North Carolina, to write a second academic book on women writers. The other was a Fulbright to Dublin to teach American literature to Irish students. Neither grant could be postponed, and I had to choose between them.

Going to North Carolina meant I'd be on the fast track in my profession. The National Humanities Center is a prestigious place. Famous people go there. I would be sure to make contacts. I might even become famous myself, because if I published a second book I would avoid the academic stigma of being only a *one-book person*. (Before becoming an academic, I had thought that publishing one book would be quite enough for one lifetime; after a few years in the profession I learned that "one-book people" were held in contempt, almost even more so than no-book people.)

I imagined myself a well-known literary scholar. I'd be in an elevator at the Modern Language Association, the national organization for English professors, where people scan nametags quickly to see if you're from Berkeley or Duke or Yale and thus worth talking to. People always passed over my nametag because it read "Dickinson Col," but maybe if I went to North Carolina and wrote another book and got a job at some hotshot place, maybe then someone would look at my nametag and instead of looking away to find someone more famous, stop with me. "Are you *the* Sharon O'Brien?" the person would ask, and I'd be pleased and embarrassed as a hush fell over the elevator.

The only problem was I didn't want to write that book about women writers at all. I'd proposed it because I didn't know what to do next, and it seemed like a good idea at the time. It was a book that I *could* do, but not one that I *had* to do, from inside, the way I had to write my biography of Cather.

J DECIDED BETWEEN North Carolina and Ireland by picturing myself in each place. I saw myself packing my car with boxes of books about women writers and driving to North Carolina and meeting scholars who'd be genuinely thrilled with their own projects, while mine already felt like a burden. Then I saw myself going to Logan Airport (because I'd have to leave from my home city of Boston) and there would be that big Aer Lingus jumbo jet, gleaming silver and rose in the setting sun, huge green shamrock on the tail. The plane would be named after an Irish saint and blessed by a priest before launching. No one on the plane would ask me what I was working on. They'd ask me what I wanted to drink, or what books I'd been reading, or who my people were.

I wanted to be seeing that shamrock, I wanted to be on that plane.

By the time I boarded the St. Columkille, in late September, I was as eager to arrive in Ireland as the jet. When we took off and I felt the power of those engines lifting me into the sky, the depression of that spring seemed to fade as the lights of Boston dwindled behind us.

I HAD A HAPPY, off-the-map year in Ireland. For the first time in years, maybe the first time since I entered first grade, I was living without the pressure to achieve. It felt like recuperating from a long illness. I felt dazed and fragile and grateful, sensing that some deep well of energy had gone dry and now had to be replenished. It wasn't until I stopped working—and feeling that I *should* be working—that I could assess the accumulated wear and tear, the way you can't tell what's happened to the hull of a boat until you take it out of the water and look for cracks.

(Even as I write this, I see how shaped I still am by American academic notions of what constitutes "work." In Ireland I was teaching two courses a semester and adjusting to a new country, but since I wasn't doing academic writing—and had let go of expectations that I should be "productive" in that way—I felt as if I were on holiday.)

In Ireland, people don't say "What do you do?" when you meet them. They don't care much about what you do; they're more interested in how you talk. I'd be at dinner parties where no one ever asked me what I did, and I learned to never ask anyone else.

I never said "yes" more in my life than that year. I'd run into friends in the street, they'd ask me to come with them to a pub, or a gallery opening, or to lunch, and instead of looking at my watch and saying "I'd love to, but I need to get back to work," I'd say *yes*. I soon learned that the Irish think Americans are "mad." It's not uncommon for some Irish people—those in the professional class—to have six weeks of vacation, and all enjoy an ample scattering of holidays throughout the year, more than making up for our Thanksgiving with bank holidays and holy days, and they can't understand why we are so driven to work. ("I'm worried about Dennis," a friend told me, referring to a brother working in the States. "He has a beeper and a fax in his car.")

Irish conversations, like Irish stories, don't travel in a straight line. They move through loops and spirals and interruptions and doublings back, in contrast to our more linear culture where the values of "progress" and "sense of direction" function as goads and reprimands. You'd spend an evening with a few people at dinner or in a pub, and you'd be interrupted more than once—not aggressively, but because someone else sparked off something you said, and the conversation would veer off in another direction.

After a while—minutes, hours, the whole evening—someone looks your way and says "And then what happened?" The seemingly broken threads of conversation are always being picked up and woven back into the whole: you just have to wait. Soon you learn how to do it too: there'll be a lull in the conversation and you'll turn to Mary, whose story about craziness at work was interrupted two hours ago, and ask, "So he really walked out in the middle of a class?" and she'll say "None of us could believe it," and she's off again.

Streets and roads in Ireland are tangled, too, just like the conversations, and I found that traveling there was more like wandering. The point is often *not* to find the thing you were looking for; you were probably meant to find something else. Space and time there are not the same as in America: the main roads are two lanes, and a cross-country trip from Dublin to Galway will take you through several towns. The best way to travel is to give in, throw away watches and be prepared to be led astray, putting aside the American notion of "making time," which only means that you got somewhere fast, not that you did anything interesting with the time it took to get there.

The spiritual geography of Ireland seemed like a web or a spiral, lines criss-crossing and interweaving like those illustrations in the book of Kells. If you enter a maze that's shaped like a spiral, like the one at Newgrange, you can't see where you're going so you have to be in the present moment: you can't look ahead to a far-off goal and not pay attention to where you are. I liked being in this maze, not having to have what we call over here "a sense of direction."

I'd had a sense of direction ever since I was five years old. In that year I took my I.Q. test, and all those points told my parents how high I was supposed to go. They looked straight up and so did I, eyes following their pointing fingers, often not seeing the ground at my feet. It was a relief to discover how much I loved getting off the track, even not having a track.

My year in Ireland, well before the emergence of the Celtic Tiger and a speeded-up Irish economy that has brought new pressures as well as possibilities, allowed me to liberate disorderly parts of myself that my American life then had no room for—my urge to play, to improvise, to digress.

*B*ACK HOME, I tried to resurrect my pre-Ireland productive self. "What is your next project?" people asked me, or "What are you working on now? Another volume of your Cather biography?" The well-meant questions grated. Sometimes I lied and said that yes, I was intending to do volume II; sometimes I got self-righteous and drenched my unsuspecting listener with celebrations of the fallow period (*so essential to the creative process!*), followed by criticisms of our product-oriented American culture.

The truth was I didn't have a next project. I couldn't imagine writing about Cather again. I didn't feel like writing about anything else, either, at least not scholarly writing—the thought of footnotes was repellent. I couldn't understand what was happening. My professional life had always been the one thing I could count on—my whole identity was wound up with being good at school—and now my desire to keep advancing seemed ebbing like air from a leaky tire.

It was probably fortunate that it was my turn to chair the English department. The heavy administrative tasks, intensified because we were going through a curriculum revision, not only kept me busy and useful, they gave me cloud cover. When I couldn't give a rapid list of publications in answer to the "What are you working on?" question, people would say, "Oh, you're chairing, no one can publish much then," and I'd nod, trying to look like someone who had hordes of books and articles inside her that would just pop out as soon as a sabbatical rolled around. "I'll bet you're looking forward to leaving the chair," they would say, "a chance to get some of your own writing done." "Right," I'd say, knowing I had no academic writing to do.

I WAS HEADED FOR a major depression during the two years I was chairing: I could sense it around the edges. I can still remember the weekend when I finally entered fully into it. It was early June, and my tenure as chair was over. I was flying to Las Vegas for a conference of English Department chairs, about to lead a workshop called "Psychological Transition from Faculty Member to Chair." I wanted to pump people up, send them back home filled with eagerness and good will and tips for handling the stressful parts of the job.

*F*OR SEVERAL weeks before Las Vegas I'd been having the oddest feeling that I wasn't really *myself.* I'd look in the mirror and the person staring back seemed to be slightly out of focus, like the blurry snapshot of a relative you can't quite recognize. I felt disconnected from a source of identity and energy—like a light bulb that hadn't quite caught in the threads, off by just a hair, and so no matter how many times you pull the switch, nothing happens.

As soon as I got off the plane an even more ominous feeling of dislocation descended. On the way to the baggage claim there were rows and rows of slot machines. Passengers ran toward them, coins in hand, ready to gamble. I stood frozen: was I the kind of woman who played slot machines while she waited for her luggage? I had no idea. I stood watching some people gamble, others walk purposefully toward welcoming relatives or toward their luggage or toward the bathroom. None of these choices made any sense.

I checked into the Tropicana, experiencing a kind of floating, out-of-body detachment. Like all the Las Vegas hotels, the Tropicana has no windows, clocks, or exit signs: the casino wants to cut you off from all references to time and place and make gambling the only reality. I wandered toward my room through spirals of blackjack tables, roulette wheels, craps tables, and slot machines, wondering if I could ever find my way back. I lay down on the bed and looked briefly at my notes for the workshop I was going to lead the next day ("Curriculum revision as an opportunity for building community," "Dealing with factions"). I couldn't imagine myself doing this; perhaps when the meeting started I would feel more like myself.

As the days passed I began feeling more and more like my blurry relative. I'd be in a session on "Writing and the Curriculum" or "Assessment in the 1990s" or "Dealing with the Dean" and I'd look around the room at everyone else, college professors seemingly content with their name tags and their lives, all nodding, listening, or looking bored, acting as if things were normal, as if they *belonged* here. Didn't they know we were on the moon?

"What are you working on now?" they asked each other at the breaks and the cocktail parties, and they answered easily. A study of the Victorian body, using Foucault. The writer and the marketplace, using an anthropological perspective from gift exchange. An edition of Thomas Hakluyt, long overdue. Editing this, researching that, just going on sabbatical, just coming off, applying for a grant, a Fulbright, a fellowship, words and sentences tumbling out easily, connected to intention and desire. I wanted to be like them, I wanted to belong, how could I tell them I didn't care about literary scholarship anymore?

What are you working on now, Sharon? they would ask. *Another volume of your Willa Cather biography? Everyone is looking forward to it! Are you doing something with that paper you gave on Three Mile Island at the American Studies Association? You really should publish that.*

"I'm still working on the Library of America Cather edition," I said, trying to fit in with my productive colleagues, dredging up an unfinished editing project on which I'd been procrastinating for two years.

I stared at my name tag. As always, it read

SHARON O'BRIEN
DICKINSON COLLEGE

There was no reason why this person couldn't talk about feminist biography or enter debates on student-centered learning—I had opinions on those subjects, even if they had belonged to me in an earlier incarnation. They had belonged to a woman who felt confident, when she attached the plastic-covered name tag to her jacket, that she was indeed that person.

When a break came we would leave rooms with names like "Islander," "Polynesian," "Aku-Aku," decorated with glossy flamingo-covered wallpaper and featuring spongy-dice centerpieces on the tables, and enter the realm of twenty-four-hour slot machines, unsleeping, constant, chirping like manic sparrows. Professors hurried to bathrooms, grabbed coffee and danish, and seated themselves before the slot machines, joking about funding their next leaves with their winnings, as happy as school children at recess. Envying them, I lurked in corners, waiting for the break to be over, waiting for things to be different.

To return to our rooms we had to stand on a moving walkway that took us past rows of parrots on perches. At first I thought the parrots were stuffed, they were so immobile, but then I saw one black eye close and open. The parrots weren't chained and I wondered why they did not fly off. I finally concluded that they were depressed: flying was hopeless, where would they go? There were no open windows in Las Vegas casinos. If they flew they'd exhaust themselves or crash into glass. Better to sit on perches and signify the South Seas to people wearing Hawaiian shirts.

After the parrots came a sign that read *Future Home of Pigmy Marmosets*. I spent some time wondering what pigmy marmosets might be. Whatever their native habitat was, it surely was not Las Vegas. I imagined a sign reading *Future Home of Sharon O'Brien*, but I wasn't sure what it, or she, would look like. I'd been living in Carlisle for fifteen years but I didn't really think it was my *home*. When people asked me where I was from, I always said "Well, I live in Carlisle, but I'm really from Boston." When I was changing planes at O'Hare and saw that red neon *Harrisburg* at the USAir counter, I would think "That's the right plane." I didn't think *home,* the way I used to when I saw *Boston* on the airport monitor.

And as for a future home, all I had were the single woman's nightmarish fantasies of a lonely life in the nursing home, being wheeled out by teenage volunteers to celebrate Valentine's Day, agreeing to eat the cake with pink frosting because it would be the high point of the day. "Now let's make Valentines for each other," the volunteers would say, and I'd obediently pick up the glue and the red construction paper and the lacy white paper doilies because there was nothing else to do.

MY FATHER'S DEPRESSION, sparked by failure, must have been a sledgehammer. Mine, slithering out of success, was creeping up so slowly I couldn't recognize it or name it, numbing me like one of those reptiles that stuns with poison so it can devour you at its leisure. By the time I left Las Vegas, headed for a friend's wedding in California, I knew that something was wrong, but I hoped being in a familiar place, around people I cared for, would help me return to life. But if there's one other thing you learn from myth and legend, it's this: people don't return from the underworld whenever they feel like it. They don't say to Cerberus or Pluto or Virgil, "Okay, fine! I've had enough now, and I think I'll return to the surface." No, they have to wait until they've undergone something frightening and dangerous, and they don't know in advance what that will be, or whether they'll survive.

California was a disaster. Seeing a close friend get married made me feel lonely, and the strain of talking with all the wedding guests I'd never seen before was too much for me. "What do you do?" someone would ask. "I teach," I'd say, striving to look dynamic. "English." Then, trying to remove the glazed expression from the other face, afraid the next comment would be "Uh-oh, I'd better watch my grammar," I'd add quickly "but I write," then realize with horror the next question would be "Oh, what do you write?"

I FLEW BACK TO Carlisle a day early, hoping I'd feel more myself in Pennsylvania's humid air, hoping that returning to the only home I had would help. I walked up to my front door, turned the key, and walked into the house. The air in the house felt different—thicker, somehow—and the afternoon light streaming in the dining room windows seemed harsher, and the pile of mail on the table looked terrifying.

"Uh-oh," I thought, "I'm in real trouble now."

215

$\mathcal{T}$HROUGHOUT THE late summer and fall, grateful for the teaching that gave me structure and responsibility, I began to experience increased dissociation, a kind of eerie numbness that separates your body from your soul. After a while my soul was hovering on the ceiling, looking down as I struggled to perform the rituals of ordinariness, like daily conversation. But I didn't want to talk because I had nothing interesting to say. Who wanted to hear about how hard it was becoming to get out of bed on days when I didn't have school?

Maybe the ultimate irony is this: depression—soul-crusher, destroyer of days, thief of life and love and time, violator of the will, unloving companion—is, at the bottom of its chill and useless heart, a ferociously *boring* torturer.

$\mathcal{T}$HE STRESS of the Christmas holidays was compounded that year because I had to attend the Modern Language Association's annual convention, scheduled between Christmas and New Year's. In earlier years I'd enjoyed the conference—it was a chance to meet up with friends—and didn't even mind the timing, although it drove my mother wild. "Why you have to go to that damn MLA at this time of year I'll never know," she would say. (It was never just "the MLA" to my mother, always "that damn MLA.") "Don't those people have *families?*"

This year I would have skipped, but I was on a committee and I had to attend. I went to a session on Willa Cather, hoping I'd feel more connected to my life and work, but the opposite happened. As I watched the audience nodding and scribbling notes, I got more and more scared. Something I once valued now seemed meaningless. Why bother to interpret fiction? What was it all *for?*

$\mathcal{O}$N THE TRAIN back to Boston, where I'd be spending New Year's, I stared out the window at the lighted houses of Connecticut and Rhode Island and Massachusetts speeding by in the dark. I was still frightened. I had hoped that the MLA session would click me back into place and make the academic world that had been mine for so long seem vital and real. Instead I felt as if I were viewing things through the wrong end of a telescope— everyone at the conference seemed diminished and very far away, separated by an unbreakable circle of glass.

School had been the place where I'd made sense of the world since I was five. If I didn't belong here, I didn't belong anywhere.

I knew that these feelings of meaninglessness were what, in Jung's view, characterized the depression accompanying the seismic midlife shift from external to internal sources of meaning. *I'm not ready for this*, I wanted to say. *Why can't I hang onto these external sources of meaning a little longer? Can't we put off the second half of life?* I tried to take consolation from my book of Jung's writings—"The dread and resistance which every natural human being experiences when it comes to delving too deeply into the self is, at bottom, the fear of the journey to Hades"—but it didn't make a dent in my dread. *You mean I can't read my way through this instead of living it?*

I didn't want to go to Hades, I wanted to stay in school.

But what I wanted didn't have anything to do with what was happening to me any more.

Getting through the Day

Often I go to bed as soon after dinner

as seems adult
(I mean I try to wait for dark)
in order to push away
from the massive pain in sleep's
frail wicker coracle.

— JANE KENYON, "Having it Out with Melancholy"

IT'S A MATTER OF SOME DISCUSSION among my friends who suffer from depression what is the worst time of day. Most of them think it's the morning. "As soon as you wake up you know you're still depressed," Jonathan says, "and there's a whole day ahead you have to get through." There are several votes for the afternoon, though—including mine—and a few for the evening.

Mornings can be terrible, particularly when you wake around four-thirty or five and know how many hours you'll have to endure before sleeping again. Depression sits on your chest, an enormous toad pushing you down into the bed, or it oozes under the door, green slime, or it's an invisible fog mixing with every particle of air and every cell in your body. It's a shapeshifter, depression, and will do whatever it needs to get you.

Your limbs have no power. You are tired, unbearably tired. Fatigue smothers your body and your soul. The air is dense as tar. To stand up and move is to combat the powers of the universe. It's as if you're living on some strange planet where the atmosphere presses in at thousands of tons per square inch.

You squint at the window, hoping the sun isn't up, but the highest leaves of the maple tree are bathed in light and so now it's almost seven o'clock, closer to the relentless energy of the day that wants to drag you out of bed. Time is your enemy and there's nothing you can do to stop it.

$\mathcal{G}$ETTING OUT OF BED on a school day requires turning your will into a derrick, lifting you from above. *Not yet. I'm not ready. Better gather my strength. Now! Well, maybe not now. I'll wait a few minutes. My class isn't until ten. If I skip breakfast that'll give me more time. . . . All right, when the patch of sunlight reaches the tip of that rug, I'm up. Up! I'll be up soon. . . . Maybe I'll call in sick but what will I tell the department secretary? I don't want to lie and I cannot tell the truth.* This is what the *DSM IV* calls "psychomotor retardation"—a pallid phrase that hardly conveys the devastating loss of physical and psychic energy depression causes.

The problem with mornings is leaving the refuge of the bed. Mornings yank you out of the comforting dark and thrust you into the unforgiving light of day. If you get up late you're already behind on the day. Other people, people who are not depressed, are already up and working. If you have your first cup of coffee at 9:30, hoping caffeine will burn off the fog, you're a straggler, a fake American. "Early to bed, early to rise," Benjamin Franklin says. You cannot rise early and that makes you feel like a moral failure. In Ireland, nine-thirty is early, but in America it's a sin to start the day this late. The sounds of human activity already percolating—traffic, the steps of the mailman, a far-off siren—and the angle of the sun tell you that you're out of step. Guilty, you want to rush to catch up, but depression paralyzes the body as well as the will.

$\mathcal{S}$OMETIMES MORNINGS are not so bad. There can be hope in the morning. Perhaps today will be better. Perhaps the antidepressants will decide to work, or you'll pay the bills, or write a letter, or answer your email, or wash yesterday's dishes, still festering and sullen in the sink.

This is a hope that unravels by noon.

$\mathcal{W}$HY DO I FIND afternoons so terrible? I think it's because I've endured many hours of waking depression already and I can't believe there are so many hours left before I can go to bed and escape. *How can it be only two-thirty? How am I going to make it until bedtime?* Time slows down in the afternoon. Seconds and minutes swell and expand. I look at the clock after ages of patient suffering. Ten minutes have passed.

Afternoons are always when I'm tempted by the attractive mortal sin of depression—the nap. "Napping is absolutely the worst thing you can do," my psychiatrist reminds me. She knows that daytime napping will mean nighttime insomnia, and I know that I always feel more depressed when I wake up. I'll feel worse later but I can't resist the short-term escape.

If I'm in a deep depression, the nasty kind that destroys your powers of concentration as well as your will, I'll try to read, but I may spend some of the afternoon hours just staring—sometimes out the window, sometimes at the rug, sometimes at the sunlight making patterns on the floor. Sometimes I listen to the furnace going on and off, or to the whirr of the ceiling fan.

Afternoons are when the mail comes. With the mail comes guilt: I know I won't be able to pay bills or answer letters, and sometimes I can't open the mail at all. Bills pile up, third and fourth warning notices come from the phone company, the gas company, the electric company, finally taking the form of telegrams with *URGENT* written on the envelopes. Once I'd let the mail go so long—weeks? months?—that I had to invite friends over for support while I opened it.

Sometimes the outside world's afternoon intrusion is so perilous I have to act. Once I came home to find a mysterious envelope pinned to my door. Was this a message from a friend, or the first contact from a mysterious lover, perhaps a college sweetheart—newly divorced or widowed—who has sought me out after all these years? The letter inside began with huge block letters.

ARREST WARRENT [*sic*]

I am being informed by the Sheriff of Cumberland County that I'm being spared the "embarrassment of being arrested at work," and I have twenty-four hours to go to the courthouse with a money order for $144 to pay parking tickets that, if I hadn't been too depressed to handle them, would have cost me twenty. I drive to the bank, get the money order, walk through the courthouse metal detector, enter the windowless office of the District Justice—fluorescent light, beige plastic chairs, and artificial plants—and pay the fine. This is an inner drama no one will ever see, a depressed person's heroic afternoon journey to the bank and the courthouse.

*W*HEN I'M depressed I never answer the doorbell in the afternoon; a stranger's energy will pierce me like a needle. I peer out through the curtains like the nutty old ladies who didn't open the door when I was selling Girl Scout cookies. I want to see who's on the porch, waiting until the paper boy, the Mormon missionaries, the UPS man give up and leave. "Be sure to check the 'Unsigned Delivery' box" I tell professional colleagues who are sending me overnight mail, "I'm going to be out most of the day," conjuring up an aura of on-the-go energy when the truth is I can't bear to open the door and sign for the package.

In the afternoon I discover times of day—now ripped from all social context—that seem meaningless and terrifying, times of day I never notice when I am not depressed. I look at the clock and it is three-fifteen. *Three-fifteen*. What are people supposed to do at three-fifteen? Why have I never noticed this time before? Can I make it until four? I think of the conclusion of Robert Frost's bleak poem about depression, "Acquainted with the Night": "The village clock / proclaimed the time / Was neither wrong nor right." And on winter afternoons, as Emily Dickinson writes, the bleak, waning light brings darkness and death even closer.

> There's a certain slant of light—Winter afternoons—
> That oppresses like the heft—of Cathedral tunes.
> Heavenly Hurt it gives us—though it leaves no scar—
> But internal difference—where the meanings are.

Afternoons. They linger and dawdle and stall, blocking the exit, cutting me off from the evening and the longed-for ending to one more endless day. If I were to kill myself, I know it would be in the afternoon.

When I think of my father's depression I always imagine him in the afternoon, sitting on the bed, looking out the window onto Lewis Road. He is dressed in chino pants and a blue Oxford cloth shirt, no tie. My mother is in the kitchen, ironing, about to make dinner, watching me in my playpen. My brother and sister are not home from school yet. It is quiet in the house. He looks out at the empty street—it's too early for the men to be returning from work—and watches the tree shadows change as the sun lowers in the sky.

EVENINGS ARE when the phone rings. Sometimes I answer, but if I'm down too low, I can't break out of isolation. The phone call's from another country. I let the machine take the message; I hear the voice of a friend, a voice unlike mine, alive and filled with tonalities. "Sharon, do you want to have lunch this week?" "Sharon, how *are* you?" "Sharon, just calling to see how you're doing, give me a call." Should I answer the phone? I cannot. Then the red message light blinks, an accusing reminder of my sloth, giving me one more obligation I will not be able to perform. "Sharon, you should have *called* me," a friend will say, days or weeks later, when I finally admit I have been depressed. I know I should have, and I wanted to, but like most depressed people I withdraw. I just couldn't pick up the phone.

ℳOST PEOPLE, when they're depressed, don't have the energy in the evening to read a book, or to watch a video or even good television. You don't have the concentration to follow a narrative, so you might watch bad television, restlessly flipping channels with the remote. You can gaze for what seems hours at the weather channel or the shopping channel, mesmerized, indifferent, watching a woman's manicured fingers, alarmingly magnified, caressing a velvet jewel case or a porcelain doll. You watch a group of people giving personal testimony for a hair thickener, or emergency operations on iguanas on the Animal Channel, or reruns of *Jeopardy!* running down the clock. Each channel-flip is another drip of morphine, deadening the pain just a bit, helping you hang on until bedtime.

𝓘 TRY TO STAY up until ten o'clock: I have my pride. But sometimes it's earlier, much earlier. I take whatever antidepressant I'm on at the moment along with Benadryl to help me sleep. I brush my teeth and try not to look at the blurry face of the woman in the mirror. Loopily triumphant, she'll win any staring contest, silently chanting *"I'm here and you're not."* I turn off the phone and go to bed, hoping for sleep, waiting for another day. I concentrate on my breathing. I stare at the ceiling fan and count its revolutions. I wait for the best part of the day. I wait for sleep.

Being in depression is about waiting. Waiting for the depression to lift. Waiting for an antidepressant to kick in. Waiting for another antidepressant to kick in. Going to work. Coming home. Making dinner. Breathing. Waiting. "Forever—is composed of Nows," writes Emily Dickinson, and what if forever is composed of the waiting Now of depression? What if this time it does not lift? Most of the people sociologist David Karp interviewed for his book on depression, *Speaking of Sadness*, mention this fear, like the person who said "I'm in it. I can't believe I'm really in it again. It's here, it's back. It always comes back. And I don't know when I'm going to get out of it. And maybe this time I'll never get out of it."

You learn to wait with the faith that comes from past experience, the faith that this too shall pass away—it always has. "But maybe this time will be different," a voice says. "This time depression has put you in a waiting room you can't leave until your name is called and nobody knows your name."

You learn to live with this voice.

MORNING, AFTERNOON, evening, night: to Thoreau, in *Walden*, these seasons of the day had meaning, telling the story of the self moving from wakefulness to contemplation to descent into the unconscious and then to wakefulness again. That's a beautiful story for the day, as it is for a life, a cycle of rebirth and renewal and descent. "Morning is when I am awake," Thoreau writes, referring to spiritual vitality as well as the literal time of day. In many cultures and religions and myths, morning is the time of rebirth, literally and metaphorically. Buddhists meditate before dawn; monks sing Matins at four o'clock. But when you're depressed, morning is when you discover, one more endless time, that nothing is different. Nothing has altered during sleep.

Perhaps this is why most depressed people find mornings the hardest. Morning is the time for change and thus for clemency, the only time when, as Jane Kenyon writes in "Having it Out with Melancholy," someone can feel "the wonder / and bitterness of someone pardoned / for a crime she did not commit." When you wake up to depression, you know your appeal has been denied. But there's nothing you can do about it, and so you put one foot in front of the other. You get out of bed, brush your teeth, get dressed. You take the antidepressant that's keeping you from feeling even worse. If you have kids you get them ready for school. Go to work, come home, make dinner or unfreeze leftovers, stay up until an adult's bedtime.

You do the best you can.

You do what others have done: you don't give up, and you get through the day.

The Great City of Lowell

I would like to find work in Boston, or in the great city of Lowell.
—statement in my father's college file

IN MY FATHER'S DAY, when Americans did not move around so much, when they did not change jobs and homes every few years, people were identified by jobs and places. My father first considered himself "an ad man," then a "radio man." My mother was an "Elmira girl," my father a "Lowell man." He was proud of his hometown, which he called "the great city of Lowell" when we went there on Sunday excursions.

The O'Brien family house in Lowell seemed full of secrets. It was dark and Gothic, with stained-glass windows on the stairs, a scary (at times delightfully so) museum of Catholic memorabilia. We would drive up there for Sunday dinner with my aunt Gert and uncle Ray, and I remember the sharp contrast between the sunny afternoon we were leaving and the somber house we were headed toward. It was filled with religious icons collected by my grandmother. You could find bejeweled Infants of Prague, cloaked in velvet robes and wearing golden crowns and holding little scepters in their tiny hands, sheltered in alcoves; lithographs of crucified Christs, sometimes the whole shot (cross, nailed hands and feet, blood dripping from the nails and the wounds in the side), sometimes just the head, in profile, always with the crown of thorns and requisite drops of blood; and—most terrifying to me—the Sacred Heart of Jesus.

Sometimes the Heart was a picture of Christ with a huge, exposed (and of course bleeding) red heart sending out golden rays of grace; sometimes the picture was just of the Heart itself, folded and contoured like a real heart, not a valentine, pierced with little spears (for the blood) and radiating grace-rays so solid they seemed three-dimensional. Usually there'd be a prayer underneath in gold script, *O Sacred Heart of Jesus, in thy infinite mercy take pity on thy sinners,* or a title, like *The Light of the World.* I used to take any excuse I could to pee, just so I could scare myself by going up the stairs to the bathroom, passing all the bloody Christs and almost-beating hearts and knowing I was a terrible sinner because I didn't really care that Christ had died for our sins.

We would have dinner on the big oaken table, covered with a crocheted table cloth, always the standard Irish Catholic Sunday fare: pot roast or lamb (roast beef for special occasions), carrots and potatoes boiled within an inch of their lives, and, in our family, Harvard beets (in my father's honor we called them "the educated beets"). After dinner Gert and my mother would clean up, while Ray and my father led the three of us outside for a walk down to the Merrimack River, just at the bottom of the street, where we could join the other Sunday strollers along the banks.

Ray and Gert were our only O'Brien relatives; our grandparents were long dead, and my father told no stories about them. All his stories about earlier times were about his undergraduate years at Harvard or his early years in radio. It seems clear to me now that the O'Brien side of the family is where the depression comes from (genetically, anyway), but there are very few clues about this family. My sister and brother can't add any more memories to mine; they don't remember my father telling family stories either.

I found out more about my father's missing past when I came across his attempt to construct an O'Brien genealogy, a couple of scrawled pages in the back of his reading journal. He had two siblings I'd never heard of, Mabel and Paul, both of whom had died young. Mabel, the first child born to his parents, died when she was six years old. Paul, born two years after my father, died shortly after birth. "2 hours" my father had written next to his name. "Did you know that Dad had a brother and sister who died?" I asked my siblings. They didn't know either.

𝒯HE TRAIL of these long-ago O'Briens may be cold, but one sunny October day I decide to return to Lowell, only a forty-five minute drive from Boston. At least I can visit the cemetery—I haven't been there since my aunt Gert's funeral, thirty-three years ago—and I can walk by the old house. I bring my one box of O'Brien memorabilia—Gert's scrapbook, family pictures, my father's reading journal—just in case anyone at the Lowell Historical Society might want to take a look.

I stop at Wilson's Farm Stand in Lexington on the way. You can pick your own flowers there, and I gather up loads of zinnias and black-eyed Susans and daisies and nasturtiums, all of them thriving in October. I've brought a vase, and I like thinking about putting these brightly colored flowers on the O'Brien grave. The Quinlans were as multicolored as tropical birds but the O'Brien ancestors strike me as dark, gloomy, monochromatic. They need cheering up, a splash of hot pink, red, yellow, orange, and purple right in front of their noses.

When I get to the cemetery I'm disappointed: I'm expecting some sort of revelation, but the modest grave just says O'BRIEN, even though the office printout says there are nine people buried here. (In addition to Ray and Gert, the grave holds my grandfather, Daniel O'Brien, and his wife, Catherine; Catherine's parents, Michael and Mary Long, her sister Mary Long, and the two O'Brien children I discovered in my father's notebook, Mabel and Paul.) The Quinlans, by contrast, had all the individual names on the headstone. Typical, I thought. The theatrical Quinlans want their own stories told, the meat-and-potatoes O'Briens don't want anybody to stand out. One last name was good enough for everybody, even people whose last name was Long. Cheaper, too.

I try to talk to the O'Briens and the Longs, a little nervous because I haven't met any of them except for Ray and Gert. I imagine them as a dour and disapproving group—except for my grandfather, Daniel, who was, my mother said, "a sweet man, very like your father." I tell them I'm wanting to know more about my father and his family, that I want to understand where my depression came from, where I came from. I'm chattering. I'm nervous. I don't think I'm getting a good reception: these Longs and O'Briens are not easily charmed.

"Well," I say, winding things up with this branch of the family, "here are some flowers for you, I think I'd better be going now," and leave for the historical society.

THE CURATOR at the Lowell Historical Society oohs and aahs over my aunt Gert's scrapbook, turning the pages with reverence. "Would you will it to us?" she asks. "We actually have very few primary documents from Irish American women." I hadn't realized that Gert's book of notes and clippings was a "primary document," and I have no idea what I want to do with it. This scrapbook is all there is of my aunt's autobiography, and I don't want it to sit in a box in my attic. But I'm not sure I want it to sit in a box in some historical society either. I'm noncommittal.

The curator apologizes for the scant collection. "People haven't been good at saving things in Lowell," she says, and sends me off to the public library, where I can find old newspapers and city records.

*I*N THE BASEMENT of the Lowell Public Library, reading obituaries on microfilm and searching through nineteenth-century city directories, I come closer to the world my father came from, the Irish world he left behind when he went to Harvard, the world he never told stories about. It becomes clear, as I read through the traces of my ancestors, that in leaving Lowell for Harvard he left one world for another.

For the Irish Catholics who emigrated to Lowell throughout the nineteenth century, landing in Boston from the famine ships and making their way north, hoping for work in the city's textile mills, Lowell was not a way station to somewhere else; the final destination, it became home. The Irish emigrated there, worked in the mills, bore children, died there; their children and grandchildren did the same. My aunt and uncle, who lived in the house their parents owned until Ray died, lived more typical Lowell Irish lives than did my father. By the early twentieth century, the Irish dominated town politics, having taken over political power from the Yankees who still owned the mills but no longer held city hall.

The Irish community was more ethnically separatist in Lowell than in other New England cities like Springfield or Worcester or Hartford. Parochial education was strong here, a way to preserve Catholic values and Irish identity in the midst of secular and anti-Irish Yankee culture. My grandparents sent my aunt Gert to Notre Dame Academy, founded in the 1850s by the sisters of Notre Dame de Namur as a sanctuary of Catholic education for girls who might well work in the mills before marriage. According to the school's manifesto, the students would learn to use "the rosary, the pen, the broom, and the needle." My uncle and father attended parochial elementary school but then Lowell High School—it was safer for boys to venture into the public schools than for girls. Along with the rest of the O'Briens and Longs, my father was a member of St. Patrick's, one of the largest and most influential parishes in New England in the early twentieth century. His father and brother Ray belonged to the local chapter of the Knights of Columbus, the largely Irish Catholic men's fraternal organization. It would have been possible, during that period, to be born, live, and die in Lowell without much interaction with non–Irish Catholics.

I stumble into this all–Irish Catholic world as I'm tracking down obituaries and funeral reports. In early twentieth-century Irish Catholic Lowell, the obituary and the funeral report were two quite separate genres. The *Lowell Sun,* then the Irish Catholic paper, catered to its readers' insatiable appetite for death news by immediately publishing a brief obituary, containing just the vital statistics—name, address, cause of death, surviving relatives. A few days later a lengthy report of the funeral appeared—who attended, who said Mass, who sent flowers, who the soloists were, how big the crowd was. What weddings are to the Italians, funerals are to the Irish, and the *Lowell Sun* didn't skimp on coverage: the editor must have assigned several reporters to the funeral beat.

My grandfather, Daniel O'Brien, who managed a men's clothing store near City Hall, hit the funeral jackpot. The *Sun* ran his photograph and gave him top billing.

MANY ATTEND O'BRIEN RITES, says the headline for his 1943 funeral. *Impressive Tribute to Retired Clothing Merchant.* Well, it *was* impressive, I can tell you, after having read hundreds of other Irish funeral reports in the *Sun.* First of all, there were four priests, not just one, and twelve soloists for the funeral mass (my grandfather was a well-known Irish tenor, and had sung "Panis Angelicus" and "Ave Maria" at dozens of Irish funerals). Then there were the usual delegations from the Knights of Columbus and the Holy Name Society, and every politician in town seems to have been there (they probably got their suits from O'Brien's Clothiers)—the mayor (Joseph Sweeney), the City Treasurer (John J. Flannery), the City Auditor (Daniel Martin), City Purchasing Agent (Martin Sullivan), City Building Commissioner (Frank O'Neill), State Representative (George Walsh), Registrar of Deeds (Daniel Moriarty) . . . the list goes on. Not a non-Irish name among them.

"There were many flowers requiring the use of an open automobile," reports the *Sun.* No wonder: John Flannery, the City Treasurer, probably called up Brendan Riley (Riley's Flowers) and said "ship enough flowers over to Dan's funeral to fill an open car," and of course Riley wouldn't have billed the city, because he had the contracts for Memorial Day and Decoration Day and the Fourth of July.

Contrast to the funeral of poor John Welch on the same day: it was "well attended," says the *Sun* politely, not mentioning any names of attendees. Clearly a face saver: everyone who was anyone in the Irish community must have been at my grandfather's funeral. Welch had a funeral mass, but no flowers are mentioned, and only one priest and two soloists. "Not much of a showing," I imagine my O'Brien relatives saying with satisfaction to each other when they checked out the funeral reports in the morning paper: after all, the major purpose of the funeral reports was to let Irish readers know *who went.* They could just as easily have been on the society page.

I'M CURIOUS about the vanished Mabel, the sister my father never knew or mentioned. With the help of the librarian I'm able to track down her obituary and funeral report, and it's almost as long as her father's, and five times as long as the funeral report for any other child who died in Lowell from 1900–1905, the years I checked.

> Although but 6 years of age, the little girl was exceptionally bright and at the Notre Dame academy, where she attended school, she was very popular among her associates, many of whom were much older. She had been ill for about two weeks, but until Saturday no symptoms were discovered that would cause uneasiness. The little one grew worse Saturday morning and died during the early part of the afternoon.

Several paragraphs are given over to the floral tributes: a pillow of roses with the inscription "Our May Belle" from her parents; a large cross of lilies with "May Belle" from her uncle Patrick and his family; other floral arrangements in the shapes of hearts, stars, harps with broken strings, a dove with six strings in its beak, a crescent and star, another pillow, a wreath or roses, a spray of calla lilies, variously inscribed with "May Belle," "Asleep," "With the angels," sent by relatives and friends as well as the choir of St. Patrick's Church and the Merrimack Clothing Company. The names, once again, are all Irish: the O'Hearns, Clunes, O'Sullivans, Hanlons, O'Malleys, Murphys, McManamas, and Courtneys were all represented.

The reporter spares no detail, including this final and—to a contemporary reader unfamiliar with late nineteenth-century mourning and funeral practices—perhaps disturbing detail:

> The little casket was borne from the house to the hearse by six little playmates of the deceased: Masters George and Harry Enright, Harold Scaries, William Donohue, Edward Leary and William Gaffney.

It's odd, reading this funeral account, never having heard of this child-aunt of mine before; what I sense from this lengthy tribute is that Mabel was the glowing light of the family, the gifted child, the special one. I've long suspected that the familial background for my father's depression came from his mother's side of the family, based on the fragments my mother gave me about my father's parents and on the few remaining photographs, in which my grandfather has a frank, open, engaging face, and my grandmother a tight, closed, strained one.

I begin to wonder if Mabel's death tipped my grandmother into depression. If so, her well-being would have been threatened again when her infant son Paul died two hours after birth and six years after Mabel. My father would have been two years old when the second death occurred, and there would be no more babies after that. Could he have been raised by a depressed and grieving mother more preoccupied with her dead children than with him?

He would have grown up in a family marked by losses that weren't talked about. Eventually his mother would have turned much of her focus to her brilliant youngest son, the high school valedictorian. And my father—he'd have wanted to please his mother, bring a smile to her face, and redeem her losses. Just the way I always wanted to redeem his.

THE FUNERAL reports lead me out of the family into the larger Irish culture of Lowell. Growing up Irish in Lowell in the early twentieth century meant being woven into a working-class community—so different from the suburban Belmont we grew up in. To belong in this world, you didn't have to do anything special—you just had to have been born there. You didn't need to go to college; if you did, a local Catholic college was the accepted choice, Holy Cross or Boston College. When my father graduated from Lowell High School as the valedictorian, he was accepted to both Harvard and Holy Cross, eventually choosing Holy Cross (according to a family story passed down by my mother) because his mother—she of the Infants of Prague and the Sacred Hearts—pressured him to stay within the Catholic world.

When my father decided to transfer to Harvard after a year at Holy Cross, he was leaving this Lowell world behind. Harvard was the elite cultural and educational institution of Puritan and Yankee Massachusetts and, as it liked to think of itself, the most elite in America, if not the world. My grandfather and his buddies at the Knights of Columbus must have been proud of my father, but he would have become unalterably different.

"So," John Flannery might have said to my grandfather, as he stood before the three-way mirror in his store, getting fitted for a new suit, "Norbert is off to Harvard now, is he? . . . Well, well." He probably wouldn't have known what else to say. He would have heard of Harvard, of course, but he would never have walked through the gates into Harvard Yard, and could not imagine what it would be like to do so. No, the Irish politicians and city hall workers who hung out in my grandfather's clothing store would have known my father was crossing a line by going to Harvard.

I imagine some of my grandfather's cronies gossiping about my father—surely his story was news!—maybe trying to put him in his place. "Did you see Norbert at Riley's wake last week, only stayed a few minutes, does he think he's too good for us now?" Criticizing anyone who excels is one of the more unappealing Irish traits. "We're a begrudging society," an Irish friend once told me. Perhaps it's a result of living with the tragic history of colonization, heartbreaking defeat, and a puritanical religion (don't *desire* anything, Irish Catholicism tells you). Maybe it's a holdover from the Great Hunger, an ethic of scarcity, a mistrust of anyone who has more than anyone else, like the "soupers" in the famine days who got fed by English missionaries because they turned Protestant. Irish begrudgingness has carried over to Irish America. As Mary Gordon observes, the central question of the Irish family, for any family member who seems too full of himself or herself, is *Who do you think you are, anyway?*

$\mathcal{W}$HEN MY father chose to become Harvard '27 rather than Holy Cross '27 he was not just entering a Protestant and Yankee world; he was choosing to stand out, and he might therefore have been seen as rejecting his Irish Catholic world. Very few Irish Catholics were attending Harvard in the 1920s, and priests often discouraged young men from attending non-Catholic colleges. He probably got some criticism for his choice, which he would have dealt with in the joky way he had, trying to dissipate envy with a smile and a laugh. He was a modest man by nature.

I wonder if instead of feeling himself a citizen of both worlds, Lowell and Harvard, my father felt he belonged to neither. In many ways he'd left Lowell behind, but he was an outsider at Harvard, unable to join in any activities or clubs because studying and commuting (two hours each way) would have taken up his time. He was poor and Irish Catholic in a secular and privileged institution. My father did not make many friends during his undergraduate days. That would come later, when he attended reunions and all the distinctions that used to matter faded. His closest companion was Dave Connors, another Irish Catholic Lowell High graduate who also commuted in.

I imagine my father put a lot of energy into convincing his family and friends that he was just the same after he went to Harvard. Of course, he wasn't the same. He'd changed social class, leaving working-class and lower-middle-class Lowell behind, except that he would never find a secure place in the upper middle class either, in contrast to his commuting companion Dave Connors, who went back to his hometown and became editor of the *Lowell Sun.*

My father would want me to go to Radcliffe, but he was concerned that I might "lose my faith" there: I still remember the (to me) humiliating trip we took to speak with the priest who headed the Harvard-Radcliffe Catholic Club, a necessary condition of my applying there. Forty years after he graduated, my father was still trying to balance the worlds of secular Harvard and Catholic Lowell.

AS I LEAVE THE library I decide I have to make another visit to the cemetery before going back to Boston. I want to find the grave of Patrick O'Brien, my great-grandfather. After a long search I locate it, and there's another mystery. Right next to it, partly hidden in the ground and grown over with grass, is another O'Brien headstone. I look up their records in the cemetery office and find another group of O'Briens I've never heard of, but they have family first names: Nellie and Mary and someone named "Pvt. Lawrence O'Brien," who must have been in the army. My brother and father both have the middle name "Lawrence," which is not a common Irish name.

O'Brien grave

Later I will discover that Lawrence fought in the Civil War and was my father's great-uncle. There seems to have been one of those Irish family feuds between Lawrence and Patrick, and so we had never known of his existence; my father, a Civil War buff, never mentioned his great-uncle, and I suspect that he was never allowed to know him.

WALKING OUT OF the cemetery I see my flowers drooping by the official O'Brien grave. I don't think these dead relatives are appreciating them. "Why the expense?" I can hear one of the Longs asking. "So extravagant." "She should have brought a plant," another says. "Something more durable." The flowers want to come home with me, I decide, and I scoop them up.

Letters from London

I wondered whether the life that was right for one was ever right for two.
—WILLA CATHER, *My Ántonia*

I'VE GIVEN UP TRYING to track down my graduate school file—too many roadblocks. I know what fiction would be in my letter of application: I would have said I wanted to go to graduate school because I wanted to study seventeenth-century English poetry, understand the connections between literature and life, and be part of an intellectual community. I'd even convinced myself that I was telling the truth.

The real truth was this: I applied to graduate school because I wanted my parents back.

WHEN I WAS A senior at Radcliffe, going straight on to graduate school was the last thing on earth I wanted to do. I'd been in school forever and I needed to get out, breathe the fresh air, explore the world, find out who I was away from teachers, assignments, and grades. I had no idea how to do this; my only desire was to find a job working for a publishing company in London, a pipe dream that seemed so unlikely I told no one about it, least of all my parents, whom I knew expected a lockstep move into even more education—law school, business school, or a Ph.D. program. There was no way I could get their support for what they would call "taking a year off"—the phrase itself showing that further education was the norm, any departure from it deviance.

In the fall of senior year I bought a little white motorcycle, a Honda 90, reduced in price because it had a splash of pink paint on the back fender. When senior year despair or panic got too high I'd hit the road, hurtling down Route 2, wind in my face, all my fears spinning down behind me like falling leaves. I'd go as far as Fitchburg before I'd turn back, and when I reached the crest of the hill at Arlington and saw the lights of Boston spread out before me, for a few minutes I felt invincible. I was no longer a scared twenty-one-year-old whose parents wanted her to go to graduate school, obediently applying even though literature now felt like sawdust in her mouth and course requirements seemed like prison terms. No—I was a woman with a motorcycle and an escape route. I'd make it to London.

I plotted and planned, obediently applying to graduate school in English. I didn't read any catalogues and I had no idea who was teaching at the institutions where I applied. I decided to go to the University of Toronto, just because it was in another country. I never imagined myself actually enrolling there. I wanted to go to Europe more than anything else in the world—I'd envied all my classmates who'd flown over for summer vacations, when I'd had to work. I had never been in a plane, never spent any time outside the Northeast. It was time to see the world.

I'd been working part-time for a small Cambridge publisher, and he set up an interview for me with Addison-Wesley's American office. I passed that test and was given the chance I wanted—an interview with the British head of Addison-Wesley in London, set up for mid-July.

All of this was done covertly. If my mother and father got wind of my cherished plan, they would keep me from my summer, a two-month trip to Ireland, England, and Italy. They assumed I would return and head off for Toronto; I hoped I would be able to stay in England.

I had my London interview, and in late August I received a telegram at American Express in Rome, telling me that I had gotten the job—editorial assistant. I would start in mid-September, and my salary would be eight hundred pounds a year. I was thrilled and terrified.

It was far too frightening to phone my parents. I knew that working in a London publishing company wasn't as bad as dropping out of school to get married, so my parents could hardly abandon me the way they did Maureen. After all, I told myself, you have your B.A. with honors from Radcliffe. A job in a London publishing company, a chance to explore England and Europe, that's okay, isn't it?

I knew it wasn't okay.

And so, like my sister before me, I wrote my parents a letter.

I HAVE THIS letter because my parents saved all the letters I wrote that year in a crumpled yellow envelope in the bottom drawer of the secretary desk; I found them there after my mother died. I took a quick look at the contents, scrawled "Letters from London" on the front, and threw it into one of my boxes of family records. I kept intending to read them, but I couldn't find the time, probably because I knew how the story came out.

I was the designated hitter, the one who needed to live out my father's unlived life and, in a way, my mother's too. That meant achievement according to the definitions of what my students call the "dominant culture." No wonder, I used to think, my first named clinical depression arrived while I was in grad school at Harvard. "The greatest burden on the child is the unlived life of the parent," Jung writes, and that's true; but it's also true that if you *do* manage to live it successfully, for a while you are the family hero, and the rewards you get make you forget, after a while, the paths you didn't take. The only problem is: other people's praise, even your parents', is not enough to save you from depression if your choice hasn't come from within yourself.

Now, in Cambridge, I find the time to read these letters, panning for clues to what happened in London. Why didn't I stay there? Why did I rush back to graduate school at Harvard, not giving my independent life much of a chance? My memory of this time is blurry: all I can remember is parental disapproval hovering over London like a scary cloud. I keep thinking I can find the sources of depression inside this bulky envelope; this twenty-two-year-old woman who wrote them, someone I don't even know any more, is going to give me some clues.

I ARRANGE my letters chronologically, without reading them; I want to see how the story evolves, to understand how my capitulation took place.

September 5, 1967

Dear Mom and Dad,

This letter is not a travel report, but the introduction of the possibility of a change in my plans for next year, and a propagandistic attempt to convince you that the change would be desirable. . . . As you know, I haven't been that sure about grad school right away, and so went to talk to people at Addison Wesley in London—and guess what, they gave me a job! Doing both editorial and production work. The job will expose me to publishing and help me decide if I want to make a career in this field, as well as giving me the chance to be in London for a year! Just think of it, a year to find out about publishing, to explore England, a year to spend in London, the most fascinating city in the world—and, most important, a year to find out more about myself, to

236

test myself in a challenging, adult situation. Travel, as they say, is broadening, but also can be somewhat superficial, while living in another country is not.

And the excitement this idea rouses in me tells me that Toronto next year while pleasant is not a positive, committed goal to which I would sacrifice all. My decision to go there was more of a negative one—I knew that it wouldn't do me any harm, that an M.A. is always useful, etc. But weighed against something that I positively *want* to do, that I consider essential to another part of my education, graduate school just doesn't hold up.

And it's not that this year rules out graduate school—far from it. Europe has made me realize how ignorant I still am, that I do want to go back to school—just not now. After exploring England and Europe more deeply I can consider graduate school more intelligently, I think, and apply to Harvard, Yale, or Stanford, if I decide that an English Ph.D. is what I want.

I realize, of course, that this is a sudden surprise (less so to me, since I have known the possibility existed for a couple of weeks). Please don't let the fact that this is unexpected, involves a change of plans, etc. set your minds against it—because this is the only time in my life when I'm flexible and *can* change plans: when I *can* live in England. I know the time is now—I won't get back to Europe for a long time.

Please remember I can go to graduate school anytime, but this is my one opportunity for London, an opportunity which I don't believe I could forgive myself for missing. I will be writing again shortly. I will end with a quote of Samuel Johnson: "When a man is tired of London, he is tired of life; for there is in London all which life can afford."

I give you time to absorb this bombshell, hoping that you will agree with me. And if distance is a large objection, remember Toronto would have been far away too. And remember that I am all too soon to be 23.
Love, Sharon

This is a letter from a daughter who knows she's in trouble. Rereading it, I can see that I tried everything—appealing to logic, appealing to academic snobbery (those shameless promises about applying to Harvard and Stanford!), appealing to patience. Appealing to almost everything except love.

What's interesting is my evident need to structure this letter like a court argument; just saying that I wanted to do this thing because of desire, or interest, or just because I wanted to was impossible. What's also clear is how much power my parents had over me, how much power I had given them. I am writing this letter to black-robed judges, not to two people whom I believe to have my best interests at heart. My telltale use of the word "bombshell"—knowing this letter was going to explode their cherished plans for me—makes it clear I knew this was an act of defiance.

I didn't follow this letter up with a phone call: too scary. I threw the bomb and ran like hell.

*W*HAT FOLLOWED I reconstruct from memory.

WESTERN UNION
SEPTEMBER 10, 1967
DEAR SHARON: CALL HOME AT ONCE.
MOTHER AND DAD

Time: The afternoon of September 15, 1967.
Place: A steamy phone booth near the Akropolis.
A young woman dressed in a purple miniskirt and a blue tank top goes into the phone booth, dials a number several times but hangs up before punching in the last digit. Finally she puts the call through.
The phone rings in Belmont.
MOTHER: Hello?
DAUGHTER: Mom, is that you? It's Sharon, I'm calling from Athens.
Silence.
DAUGHTER: Mom, are you there?
Sounds of sobbing.
DAUGHTER (fearfully): Mom, what's wrong? Is anything wrong?
MOTHER (tearful and angry): How could you do this to me?
DAUGHTER: Mom, I'm not doing anything to you, I don't understand.
MOTHER: How could you do this to me? To us? After all we've done for you? Throw away a brilliant mind, a fellowship, a future, just so you can go to that Carnaby Street and wear miniskirts and be with those hippies?
DAUGHTER: Mom, I'm going to be working in a publishing company, it's nowhere near Carnaby Street. And I don't wear miniskirts.
MOTHER: You've just gone and done it, without a by-your-leave, without giving any thought to us. To your future. It's a criminal waste of an opportunity.
DAUGHTER: Mom, I only wanted to do something I cared about. I just don't want to go to grad school right now, I—

Mother hangs up. Father is not heard from.
Daughter stays in booth, leaning against the side, staring at the incomprehen-
sible language on the phone box for a long time.

I do not remember speaking with my father during that conversation, although I may have. It would not have been unusual if I hadn't: he always
hung back during my mother's outbursts, waiting for things to blow over.
I waited for word from him, hoping he would be persuaded by the logic of
my letter, hoping that I had won him over with my Samuel Johnson quote
and my practical observation that I would be able to explore a career in
publishing.

He wrote me a week later. (My mother would not write or contact me for
six months.)

When I opened my father's letter I must have been trembling: he was
my lifeline.

September 22, 1967
Dear Sharon:
Your mother and I are very disturbed by your decision to postpone graduate
school and stay in London. You have never shown much interest in a career
in publishing before, and I cannot help but wonder where this sudden enthusiasm came from. I am concerned that your impulsive decision shows an
immature desire to run away from the responsibilities of Life as well as fuzzy
thinking. The office of Addison-Wesley you describe sounds like a mere ex-
port facility and not a place where you can gain considerable knowledge of
publishing. I am not persuaded that this year will contribute in any way to a
career decision. Your choice of graduate school was, I think, far more sound
and rational. However, I wish you luck in this venture, and hope that you can
extract from this year the kind of wisdom you will need in the future.
Love, Dad

Looking back, I keep wanting to cheer myself on—don't capitulate! Your
father's criticism is far more devastating than your mother's meltdown, but
just know you're doing something brave—running toward life, not away
from it. Hang in there. Just remember, he's not God.

26 October 1967

Dear Dad,

Your expressed reservations are, I think, well taken. Certainly my staying here reveals a certain amount of emotional indirection as well as rational direction; I think that any sudden departure from a scheduled plan does. I just want to say that this hiatus in my graduate school plans is not evidence of a desire to run away from the responsibilities of Life, but of a desire to face them more intelligently in a year's time. My decision to go to graduate school is becoming more solid every day.

I had thought of the young woman as a free spirit for most of the year, finally caving in around February or March, but looking at the date on this letter I can see that she had almost immediately committed herself to returning to graduate school, and the juxtaposition to parental disapproval makes it clear that her choice of a career—then—didn't spring from strength. She does manage one moment of resistance—this "hiatus" in her graduate school plans is not "running away from Life," she protests—but then she accepts her father's view of her life lock, stock, and barrel, agreeing, for example, with his assumption that to face the "responsibilities of Life" is equivalent to enrolling in graduate school, because she promises to do so "in a year's time."

I can remember what she was doing that fall, and how hard it was, and how proud I would have been had I been her parent. But there's no way she can see how well and bravely she was facing Life by securing a job in London on her own initiative, finding a British roommate, moving into a flat, commuting to work every day, feeding and clothing and housing herself, and exploring the social and cultural world of a different country. There's a grave limitation and a puritanism in her father's view—his use of the word "responsibilities"—that she cannot see or challenge, just as she cannot ask him the question that's now obvious to me: *do you think that attending graduate school is my responsibility not to Life, but to You?*

2 November 1967

Dear Dad,

I want to acknowledge the receipt of your letter and check, the size of which made me uncomfortable. I will try to conserve most of it for more worthy causes than living expenses, like telephone calls home and graduate school applications (I'm going to try Harvard and Yale this time). It was immensely cheering to know that your disapproval and disappointment didn't prevent the expression of well wishes, which I really need at this point. It's difficult, isn't it, starting out in a foreign city where you don't know anyone. The excitement of London doesn't always compensate for loneliness. When I got to Victoria Station, after a long ferry and train ride, I had never felt such complete isolation, being surrounded by crowds of people who belonged where they were when I didn't belong at all. But, strange as it may sound, I really want the challenge of entering a strange environment and making myself happy, useful, and fulfilled. I have decided that I need to prove myself by a sort of Spartan exercise, throwing myself onto the cold hillside and see if I survive. London is beginning to take on the warmth of human contact, without which any city is meaningless. I have made one firm friendship with a girl from the North of England, here to study medical social work: she's as new to London as I am and we're seeing the sights together. We've already seen one play together, Olivier in Strindberg's *The Dance of Death*, for 2 shillings (28 cents). I have decided to take a course in British history and to join the Samuel Johnson society, which sponsors lectures by university professors.

Please reassure Mother that while my decision to stay here may be ill-advised, it was not to indulge a furtive taste in mod life and swinging London. (I am not a flower person, in case there was doubt.) I thank you for your expressed forbearance to your errant (in both senses) daughter.

Love, Sharon

11 October 1967

Dear Mom and Dad,

I have spoken to an English professor at London University about applying to graduate school after a year off—he says it's no problem, and might even be an advantage, and no affect on financial aid. So it's good to know there's no stigma attached to applications after a year. I have sent away for applications from Harvard, Yale, Stanford, Chicago, and Berkeley; I find that my decision to apply is built on a much firmer basis than last year, when it really came out of habit and fear of doing something different. I do want to be an academic; my only uncertainty is whether I will be any good. Thank you once again for sending my winter clothes and my flute.

Love, Sharon

15 November 1967
Dear Mom and Dad,

I am finding that my major adjustment is not to a new country but to living without the support of friends and family. It is terribly difficult to meet people here. But even these first months of loneliness I value, since what I realized I needed to do was to withdraw from all the props which had supported and defined me—family, friends, school—close the doors, turn off the lights and the television, put away the books, and see if there was anybody left, namely any ME. I'm not yet convinced there is, but I know that this is the way to find out. I hope that, despite everything, you will be behind me this year.

I find that I have a great need for—if not your approval—at least your acquiescence and understanding. I miss you and home very much.

I have by now received all my application forms and am composing an essay "Why I want a Ph.D. in English." I will be attending a concert and a lecture this weekend, and have to say I have found London a university in itself.

Love, Sharon

3 December 1967
Dear Mom,

I hope that you have not been writing me because you are too busy—and not because you are boycotting me—I really can't see that my offense would be so grave as to warrant silence. And if it is, I wish you would still write me anyway—I do miss you and would like to hear how things are going with you . . .

Love, Sharon

February 25, 1968
Dear Dad,

My thoughts and feelings about graduate school are all a-jumble—perhaps your objective good sense and reasoned judgment can discern a pattern. I'm afraid I may have made a false equation between intellectual stimulation, which I miss, and going to graduate school. Is it a delusion to go to grad school just to get my mind recharged? Would I be retreating to the womb? I do want to learn more—I've become acutely aware of how ignorant I am this year—but I am not at all sure that I want a career in university teaching. It is so difficult to imagine myself teaching college students, as I am so far from possessing either the necessary knowledge or confidence. It seems wasteful to attend graduate school without being devoted to the idea of teaching—or do you agree?

I'm also not at all sure I possess the necessary brain power. I was a capable student at Radcliffe but no great creative genius, and the competition in grad school will be fierce. I don't feel myself good enough.

On the other hand, if I didn't go, what could I do? I like publishing and could be happy in it, but it doesn't provide the same kind of mental excitement that college did. But then, should it? Am I expecting too much?

I'd be interested in knowing how you feel, since I think we have similar literary minds. You made the business choice—do you feel culturally starved? Do you wish you had gone to grad school in English? Or is it possible to satisfy yourself by private reading?

I hope I haven't been too jumbled in presenting my dilemma. I would like to hear your thoughts, which will no doubt be of help.

Love, Sharon

March '68

Dear Mom and Dad,

I have become more militantly anti-war lately; the events of the last weeks have been terrible, the Hue devastation, the bloody defense of Khe Sanh, where I was horrified to hear that an American general would not definitely rule out the use of tactical nuclear weapons. "Tactical nuclear weapons!" What a euphemistic phrase. I think the smallest "tactical" weapon in the American nuclear arsenal is about 10 times the size of the Hiroshima bomb and powerful enough to obliterate Hanoi.

I'm working with some people at LSE who are trying to unite war opposition in London. There's a flurry of activity this week—we're handing out leaflets for the large demonstration on March 17, a march from Trafalgar Square (peaceful, hopefully) to the American Embassy. It may not do any good but that is no reason for not expressing opinion.

I can't help wondering with the world the way it is whether it's escaping from reality to go to graduate school.

Love, Sharon

April 1968

Dear Mom and Dad,

Well, the results are in—sort of. Rejected at Yale, accepted at Stanford and Berkeley (no money, though), and accepted at Harvard, although they won't tell me about money for another couple of weeks.

I would like to change schools for graduate work, and it is not very adventurous to return to the place where I spent most of my life. But if Harvard gives me money, I know I'll need to go there, and I admit the thought of a Harvard Ph.D. is alluring. I'll let you know.

Love, Sharon

June 1968

Dear Mom and Dad,

I wonder though if the United States is worth returning to: the country seems to be sick. I had always criticized Ireland for persecuting her heroes, but what can you say about a country who murders hers? How appalling and inconceivable that we now have to distinguish which assassinated Kennedy we are talking about. McCarthy's polls seem to be climbing—do you think there's any hope?

No, no news from Harvard on money yet,

Love, Sharon

June 1968

Dear Mom and Dad,

I've just heard from Harvard—they've given me a really magnificent fellowship which should take care of all my expenses: I'll never cost you another cent.

Love, Sharon

*I*T IS PAINFUL to reread these letters. Here and there I see the young woman's authentic voice, as when she writes of her need to go into a room, shut off the lights, and "see if there is anybody there." She knew intuitively what the problem was: she had shaped herself to win the approval of parents, teachers, social authorities, and now she wanted to remove herself from this field of force and find out what was *real*. She's all tangled up in the dilemma my students—now just the age I was then—confront during their senior year: how can I ever discover who I am or what I want, separate

Sharon in London, 1968

from my parents' influence and social expectations? Generally I say to them, "you have to *act* in order to discover who you are and what you want," or "try it for a while and see how it feels."

I tried my adventure and it didn't feel good. Other daughters might well have stayed in London—which I loved—and coped with a mother's silence and a father's disappointment, but I couldn't. Perhaps the patterns of abandonment in my family were simply too strong, and unlike Maureen, I was alone in my rebellion: loneliness threads its way through all those letters.

So I got scared and returned to safety. By the late spring I had convinced myself that I wanted to study Renaissance poetry back in Cambridge rather than take on the new job Addison-Wesley was offering me—assistant production manager. I never asked myself why I kept putting off my departure date, finally flying back the very day of Harvard registration.

Some passages in those letters make me proud. I hear the voice of a young woman straining for independence: she knows this year is a turning point and wants to ride out the storm. She's honest in speaking about her confusion; she's seeking parents who will reflect her back as herself, rather than as their image of what they want her to be. Briefly I imagine history rewritten—*what if?*—but I can tell even from the early letters that she is doomed. It's not just the pleading tone, the almost cringingly deferential stance she takes toward her parents that bothers me now: it's the false, stilted language she uses to convince her parents she's still a good daughter. I read "I thank you for your forbearance to your errant daughter," the distancing third person, the Latinate language, and I know what she doesn't know: behind that sentence is the fear she'll be abandoned if she follows her own desires, a fear she's in no way ready to handle.

I used to want to shake her and say *Forebearance? Why are you thanking him for that, you deserve that and much more, there's nothing wrong with not going to graduate school right after college, nothing wrong with not going ever. Stop writing in that awful don't-hurt-me voice, stop telling them you're joining the Johnson society and London is your university, stop backing off from all the brave things you want to do! Don't cave in, you're going to fuck up both our lives.*

Then I was blaming her for the depression that would come later, in graduate school. This was before I realized that even though it had been a forced march to an English Ph.D., the academic life I would shape over time was a good one, involving the heart and soul as well as the mind, and if I could choose again I'd go to graduate school. Not right away, and not in English—most likely American studies, which I didn't know existed then. But this understanding would take a long time to evolve.

Sometimes I'd stop blaming the young woman for her capitulation and say to myself, Sharon, she's only twenty-two, she's alone in London, she can't survive without some connection to her parents, she's doing the best she can, so why are you getting angry at *her?* The answer was easy: *because it's still easier to get angry at her than at them.*

*T*HE TIME DID come when I could get angry at my parents—I had become the age they were then, and saw all around me, in my students, versions of the self I was then. I couldn't imagine, if I were a parent, cutting myself off from my twenty-two-year-old daughter who'd snared a job in a London publishing company instead of going to graduate school in English. I probably would have envied her, and asked if she minded if I flew over at Christmas for a visit, and could she get us some theater tickets? I hope that I wouldn't have cut myself off from her, as my mother did, or written her a disapproving letter, telling her how immature and irresponsible she was, as my father did.

I know what Alice Miller would say about my younger self: that I was setting myself up for depression, bargaining away my authentic self for my parents' approval, and that my parents, in turn, were all unknowingly projecting their needs onto me. My mother needed me to succeed in the public terms she valued; she was personally invested in my achievements. My father's reaction to my defection from graduate school is more complex. I can see him wanting to live his unlived life through me, the life as a teacher and literary critic he hadn't attained himself. Once he knew I was going to graduate school in English, he started writing me about how *he* would teach an introductory literature course, going so far as to design a reading list and syllabus and course description; he wrote me about his views on literary theory and criticism, often copying out two or three pages of single-spaced passages from critics he liked, like Bernard De Voto.

But there's something else in his letters to me that year that I think goes back to the time he took his big risk, made his Big Move to Boston, and it didn't work out. I remember his confession in his twenty-fifth reunion report that he sometimes envied classmates who had "hewed to the line," sticking to one profession, instead of being buffeted about by chance the way he had. He wanted me to "hew to the line" as he had not been able to, he wanted me to be safe, all unaware that his hopes and expectations and fears were becoming, for me, part of those external forces that can, for a time, constrict our choices.

THERE'S MORE to the story of the year in London, though: letters, shaped for an audience, always tell only part of a story. The year wasn't all capitulation and attendance at the Johnson society. (I never went.) I see the gaps in the letters and remember what the young woman didn't write home about.

1. Buys a used motorbike and drives to work, cautiously at first, then weaving in and out among the red double-decker buses, passing Westminster Abbey and the Houses of Parliament and Piccadilly Circus on her way to work in Oxford Circus. On the way home, Hyde Park Corner and Sloane Square and the Kings' Road. Only has one accident, taking the turn at Hyde Park Corner too fast and tipping over, but the British drivers are courteous—a whole line of traffic stops and people get out to see if she's okay. She picks herself up, waves, gets back on the bike, and putts off home.
2. Moves into a flat in Parson's Green with her English friend Judith, where they talk about men and sex and parents and longings, and where, one long summer twilight, they throw a terrific party.
3. Decides it's time for a love affair (by now, notions of mortal sin have faded to acceptable levels) and goes on the pill "just to be ready," she tells Judith, who couldn't agree more.

247

4. Buys a notebook and starts writing poetry that's both derivative (some Tennyson, some T. S. Eliot) and heartfelt. Her themes are love (the impossibility of it, the yearning for it), repression and freedom, the power of words, death, and memory.

5. Learns to recognize eighty different kinds of typefaces by sight, and to tell the difference between books printed by letterpress and offset.

6. Goes to Carnaby Street and buys a purple velvet mini-skirt, a crocheted chartreuse tank top, and shiny black patent leather boots.

7. Copyedits a 400-page statistics textbook entitled *Elements of Continuous Multivariate Analysis,* and in her eagerness to be of use changes all uses of the term "non-normal number" (more than a hundred) to "abnormal number," glad she is saving the author, a distinguished statistician from Harvard, an embarrassing mistake. After her boss fields an explosive phone call from the author, she changes them all back.

8. Gets her ears pierced on the Portobello Road.

9. Smokes pot for the first time.

10. Gets a promotion at work, to assistant production manager, and handles the office for a month while her boss is on vacation.

11. Flies to Paris to be part of the Spring '68 student revolution, hitching in from the airport with groups of students because all the strikers have closed down all public transportation. Stays up all night talking in cafes, goes to demonstrations, learns to chant the Internationale.

12. Marches on the U.S. embassy in London, with crowd chanting "U.S. out of Vietnam now," and "Ho Chi Minh, Ho Chi Minh, He will fight, He will win."

13. Reads most of Hemingway, Durrell, Orwell, and Greene (these authors she mentions to her father) and Camus, Anaïs Nin, and Henry Miller (these she does not).

14. Goes to Greece for a month with Judith—they hitchhike around, pick up guys, give blood in Athens for money just for the hell of it, sleep on beaches in Crete and Corfu, drink cheap retsina. Judith is romanced by a *taverna* waiter who takes her to cock fights, and she falls in love with a nineteen-year-old Oxford student named Peter who loves her back. They promise to write.

15. Postpones her return flight three times, finally leaving on the last Icelandic flight that will get her to Harvard in time to register. Hugs Judith good-bye in Luxembourg. Both young women are weeping and she wonders why on earth she is leaving.

16. Smuggles a joint through New York customs, hidden inside a fountain pen, just to show the world and herself that she's not going to conform.

𝓗ER FATHER picks her up at the airport in Boston that September day and drives her straight to Harvard's Memorial Hall. Standing in line to register, seeing the same posters and banners for the Glee Club, the Outing Club, the Gilbert and Sullivan Society that have been there since she was a freshman, reading the same names of the Civil War dead engraved on the wall, signing up for courses on Chaucer and Restoration drama and Dante that she had seen in the catalogue before, she fears she has made the wrong choice. She had wanted to start a new life but all her adventures seem to have brought her back to the same place.

Her father waits outside and drives her back to Belmont, chatting about graduate school and the courses she's signed up for. Her mother is waiting near the door, tearful and overjoyed to see her daughter, and when they hug all she feels is gratitude for being taken back into the family.

Her parents do not ask her about her year in England—the talk is all of Harvard, and of the past year in their lives—and she does not mention it, not wanting to disturb the fragile equilibrium of her return.

They never will speak of it.

Depressives in the Lounge

Depression—It's an illness, not a weakness.
—slogan of the Manic-Depressive and Depressive Association of Boston

I'M DRIVING THROUGH BELMONT, on my way to McLean's Hospital and my first meeting of MDDA, the Manic-Depressive and Depressive Association. It's an advocacy and support group, the local chapter of a national organization. I've known of its existence for a few months but haven't been ready to go. Attending this group has represented defeat, a sign that depression would be a permanent part of my life instead of a mind storm just passing through. Surely the people who attend are much sicker than *me:* as long as I don't go, I can maintain my separateness, and the story that I will, some day, recover.

But I'm still stuck in my midwinter doldrums and desperate for change. Tonight I walked home from Harvard Square in the five o'clock dark of mid-December, threw down my backpack, fed the cat, and sat on the couch for an hour, watching *Frasier* reruns I'd seen twice before. I knew the MDDA meeting was at 7:30. At least it would pass the time.

I DRIVE UP Belmont Street, past the funeral home where my parents were waked, past Lewis Road, our old street, past Our Lady of Mercy Church, the site of my first communion and my parents' funeral masses. On the left is one of the few remaining Brigham's, the ice cream store where my father would stop in for his coffee milkshake, and where I lurked on Sundays during college, too afraid to tell my parents I was no longer going to Mass. At Waverley Square I take the right fork—the left fork would take me to the small apartment my mother moved to after my father died, the apartment where she herself died, in her own bed, all three of us there, the way she wanted. I drive past the Duck Pond and past all the long-ago Thanksgivings, the mornings when my father took me and my brother to feed the

250

ducks so my mother could have "room to breathe." Then the right turn into McLean's.

McLean's is a famous, and privileged, mental hospital associated with Harvard University. When I was in high school, kids went there to park; undisturbed back lanes would be dotted with parents' cars and entwined couples on Saturday nights after a dance. McLean's is also the celebrated place of incarceration for writers I've taught—Robert Lowell, Sylvia Plath, Susanna Kaysen. I've been here once before: a visit to a psychiatrist more than twenty years ago, the summer my father lay voiceless and dying in the intensive care unit at Mass General. I must have had to tell somebody what it was like to not be able to tell the truth to your dying father who could no longer speak or write. So I drove up to a mental hospital and told the truth to a stranger. "Families only become more themselves during a crisis," the psychiatrist said.

I feel nervous going to McLean's. This venture brings out my native shyness: walking into this unknown group makes me feel like a kid starting camp in the middle of the month, knowing all the experienced campers have been there for two weeks. I'm somewhat reassured by a check-in line for nametags: at least I don't have to walk, all unprotected, into a horde of strangers who know each other. As I write my name on a red-bordered tag (blue is for regulars) and look around a cafeteria filled with more than a hundred nametagged people I have a strange sensation. I scan some of the nametags near me—Mary Ellen, Robert, David, Barbara, Karen—and think *All of these people suffer from depression or manic-depression, and they don't look any different from anybody else, any different from me.* Of course I've know this in my head, but somehow seeing so many people in the same room—it could be any group—announcing by their presence and their names that they have—well, *suffered*—is oddly exhilarating.

*A*FTER I SIGN my nametag (just "Sharon," no last names or professional affiliations here), the woman in charge advises me to attend the Newcomers group. I join the other red-nametagged people while the older blue-tagged campers go off to their own discussion groups. An old-timer named Charlie is our discussion leader. He gives us the MDDA rules: our discussions are confidential, no outside observers unless everyone in the group agrees, give support but not advice. He introduces himself by telling his own depression story. "I'm sixty-six years old and I think I've been depressed since I was four. I've lost more jobs than you can count and spent more years

251

than you'd like to think looking into a bottle. Now I'm not doing so bad, on a new medication, sometimes the docs can't keep up with me, and thanks of course to this group." He pauses and nods to the man next to him, who's wearing stained carpenter's pants and staring straight ahead. The nod is a sign that he should introduce himself, but the man keeps staring and finally Charlie picks somebody else to go first.

It is unexpectedly moving just to listen to the check-ins and introductions. "I'm John, I've been struggling with depression for twenty years." John is dysthymic and hasn't found a medication that works. "I'm Stuart," says a man gripping the seat of his chair. "I'm in McLean's right now. I'm pretty suicidal, I guess. Lithium isn't working and they haven't been able to find meds that work." Stuart doesn't speak during group: he's barely hanging in, trying to make it until 9:00 P.M. and his sleeping medication. "I'm Anne," a woman says. "I'm still working on trying to regain custody," and people nod sympathetically. "I've been out of the hospital about three weeks now, no panic attacks, so I can be grateful for that." I will later realize such comments are typical; people in MDDA are always finding what they can be grateful for. "The rapid cycling is pretty bad right now, but I'm in the day program here and I think it's helping." "I've been pretty down for the last few weeks"—here "pretty down" doesn't mean "somewhat dispirited," it means "practically leveled"—"but I'm still able to go to work, so that's good."

When professional colleagues introduce me at talks and conferences, they list my accomplishments and honors and merit badges. Here everything is reversed as I introduce myself by what is silenced out there. "I'm Sharon, and I've suffered from major depression on and off since I was a teenager, pretty intensely for the last ten years. I've tried almost fifteen antidepressants but nothing's really worked yet." People look at me, one or two gasp in sympathy, everyone's faces are welcoming and I have an unfamiliar feeling of belonging. They understand what's below the surface of those few words, just as I understand the unspoken months and years of suffering when they speak. When we use the word "depressed" we all know we're not talking about the ordinary lows that everyone experiences, we're not talking about feeling down. We have a common language, and we know we're talking about the untranslatable depths. "I'm not doing too well right now," I add, and people nod again.

They know what "not too well" means.

As I say the words "I'm Sharon" to a group of strangers, I know I'm doing something that some people, including many of my academic colleagues, would satirize. Support groups are easy targets for people who find the verb "share" humorous. I've heard the phrase "Thank you for sharing" used ironically hundreds of times; I've read Wendy Kaminer's witty, detached debunking of the recent epidemic of "codependency" and "recovery" groups; I've listened to many jokes beginning with "I'm [name]" that mock the classic support group introduction, and in the past I've probably laughed at them. Maybe right now I'm doing something that other academics would find self-indulgent or laughable or politically retrograde.

I have to say, I really don't care.

After me it's the staring man's turn. "I'm Don," he says in a flattened voice, his eyes dull chips of coal. "I'm bipolar, been in and out of hospitals maybe twenty times. I don't hold out much hope for getting better but I thought I'd try this group." He is wearing a long-sleeved jersey, but it's shrunk from many washings. His wrists are ropy with scars.

"We're glad you came, Don," Charlie says. Don doesn't look at him. He leaves during the break.

Driving home, I feel like I'm a new recruit in a war that's been going on a long time. I'm going to go back and get my blue nametag.

*I*T DOESN'T take long before I get to know the MDDA routine. Every other week we listen to a talk before we have groups—topics like "Health Care Parity," "Dual Diagnosis in Children," "Electroshock Therapy," "Side Effects." The speaker stands behind a podium that carries the MDDA logo—the words "Unipolar/Bipolar" and two polar bears, one seated and shivering, paws over its eyes, the other cockily prancing in the sun, waving a walking stick, about to burst into a soft-shoe routine. When the question period is over an MDDA officer comes to the podium to announce where the support groups are meeting. "Okay," he says, "tonight it's Newcomers in 112, Friends and Family in 113, Employment in 114, Women's in 115, Wellness in 116, Manics in 117—don't make too much noise, you guys—and depressives, you're in the lounge outside." He pauses. "We all know *you'll* be quiet."

At first I thought the list was just plain funny, but I come to appreciate and respect the straightforward room assignments, the willingness, which I find everywhere in MDDA, to avoid euphemisms. People don't stumble and trip or lower their voices when they say words like "manic," "depression," "suicide," "hospitalization," the way they often do in the outside world.

Some of us shift around among the groups, depending on our moods and needs. It might be Employment for two weeks, then Women's, then back to

Employment and on to Depressives. Officially we're not supposed to go to Friends and Family just to find out what they think about us: you're required to have friends or family with mood disorders to attend this group, but most of us do so the point is moot. Other people pick one group as home base.

At first I attend Depressives but after a few weeks I switch to Wellness. I'd been resisting because I hate the word "wellness," but I'd gotten to know the facilitator and he invited me to sit in. My depression was lifting a little and I wanted to start focusing more on prevention and coping. Besides, all the bipolars in Wellness gave the group a lot more energy.

Most people in Wellness were suffering from chronic mood disorders and were working on managing them. They were all acquainted with grief but weren't giving up, so there was an atmosphere in the room of, if not hope, at least stubborn persistence, and sometimes a cathartic black humor.

"I'm sorry for interrupting during check-ins again," says Bill, a bipolar who's in the day program at MGH. "I know that's one of the things I need to work on."

"And as we know, that's the least of your problems," observes the facilitator, who's shared hospital time with Bill.

The check-ins continue. "I think I've been depressed all my life." "I was diagnosed manic six months ago and I think I'm still adjusting." "I'm feeling normal for the first time in years, and it's great, but I keep looking over my shoulder. I don't trust it." "I'm just recovering from a manic episode and I'm feeling so bad about all the stupid and hurtful things I did when I was high." People nod. We all *get* it in our bones, no matter where we are on the spectrum right now, whether we're high functioners like the facilitator— "high functioner" is MDDA lingo for somebody who's either in a good space or whose illness isn't too bad—or working every minute just to stay alive.

Nobody's passing here.

AT THE break I'm startled to hear people make mood disorder jokes. "How many ECTs does it take to screw in a light bulb?" asks Don, the group leader.

I haven't heard the abbreviation before, but I catch on: ECTs must be people who've had electroshock treatments.

"I don't know. How many?"

"I forget." Everybody laughs.

"I don't get it," I whisper to Charlie. "Memory loss, a side effect," he whispers back.

"How many depressives does it take?" Don asks.

"I give up," everybody says, playing the game.

"None. They haven't noticed that the light has gone out."

People say things casually to each other they'd find insulting in the outside world. Here it's a form of teasing. Phil, an earnest depressive who's intrigued by the diagnostic codes of the DSM, wants to know if it's true that only one manic episode can qualify you as bipolar.

"In your *dreams*, Phil," says Marybeth, who's bipolar. "What are you, a wannabe?"

People can make the kind of demeaning remarks about the mentally ill they would never, in these politically correct days, make about blacks and gays. Making jokes is a way to take our power of naming back from the culture. It's also a way of reinforcing our momentary "outness." All of us possess many identities—we're bipolar or unipolar, yes, and we can also be teachers, social workers, parents, cooks, wine-lovers, Italian and Irish and WASP, Little League coaches, journal keepers, Buddhists, soccer players, poets, aunts, madrigal singers, gardeners, and citizens. The only thing is, none of those other identities are deviant. So when we play with the language the medical profession uses to define us it's a way to resist the stigma.

We can tease each other because, in an odd way, we're family. I've never known anyone who was manic-depressive until I got involved with MDDA, and now it seems that we unipolars and bipolars are first cousins.

There's a place for humor because there's so much sadness to be borne. During the year a woman from Wellness, one of the sparkplugs, commits suicide. None of us can believe it. We all can believe it.

I STAY WITH the group for the rest of my year in Boston, soon finding myself one of the "regulars" in the Wellness group. A ritual develops—organized by one of the bipolars—of adjourning to the Ground Round, a local restaurant, after the meeting, for snacks, conversation, and drinks—usually coke, sprite, or coffee, since people are either in recovery or taking meds that don't mix with alcohol. Under normal circumstances I'll allow myself a glass of wine, but during my year in Boston I give up alcohol entirely—it's a depressant—and join the decaf coffee drinkers.

I come to look forward to my Wednesday nights. For me, attending this group—and so admitting openly to depression—is about accepting the ongoing reality of the illness. And accepting depression, as I finally will understand, is a process, not an action. The more times I attend this group, the more times I name myself as a sufferer from depression, the more times I go to the Ground Round and tease the bipolars ("Thank *God* for your energy, without you we depressives would just creep right home to bed"), the more times I fight denial. If I gave denial a chance, I'd be checking the news for the latest wonder drug, the newly unveiled antidepressant that, this time, is going to work for sure.

I make friends with Annette, diagnosed with manic depression a few years ago. She's got one of the best reasons for coming to MDDA. "If I'm hospitalized again," she says, "I want lots of people to visit me. I mean *lots.*" Annette's first (and so far only) hospitalization was very successful. She wants to be sure that any subsequent ones measure up. "I didn't even know there was a stigma about manic depression," she says. "I was in my twenties, a complete innocent. Didn't know there was anything wrong with being bipolar till later, when everyone was telling me how brave I was to be so up front."

When she was hospitalized Annette called everybody she could think of to tell them, family, friends, faculty at her graduate school. "I had fourteen people visiting me the first night—most people didn't have anybody—and they could hardly fit into my room. Balloons, candy, flowers, the works. It was worth it."

I like the image: lots of cheery, gift-laden visitors crowding their way onto a locked ward. "If I'm ever hospitalized that's what I want too," I say. It's a revolutionary idea. I've always feared hospitalization for depression. I've imagined being in some back ward, trapped, desperate, forgotten, and alone. I never thought about visiting hours. I'd probably be taken to Hershey Medical Center, thirty miles away—but there's no reason why my friends can't make the drive, bringing me *People* magazine and the Sunday *Times* and cafe lattes. Balloons, too. When you read *One Flew over the Cuckoo's Nest* or *Girl, Interrupted* it never occurs to you that if you were in a mental hospital your friends could bring you balloons and good coffee.

"If I'm hospitalized I definitely want balloons," I tell her.

"I tied mine to the bars in the window and they lasted for two days," Annette says. "If I have to go to McLean's, I want everybody in the group to know, everybody to visit. I'm committed, I'm networking."

I LIKE GOING TO the meetings because I know I don't have to be upbeat, the way I am sometimes with friends whose patience I fear is running thin. Maybe I've asked for too much, maybe I haven't given enough back;

you start thinking in terms of emotional economy when you have a chronic illness. Have you invested enough to be able to make a withdrawal? Have you overdrawn your friendship account? Sometimes your well-intentioned friends who've never been depressed say "It's going to be okay, don't worry," not knowing—how could they?—that sometimes that feels like a dismissal. "Sometimes I just get sick of people telling me 'it will be all right,'" a man says at a group meeting. "I mean, I'm not going to give up, at least I don't think so, but things are never really going to be all right." Strange as it may seem, sometimes that's just what you want to hear, someone else saying that things are not ever, really, going to be all right. Because as long as you feel there's a happy ending up ahead you're not reaching, you cannot be content with your life.

People at MDDA, I notice, never tell each other that everything is going to be all right. They listen to your story and give you understanding, and they tell theirs and you give understanding back. After meetings they say "See you next week," and "Are you going to the picnic?" and "Hang in there" and "Call me if you need to."

So do you think there's such a thing as recovery?" a man in my depression support group asks. "A permanent breakthrough?"

No one speaks for a while, and then a woman who's bipolar—"not doing too bad this week"—says "even if I felt good for a long time, I mean a *long* time, I wouldn't trust it. I'd be waiting for the other shoe to drop," and several people nod. "Waiting for the other shoe to drop" is a phrase that recurs often in my group when people go through stable periods. Another is "looking over my shoulder," as when someone says, "I've been feeling quite good lately, for a few months now, but I keep looking over my shoulder," laughing apologetically, "wondering what's gaining on me."

"So how do you feel when you have good days?" someone asks the bipolar woman.

"Like they're a gift," she says, and people murmur assent.

Like most of the people who attend my support group, I'm not just learning how to manage a chronic illness. I'm working on finding a new story for my life, a story that gives me hope but doesn't require the happy ending of recovery. This is a struggle in America, a culture that celebrates and practically requires individual achievement, a culture where we don't have enough stories for imagining lives that do not fit, in one way or another, the success plot.

$\mathcal{T}$WO YEARS AGO I attended a panel at the annual Modern Language Association conference called "Professors on Prozac." Would any of the speakers or attenders "come out" as a depressive? Would I? This was unlikely, since at academic conferences intellectual expression is the norm. Saying something emotionally risky would be like interrupting a Catholic Mass with a fervent "Hallelujah"—it just isn't done.

Would this session be different? Some academics, particularly English professors, had been publishing memoirs and using the first person in their scholarly work. So "Professors on Prozac"—the pun suggesting professors might be taking the antidepressant as well as talking about it—might offer an environment where people could reveal themselves.

The leadoff speaker did so, and I was impressed with her courage. She was a graduate student, perhaps on the job market; how bold and honest to include her story along with an academic perspective. The chair of the session and the other speakers took more detached and theoretical approaches to the rise of biochemical theories of depression's origins and the proliferation—and corporate advertising—of Prozac, the antidepressant icon. Drawing on Michel Foucault's theories of power and knowledge, one speaker portrayed Prozac as linked with Western capitalism, cheering people up so they wouldn't work for social change.

Another speaker acknowledged that antidepressants could be useful for people with clinical depression but argued that we need to analyze the "discourses" of Prozac in the culture. "Why is the subject of Prozac so popular that it comes up at seemingly every social occasion?" she asked. "What cultural authorities and discourses have been promoting Prozac, and what do they gain from it?" *People talk about Prozac because they are afraid to talk about depression,* I thought, but I didn't say anything.

This speaker was raising some interesting questions, my academic self said. Of course we can't think about the popularity of Prozac without also thinking about the corporate power of the drug industry, and about health insurance that will fund antidepressants but not therapy, because therapy takes longer. Then my depression reminded me that words like "pathologization" and "Foucauldian theoretical approach" and "social subject" can mask unease. No one, including the speaker who revealed her own illness, used words like "despair" or "suffering" until a therapist in the audience spoke during the question period.

"I don't dispense pills all the time," he said, "but I just need to remind all of us of the anguish depression can cause, anguish that antidepressants can, in part, alleviate." He paused, and the room was silent. "We need to remember that most people who commit suicide are suffering from depression."

After he sat down the room was silent. I felt like applauding, but I didn't. I was afraid to be the only one.

*W*HEN I LOOK back on this session, now that I have been speaking more honestly with people about depression, I am sure that many people in that room besides me knew what the word "suffering" meant. Many must have been taking Prozac as well as thinking or writing about it, many must have understood depression from the ground up. But in the context of an academic conference, where speech was supposed to be intellectualized and theoretical, they—like me—could find no way to speak.

I know at least one other person there understood suffering—the organizer of the session, a brilliant scholar who had just published an important book. A few months later she would kill herself. At the next conference I attended people entered a session room exactly like the one where I'd heard "Professors on Prozac," but this time they were not going to hear academic papers. They were going to a memorial service.

I can't forget these two events, both held within the same year. I can't help wondering whether it's not just the suffering of depression that leads to suicide—it's also the isolation. And yet the ultimate sadness, the ultimate irony, is that the potential for community is there all along. But it's hidden, and we cannot find it unless we challenge the stigma and speak.

*I*N THE SPRING THE *Boston Globe* runs a story on Anne Sexton, who once taught creative writing to inpatients at McLean's. We discuss it at Wellness. "She was a McLean's wannabe," Charlie says—he's our historian. "She never could get in here and it bothered her." Sexton's psychiatrist sent her to the less fashionable Glenside, over in Jamaica Plain, and it seems she had always wanted the distinction of a stay at McLean's. The grounds of the hospital are referred to as the "campus," and the landscape design was created by Frederick Law Olmstead, nationally known as the designer of Central Park, locally known as the shaper of Boston's "Emerald Necklace" of parks, and MDDA-known as an inpatient, for a time, at McLean's.

Current inpatients might be surprised to learn that Sexton actually *wanted* to go here. But back in the 1950s, before health insurance regularly covered stays in mental hospitals, McLean's was pricey and prestigious— "very much the bastion of those old WASP families," according to Sexton's

259

friend Lois Ames, "*the* mental hospital, the place to go if you were in trouble in those days. It was like going to Shreve, Crump & Low." These days going to McLean's is more like going to Filene's Basement: you don't need to be in the Social Register to be admitted. Being hospitalized here is no picnic; to the people on the locked wards, McLean's does not have any artistic or academic panache. People who suffer from bipolar and unipolar "mood" or "affective disorders," as the psychiatric trade now calls them, come from all class and educational backgrounds, and college professors from Newton can find themselves McLean's roommates with laborers from South Boston or bus drivers from Mattapan.

MDDA meetings are similarly democratic: mental illness is the great leveler, and the class distinctions that privately obsess American society, despite our public ideology of classlessness, are momentarily erased here. In the "Depression" group you can see a Harvard grad student sitting next to a Vietnam vet who's living in subsidized housing, a therapist who's having a bad reaction to a new medication being encouraged by a nurse's aide whose week has been "pretty level, thank God." Sometimes I think that John Winthrop's long-ago utopian vision of Boston as the "city upon a hill," where people would gladly help others in need, is realized not in space but in time, every Wednesday from seven to nine o'clock at McLean's.

People are drawn together by their illnesses—nobody here calls what we have a "disorder"—and by their struggle to let go of the story that depression *is their own fault.* Yes, intellectually everyone in MDDA knows that depression and manic depression are inherited, genetically structured illnesses, everyone knows that our brains are "wired differently" from other people's, everyone knows that we should compare our illnesses to diabetes and equate antidepressants with insulin. Yet at the same time, emotionally most of us are still afflicted by the contradictory belief that we're weak-willed. We're just not strong enough to overcome our illness: if we were only better people, we'd be normal. "I can't get over thinking that I just can't lift myself up by my bootstraps," a man recently diagnosed with major depression says. The bootstrap metaphor recurs frequently at MDDA meetings. Sometimes it's said self-condemningly: the speaker accepts, momentarily, the social judgment that depression or manic depression is her own fault. Sometimes—when the speaker wants to challenge that same social judgment—it's said defiantly: "People think you can just lift yourself up by your bootstraps, but you can't, you just can't." "My father is one of

260

those people who think you should be able to lift yourself up by your own bootstraps. He just doesn't get it about depression."

Even when MDDA members use the phrase to suggest it's *other* people who think self-reliance and individualism should be able to overcome depression or mania, I know that at another moment, in another time they'll confess that they think so too. "Deep down," someone will say, "I think I should be able to get better by myself," and the group—which minutes before was defying the notion of individual control over illness—will nod agreement. A few days ago Don, who's been dealing with bipolar illness for thirty years and knows that it's biochemical at its base, admitted that he's been thinking about going off meds, "just to see if this time I can do it on my own." I'm familiar with the impulse: I've stopped taking medication countless times, each time thinking *this time I'll do without the training wheels*, each time finally, after a few weeks or months, spiraling down again, each time having to go back to my psychiatrist and say "I give up."

The more time I spend with people here, though, the more I realize the group is much more about resistance to cultural stereotypes about mental illness than about accommodation. Of course we've all internalized the belief that our illnesses are our own individual fault: you can't grow up in American society without doing that. But we're all fighting against that, and the group helps me to make progress. The whole organization is committed to fighting the social stigma attached to mental illness as well as to providing education and support, and the drop-in center is filled with buttons saying "Depression: It's Nobody's Fault," and bumper stickers asking you to "Honk If You're on Lithium," T-shirts and sweatshirts that feature the MDDA mascot polar bears and the words "bipolar/unipolar," and an array of stuffed polar bears in various sizes and shapes.

A FEW WEEKS AGO I went to "MDDA Night at the Pops," wondering just how "out" we were going to be at Boston's Symphony Hall. Unlike race or gender or certain physical disabilities, mental or emotional illness is an invisible form of deviance within our culture, and so—as with homosexuality—it's possible to pass. Would MDDA-Boston have any visible signs of its identity, or would we blend in with the crowd? Looking out from the second balcony, I saw a banner across the way proclaiming "Matignon Alumni Association," and another, way in back, saying "Raytheon."

"Do we have a banner?" I asked, hardly daring to hope. Would MDDA really be that bold, to have a banner spread out over the second balcony in snooty Symphony Hall, flaunting right out there for all the people sitting in the pricey cafe seats to see? "Yes we do," Charlie, now the chapter president, said proudly, "right heah," pointing to the railing, where I can just see the banner attached.

"What does it say?"

"*Depression: It's an illness, not a weakness.*"

At intermission I go over to the other side of the balcony so I can look back at the MDDA section. There's the banner, purple with gold lettering for the slogan and the name MDDA—Boston. It's just as big as the Matignon and Raytheon banners.

"I'm really glad we have a banner," I tell people when I get back. "I was worried we wouldn't."

Ellie, who's in charge of the drop-in center and all MDDA paraphernalia—the greeting cards, the posters, the cuddly polar bears—turns to Charlie. "See," she says, "I *told* you it was a good idea to bring the bannah," and he nods.

*I*T'S THE annual MDDA picnic—a summer evening on the grounds of the hospital, an all-American cookout with burgers, potato salad, chips, ice cream. Some bipolars have organized a volleyball game, and later there will be Frisbees sailing through the darkening sky. I get there late and walk over to the drinks table, which features a small polar bear centerpiece. The polar bear is wearing sunglasses and has a celery stick in its paw. A guy from Wellness hands me a can of soda. I look at it for a while before I get it.

"Oh," I say, "it's Polar Cola."

"Of course," he says. "What else?"

*I*T'S THE Wednesday night meeting. "The stigma," a woman in my group says. "If it just weren't for the stigma." It could be anyone speaking. Everyone nods, and as we do, we look at her and then we look at ourselves around the circle. The stigma shimmers and fades in the light of our eyes and we sit there, a visible community, fragile and temporary and real.

Recovery Stories

If many remedies are prescribed for an illness, you may be certain that the illness has no cure.
> —ANTON CHEKHOV, *The Cherry Orchard,* quoted in Jane Kenyon's "Having it Out with Melancholy"

Who would have thought my shrivel'd heart
Could have recover'd greenesse?
> —GEORGE HERBERT, "The Flower"

I BROUGHT WITH ME TO CAMBRIDGE a box crammed with books on depression—books approaching the illness from biochemical, psychoanalytic, psychological, cultural, historical, and literary perspectives. I'd read them all, and had learned one maddening fact: no one knew for sure what caused the illness, or how to cure it. There were different discourses giving meanings to depression, different theories created by different experts, but no fully shared story of origins.

In contrast to my father's time, though, by the 1990s there was a much clearer understanding of the biochemical and genetic components of the illness; I was lucky to be living in a time of such medical progress. It had become clear that people could inherit a biochemical predisposition toward depression, as my father likely did, as I and my siblings surely did. Neurotransmitters in the brain, like serotonin, had been linked with depression, and antidepressants seemed to increase the amount of serotonin and other neurotransmitters and so alleviate, or even erase, depression.

This biochemical model was, and still is, the dominant one for understanding and treating depression, and that's not a bad thing, because depression *does* have physical—often inherited—sources. This model may also have achieved dominance because it fits so neatly with the marketing power of the drug companies, and because it keeps the focus on the individual rather than the larger society. That doesn't mean it's not valid—only that if you believe in it too uncritically you don't explore other sources of the illness.

On the other hand (I always find myself qualifying statements about the sources of depression), medication is a blessing many Americans can't accept. Depression is the most under-medicated illness we have. Most Americans simply do not want to take medication for depression because they view such a choice as a weakness. Our cherished ideologies of individualism, self-reliance, and "by-your-bootstraps" Horatio Alger upward mobility clash with a reliance upon medication for depression. "I should be able to get better all by myself" is common wisdom, or "I should be able to get better only through exercise, prayer, acupuncture, St. John's Wort"—anything but an "artificial" medication manufactured by a drug company. "I'm not going to be one of those Feel-good Freddies," says a friend's mother, refusing medication for her depression. The drug companies and medical establishment have done the best they can to stress the physical bases of depression and to make parallels between taking antidepressants and taking insulin for diabetes, but many people cannot accept this parallel—understandable given that our culture separates illness into two categories, "Physical" and "Mental," refusing to acknowledge the interplay between mind and body and placing a stigma on any illness that falls under the latter category.

EVEN THOUGH my American studies training has led me to sniff out ideology like a bloodhound, seeing reflections of the simplistic American belief in the power of the individual will in the views of those who think people with depression should just "shake it off," I've shared in this belief too, as has my sister. Both of us have taken medication when we've been depressed and then stopped it when we felt better, against the advice of doctors, because we felt like we would be *better people* if we didn't take medication. Stronger, more virtuous, more moral. Maureen has been on a dosage of 20 mg of Prozac, the standard, but has attempted to lower it as much as possible—trying to get to 15 mg, then 10, then having to accept, as depression fogs its way into her life again, the need to go back to 20 mg.

"So," I asked her a few years ago, "let me get this straight. You think that if you take 10 mg of Prozac a day instead of 20 mg, you'll be *twice as good* a person. And if you ever had to take 40 mg a day instead of 20, you'd been *twice as bad* a person."

"That's it," she said.

"And on 40 a day, would you be four times as bad a person as someone on 10?"

"You got it."

"But taking medication for your high blood pressure doesn't make you a bad person."

"No."

"And you do know that depression has a physical component, and that high blood pressure has an emotional one."

"Yes."

"Okay. Just checking."

For me, *beginning* to take medication was not so hard: in fact, I initiated the decision, making an appointment with a local doctor and asking him to prescribe an antidepressant. I did not interpret this initial choice of medication as a sign that I was ill: only that I was suffering from a depression I assumed to be a self-contained episode. *Continuing* to take medication when depression did not lift permanently was a far more problematic process.

"So let me understand this," Maureen said to me during my early history with medication. "Taking medication for a short period of time did not make you a bad person."

"No."

"But taking the *exact same* medication and dosage for a long time *would* make you a bad person."

"Yes."

"So, let me understand you. If you had to take Prozac for two years, would that make you twice as bad a person as someone who only had to take it for a year?"

"Exactly."

"And taking it forever—"

"That would make me a very, very bad person."

I NO LONGER attach any moral significance to taking, or not taking, medication, and I often recommend it—perhaps too soon—to people who are suffering from untreated depression, often advocating it much more strongly than my understanding of depression as having complex sources might suggest because I know I'm combating our fierce cultural resistance to medication.

I remember combating various forms of this cultural resistance myself, in various stages over the last several years. When one of my doctors—who thought my illness might be what the DSM calls "Bipolar II," bipolar without the highs (this turned out to not be the case)—recommended lithium as an additive to the antidepressant I was then taking, I felt threatened and insulted. The word "lithium" really hit a nerve. Lithium seemed like a heavy-duty, industrial-strength medication, meant for people with *real* mental illness. Contemplating taking it raised all kinds of unpleasant possibilities. *Am I really sick enough for lithium? Does this mean I have to view myself as mentally ill?*

My battle was not with the medication itself, but with the meanings I, and my culture, gave to it. Part of my resistance was simply snobbery. Prozac was a medication, but lithium was a *drug*—heavy and crude. Prozac had been featured on the front cover of *Time* and *Newsweek*—even if it didn't work for me, it was the hot remedy of the nineties, the only antidepressant that kept popping up in *New Yorker* cartoons and movies and greeting cards. Lithium seemed an old-fashioned, lumbering drug, a fifties throwback, like black-and-white TV. How could it be meant for a baby-boomer depressive like me?

Lithium also sparked off my quarrel with language, terminology, and diagnostic categories. In part I resisted lithium because I didn't want to define myself by the word "bipolar." I knew this was a socially constructed category, invented by psychiatrists, that did not "naturally" describe me, but I still didn't like it. I didn't want to belong to any category, not even the slightly less stigmatized "unipolar": I wanted to think of myself as an individual, not a generic. Besides, why did I have to have a label? Wasn't there any *me* here?

My quarrel with lithium brought to the forefront a struggle many people who suffer from depression confront: with naming and diagnosis. Do I have a "mental illness" or a "mood disorder"? Do I want to resist categorization entirely, viewing it as oppressive rather than useful? Do I view myself as "a depressive" or as someone who "suffers from depression," a small but telling distinction? Do I invent my own term for depression—perhaps "mood affliction"—trying to name myself, instead of being named by the DSM-IV? Do I ignore categories entirely, not caring what term the psychiatrists check on my chart—generally "296.32 *Maj. Dep. Recurrent*"—saying to myself "Render unto Caesar the things that are Caesar's, and unto God the things that are God's?" (Yes.)

These questions cannot be answered quickly. Accepting depression as part of your life—something that can be managed, but that, as in my case, still appeared particularly in stressful times—is a long journey, marked by shifts in identity along with ever-deepening stages of rebellion and acceptance. Like many people with depression I kept drawing lines in the sand, me on one side, my illness and some form of medication on the other.

By now I've stepped over enough lines that I don't need to draw them any more. In fact, I've become an aggressive, knowledgeable consumer—I keep up with the latest research news on depression and medication, and I sometimes come to my doctor with requests or suggestions. I've given up the notion that complete recovery is possible, but not on the notion that some combination of drugs may work better than the one I'm on at the moment, and I'm stubborn enough to keep trying new versions. I've become pragmatic: whatever works.

THE OTHER dominant story of depression's origins—now less popular than the biochemical one—is the psychological story, congruent with our therapeutic culture. There are different versions of this narrative, but most center on the dynamics of loss. This is the one I was tracking, in contexts that became larger and larger, as I traced my family emotionally and spiritually back to the Famine and unchosen emigration.

What tends to get obscured by these stories—the biochemical one in particular—are the cultural and social sources of depression. In his book on depression *Speaking of Sadness,* the sociologist David Karp explores the social sources, pointing in particular to issues of poverty, oppression, and discrimination.

For those in the relatively privileged middle and professional classes, like myself, I think the cultural sources are also strong. Cultures give meaning to illnesses: they provide the frameworks through which we view and understand them. But they can also give rise to illnesses. Sometimes an illness seems to embody the spirit of the age, and it had seemed strange to me that during the 1980s and 1990s when the American economy was flourishing and the cold war finishing, depression seemed more and more the illness that signified our time. I might have been suffering in private, but I was, it seemed, part of a mass movement.

The booklets put out by drug companies and depression support groups do not mention American cultural systems and values as contributing to depression. George M. Beard's theories no longer seem relevant, which makes sense. We prefer to offer individual solutions to what are social and economic problems. (That way nothing really has to change.)

In her powerful poem "Having it Out with Melancholy," Jane Kenyon contrasts what she calls "ordinary contentment" to depression. I like that phrase, and I think she's right. But in American culture ordinary contentment is a hard state to achieve: we're supposed to be shooting higher, for success and happiness, which we equate. The Declaration of Independence does not imagine the goals of American life as "Life, liberty, and the pursuit of ordinary contentment."

$\mathcal{B}$ACK IN the fifties, my father didn't have such a range of stories for understanding his depression. But he did have one important belief that I think helped him considerably: the explanation for suffering and depression offered by Catholic spiritual traditions.

I find my father's reinvention of his life and his handling of depression— interconnected enterprises—in his reading journal, filled with quotations from spiritual and religious sources. Reading and writing clearly were spiritual practices, helping him to give meaning to his life beyond the economic values that dominated his culture. His reading helped him become more attuned to the reality of the invisible world and, I think, may have helped him accept a life more limited in material and professional success than he had hoped for.

Throughout the late 1940s and 1950s, while he was adjusting to diminished economic and professional goals, my father was reading St. Thomas à Kempis, St. Thomas Aquinas, St. Augustine, Cardinal Newman, and the Catholic poets Gerard Manley Hopkins and Francis Thompson (who also suffered from depression). One of his favorite poems, Thompson's "Hound of Heaven," portrayed Christ as the hunting dog who pursues the fleeing soul. I can remember him quoting the thrilling opening lines "I fled Him, down the nights and down the days; / I fled Him, down the arches of the years; / I fled Him down the labyrinthine ways / Of my own mind." Raised in an Irish Catholic culture that stressed submission to the priest's authority, my father became a searching, intellectual Catholic, and his access to spiritual narratives helped him to place his life in a larger context than the American success story. St. Thomas à Kempis's *Imitation of Christ*, a meditation on the spiritual life, was one of his favorite books—he would take it with him to the hospital when he was dying, when he probably turned to a section he had read many times, "The Uses of Adversity."

Sometimes it is to our advantage to endure misfortunes and adversities, for they make us enter into our inner selves and acknowledge that we are in a place of exile and that we ought not to rely on anything in this world.

His reading journal is full of quotations that place the meaning of life in a spiritual context, like this excerpt from a biography of Cardinal Newman:

Newman shared with the saints one pre-eminent gift, given only to a few, the gift of kindling in the minds of others the sense of God's nearness; and humanity will always revere, as in a class apart, those chosen souls who through the veil of the visible behold the invisible that lies beyond and reveal to others a glimpse, although only a glimpse, of what they themselves have seen.

All the quotes my father chose focus, in one way or another, on the reality of the invisible, and the importance of the spiritual, creative, and intellectual worlds. His reading notes do not include quotations that exalt the spiritual over the material; rather, he likes passages in which the unseen and the seen cross over each other, points of intersection, as in this passage from Newman:

As we dwell here between two mysteries, of a soul within and an ordered universe without, so among us are granted to dwell certain men of more delicate fibre than their fellow men whose minds have, as it were, filaments to intercept, apprehend, conduct, translate home to us stray messages between these two mysteries, as modern telegraphy has learnt to search out, snatch, gather home human messages astray over waste waters of the ocean.

My father was drawn to writers who imagined some way of honoring spiritual realities and interweaving them with the everyday realm of the senses. My guess is that he also identified with the "chosen soul" imagined in both passages, the man of "delicate fibre" who exists between the worlds and "translate[s] home" the messages wandering between the worlds. He was a man of such delicate fibre, but unlike Newman he did not find the vocation that allowed him to translate to others the messages he received. They stayed private, handwritten in pencil in his notebook.

WHEN MY own midlife depression began, I didn't have the spiritual resources my father had forty years earlier. I was a lapsed Catholic, having left the church for the usual reasons people did in the sixties—the condemnation of premarital sex and birth control, the antifeminism, the preoccupation with sin. I wasn't drawn to Aquinas or à Kempis for spiritual assistance—the constant emphasis on suffering seemed too close to the traditional Irish Catholic way of dealing with adversity, "offer it up." So, unlike my father, I did not inherit a narrative for understanding depression from my religious life.

The appearance and marketing of Prozac in 1988 and, later, other SSRIs (like Zoloft and Paxil) did give me and other Americans a quasi-religious narrative for depression: the recovery story of illness and cure, which mingles spiritual and medical languages and connects to both the upward mobility story and the conversion narrative (*I was blind, but now I see).* One reason why Peter Kramer's *Listening to Prozac* was so popular was its recounting of antidepressant "miracle" stories, the same kind of ecstatic transformations we see celebrated in advertising, in makeovers in women's magazines, and in infomercial testimonies to the new lives granted by hair thickeners, teeth whiteners, and weight-loss products.

You can see the spiritually transformative power Eli Lilly wanted to attach to Prozac in the series of advertisements published in the mid-1990s in mass market magazines like *Time, Newsweek, People,* and *The Ladies' Home Journal.* On the left is a dark page with a cloud dripping rain and the words *Depression hurts.* On the right is a light blue page with a bright, childlike sun radiating heat and light and the words *Prozac can help.* At the bottom is the PROZAC brand name with the "O" transformed into a yellow, beaming sun. Another ad in this series shows, on the left, a stark winter tree, stripped of leaves, against a blue-purple background. On the right is the tree, blooming greenly on a bright yellow background.

The written text gives only modest promises: it's Prozac *can* help, not Prozac *will* help. But the iconography, always drawn from nature, tells a miraculous story of the seemingly instantaneous journey from illness to health. The images of suns and blooming trees promise the same renewal and rebirth Thoreau prophesied in the "Spring" chapter of *Walden.*

Such advertisements offer a remedy and also reflect a cultural pressure that my father, who relied on *Imitation of Christ,* did not experience in the late 1940s. Now, it seems, if we want to speak about depression, we are encouraged to use the narrative form of the recovery story. Even William Styron, in his groundbreaking memoir of depression *Darkness Visible: A Memoir of Madness,* ends with an image of transformation. Wanting—

understandably!—to provide hope for the reader, he gives us a parallel to Dante's *Paradisio* in his concluding sentences. "For those who have dwelt in depression's dark wood, and known its inexplicable agony, their return from the abyss is not unlike the ascent of the poet, trudging upward and upward out of hell's black depths and at last emerging into what he saw as 'the shining world.' . . . *And so we came forth, and once again beheld the stars.*"

I love reading Styron's last words: after all, they are mythic. I am reading the end of *Walden* as well as of *The Divine Comedy*; I am reading the story of death and rebirth, one of the great structuring stories of myth, legend, and religion. I am reading Shelley's "Ode to the West Wind"—"If winter come, / Can spring be far behind?" I am seeing Aeneas and Orpheus and Persephone emerge from the underworld, blinking in the sunlight. I am reading Horatio Alger, I am seeing Rocky run up the steps of the Philadelphia Museum of Art, I am remembering the rising sun replacing the thundercloud in the Prozac ad.

And so, if I suffer from a depression that does *not* yield to a miraculous cure—as I do—then I am reading a story that can seem elusive, reproachful, silencing. If you suffer from a chronic illness in our culture, the recovery narrative—if by "recovery" we mean a return to an unblemished state—simply does not apply. You need other deeper, more complex stories in order to imagine your life over time.

My reading journal—lacking, I admit, my father's references to Browning and Newman—contains quotations from such stories. I was fortunate to find solace in the memoirs of depression not available to my father—those by writers like William Styron, Martha Manning, Kay Redfield Jamison, Andrew Solomon—and in revisionist Catholic and Christian writing (Marcus Borg, Kathleen Norris, Thomas More). Reading these books gave me a sense of companionship and reminded me of C. S. Lewis's answer to the question "Why do we read?" *We read to know we are not alone.*

I'm thankful, too, for my love of literature, which has given me more treasured quotations for my reading journal: passages from writers like Herbert, Thoreau, Dickinson, Kate Chopin, Fitzgerald, Jane Kenyon, Willa Cather, William Trevor. One poem I copied out is an excerpt from Mary Oliver's "The Journey":

little by little,
as you left their voices behind,
the stars began to burn

through the sheets of clouds,
and there was a new voice
which you slowly
recognized as your own,
that kept you company
as you strode deeper and deeper
into the world,
determined to do
the only thing you could do—
determined to save
the only life you could save.

I imagine talking with my father about this poem, wondering if he would like it. Would he think the ending was selfish? Would he be disappointed that the poem doesn't allow for a divine voice? Perhaps. But I think we'd agree on one thing: the best words here are *little by little* and *slowly.*

The poem gives us hope because it reminds us that things take time. Journeys can be long, outcomes uncertain, recoveries incomplete. Beginning the effort is important, though, as is remembering that we make our way through the world with wandering steps and slow.

Baby steps.

You'll Never Work in This Town Again

A loving heart is the beginning of all knowledge.
—Carlyle's "Essay on Biography," quoted in my father's reading journal

MCLEAN'S IS ONE OF THE TEACHING HOSPITALS associated with Harvard Medical School, and as I'm weaving back and forth between my MDDA support group meetings at McLean's and my days in Harvard libraries, I'm wondering if these two parts of Harvard are connected. Does the stress of Harvard send you to McLean's? Does McLean's patch you up, send you back to Harvard, ready to pass as normal and achieve, until you're back in McLean's again?

Maybe there's an underground passage between Harvard and depression.

Andrew, one of my MDDA buddies, thinks so. Harvard's a breeding ground for depression and manic depression, he tells me. "It's in the air," he says. "Practically contagious." He's a grad student in visual studies, and he had his first manic episode two years ago, after a particularly stressful set of oral examinations before a tribunal of five full professors, in a big room with other people watching. "Two weeks later I was paranoid," he said. "I thought there was a conspiracy, with Harvard targeting me."

"You don't have to stretch to see where that came from."

"Yeah, but wait'll you hear what comes next. I have to find some woman and save her too, before Harvard destroys her—it all gets mixed up with the Lord of the Rings. Eventually I have to save the whole world from the forces of evil. I was a little grandiose. Finally, when I was staying up all night calling people at random in the Cambridge phone book, telling them they had to meet me in Harvard Square the next day so we could evacuate the city, my roommates called the Harvard cops, and they took me to McLean's."

A FEW DAYS AFTER hearing Andrew's story, I give a talk at Harvard's Pforzheimer House—this used to be Radcliffe's North House before the merger. As a Radcliffe student I lived in Comstock, one of the dormitories. Here I am in the living room of my old college house, looking at an audience of Harvard undergraduates—now male and female, almost evenly mixed between white students and students of color—reading a story I've written about being diagnosed with depression at Harvard in 1969.

Afterward several students come up to me and tell me they're on antidepressants, but they don't want anyone else to know it. "I almost dropped out," one young woman confides, "but I really want to make it until graduation."

"Do you think the atmosphere here contributes to depression?"

"Absolutely," she says. "It's the pressure. And it's knowing how smart everybody else is, and feeling like you're the one who doesn't belong."

"Everybody else feels like that too."

"Knowing that doesn't help."

A FEW MONTHS AGO I buttonholed my new meds shrink, who works for the Harvard Community Health Plan. He had a complex view of the multiple sources of depression—culture, genetics, biochemistry, family, life events—and we spent most of our sessions, after he'd tweaked my medication, just talking. "But what if you had to pinpoint the major source," I asked him. "For my clients—they're mostly professional, white-collar—it's the pressure to achieve," he said.

Harvard symbolizes, concentrates, expects, and venerates the pressure to achieve. Harvard thinks of itself as the best, and you're supposed to be and to produce the best to belong here. The problem is, there are thousands of students and faculty members in the university—not every one of them, not many of them, can be the best, if we define "best" by external signs of success. What happens to the rest? What happens to those who fail to excel?

I WAS DIAGNOSED with clinical depression when I was a second-year graduate student in English at Harvard. Harvard didn't cause the depression—coming out of my family, going to graduate school in response to what felt like parental expectation, I was a depression waiting to happen, and if I'd gone to Berkeley or Stanford instead, it probably would have happened there. But Harvard was, as Andrew put it, a breeding ground for my depression, which emerged fairly quickly once I got there.

*I*N MAY OF MY first year I applied to teach expository writing to freshmen in the fall of my second year. This was early—most graduate students waited until their third year to teach—but I continued my pattern of dealing with scary things by throwing myself into the midst of them as soon as I could.

The future teachers had a short meeting with the director of the program, Professor K, who gave us a list of twenty books from which to construct a syllabus, and told us we should select three. This was the entire extent of our introduction to pedagogy. Before leaving for the summer I selected *The Tempest* and a collection of George Orwell's essays, both of which I had read, and *The Autobiography of Malcolm X,* which I had not. It was the summer of 1969, after the assassinations of Kennedy and King, and I thought Malcolm X's story would be relevant. I thought that all three books would relate to issues of language and politics and power; I just wasn't sure how.

I'd been nervous about the course, unsure of my abilities as a teacher, but when I read *Malcolm X* in August nervousness tipped over into terror, and terror into panic. I was stupid. I was a fraud. I was white. I had no idea how to teach. How could an Irish Catholic girl from Belmont High teach an autobiography by an angry black man to Harvard undergraduates? The black students would scorn me. The white liberals would side with the blacks. My only supporter would be a polite young woman raised by the nuns. The only question I could think to ask about the book was "So, what did you think of *Malcolm X?*"

I had no idea who they were, and I was already afraid of my students.

I DID NOT TELL anyone in authority about my fears. There was no one to tell: none of the professors I'd had classes with had ever spoken to me personally, or even made eye contact or smiled when we passed in the halls. Professors in the English department were rumored not to want to have anything to do with you until you were writing a dissertation, and sometimes not even then. The head of Expository Writing, the celebrated Professor K, wafted in and out of the department offices in the English headquarters in Warren House on a golden cloud, followed by a retinue of assistant professors and graduate students seeking favors. Going to see this deity and telling him I was afraid to teach was impossible.

At Harvard, you were supposed to be competent; you were not supposed to ask for help; you were not supposed to have panic attacks about facing your first class with no support and no guidance. My anxiety was shameful, a sign of weakness and failure. I could not even tell my friends. I had to keep up the façade that I, like them, belonged at Harvard, even though it was now clear that I did not.

I went to the program secretary and told her I could not teach, explaining that I had overextended myself and had to study for my orals (which at least was true). I waited for her shock and disapproval, but she'd seen a million graduate students come and go, and she could have cared less if I taught or not. "Then we'll just have to get someone else," she said, while she crossed my name off her list.

I walked home and made light of my decision to my roommates, telling them the same lie I told the secretary. "I just decided not to teach," I said casually. "Too much work preparing for my orals," and they nodded, accepting my story. I told my boyfriend the same thing. No one could know why I'd backed out.

THE NEXT morning the telephone rang. It was Professor K. "This behavior is completely unprofessional," he said. "Did you know that classes start in three weeks? I'll see to it that you never get to teach another section at Harvard, in my course or anyone else's."

He did not ask me what was wrong. The only words I said during our conversation were "hello," "I'm sorry," and "good-bye."

Professor K had confirmed my own worst view of myself, and the result was what I now call my "You'll Never Work in This Town Again" depression. It never occurred to me that with a little support and coaching I might have been able to teach, or that Professor K might have asked me what the problem was before he judged me. I gave him all the authority to define me that he so easily assumed.

Within minutes of this phone call I was in a deep depression. I would stay in bed each day until noon or one o'clock, getting up only to attend my afternoon classes.

Then I'd drag myself to the library, then home, eat peanut butter out of the jar and go back to bed. It went on like this for weeks. I had told my boyfriend about Professor K's phone call but no one else: I was too ashamed.

I was not suicidal in the sense of actively planning my own death, but I had what the psychiatrists call "suicidal ideation." That just means I fantasized about killing myself. Suicide would be a form of travel, a way to move on.

My boyfriend was a graduate student in clinical psychology. I tried to mask the worst of my distress and pass as normal even with him, but he could tell something was wrong and urged me to see a psychiatrist. He wanted me to see Dr. F, the head of psychiatric services at the Harvard University Health Center. Dr. F taught in the clinical program and my boyfriend knew his reputation. "He's a god. You'll love him. Make an appointment."

"Okay," I said. I didn't want to see a psychiatrist, but I knew I had to do something. This was no way to live.

DR. F WAS A TALL, rangy man in his late thirties, wearing one of those combinations—a tweed jacket, dark blue shirt, and red tie—that say "I'm professional and laid-back at the same time." He gave my lifeless hand a warm handshake and asked me how I had been feeling. His voice was rich and textured and he looked at me intently, still holding my hand. I could tell that he really wanted to know about me, that he cared.

I felt as if I'd been wandering in a desert and had finally stumbled on an oasis.

I told Dr. F about my failure to teach the course, Professor K's phone call, feeling worthless, not wanting to get out of bed, and fantasizing suicide. He nodded, calm, accepting, un-judging. "You are in a clinical depression," he said, "probably brought by the horrors of graduate school, not uncommon, Harvard can do this to people," and he smiled at me to say he knew how heartless Harvard could be. Thank God for Dr. F. Someone understood. Someone was on my side. He and I had bonded together against the terrors of graduate school, against the unfeeling Professor K.

Being told I was in a "clinical depression" actually felt good. I was relieved to know I *had* something, a condition, an illness, as in childhood when the family doctor said "You have the measles." "Clinical depression"— the term used then for "major depressive episode"—sounded like a category that other people had occupied, and so instead of feeling erased by the classification I felt consoled. I was part of a community of sufferers. Doctors knew about dreadful illness, and I would be cured.

It was not until Dr. F gave me my options for therapy that I began to feel uneasy.

"My therapy schedule is booked," he said, "otherwise I could take you on myself." *Oh no.* That was what I wanted, therapy with Dr. F, and I couldn't have it. Of course he was a busy man, head of psychiatric services, how could he possibly have time for me? He paused, then leaned closer to me, kindly, confidential.

"But I could fit you into my teaching schedule," he said, as if he were offering me a homemade Christmas present, something just from him to me.

"Teaching schedule?" I asked. I didn't understand, but there was hope.

He was teaching a graduate course in clinical psychology, he said, to students like my boyfriend, students like me. He would do therapy with me, just the same as if I were his regular patient, except we would be viewed through a one-way mirror by his graduate students. He needed a subject. "You'll never know they're there," he said. "It's just like a wall. You can only see through it from the other side."

I did not know what to say. "The other option," he added, "would be for you to see a private therapist in town. I can recommend someone, of course. It'll run you about thirty dollars an hour. Your work with me would be free."

I did not feel betrayed or angry with Dr. F for suggesting that my despair could become a teaching text. I was the good daughter, and I felt that he was doing me a favor just to be talking with me. It didn't occur to me that there could be other psychologists on the staff with open schedules; later I would realize that Dr. F didn't mention this option because he wanted me for his class.

Maybe it would be okay, I thought, having therapy surrounded by silent, invisible watchers? But some voice of self that had not been silenced by depression told me that this arrangement didn't really feel okay. It just didn't seem right to be telling this doctor your most intimate story while anonymous graduate students you couldn't even see but who could see you would be taking notes on what you said. On the other hand, I was desperate. I wanted Dr. F to be my therapist, not some stranger I would have to pay.

I was tempted. It would be so easy to say yes.

"No," I said. "I just can't do that." Then I added "I'm sorry," because it felt like me who should be apologizing.

Dr. F leaned back in his chair, opened a drawer, and took out a black address book. "Then I'll give you a referral," he said. He gave me the number of his colleague Dr. L in a voice that seemed crisper and less kindly. "Well," he said, "I guess we've done all the work we can do together," extending his hand, and I knew this was my sign to leave. No help could be found for me at the Harvard Health Services, and I would have to pay a private therapist, although I didn't know how I'd manage. Thirty dollars a week was a lot of money for a grad student on a small stipend.

I GOT A PART-TIME job to pay for therapy with Dr. L, whom I remember as cold, distant, unsympathetic, and short. Dr. L sat in his leather psychiatrist's chair next to his desk while I sat on a leather couch separated from him by oceans of space and a substantial coffee table. At the beginning of a session he would roll his chair toward me an inch or two, fold his hands in his lap—his gesture of openness—and wait for me to speak. When the session was over, he would twirl his chair back to the desk and write out my bill while I signed a check for thirty dollars.

He fingered his beard while I talked. Mainly he stayed silent. Occasionally he would make a note on a pad of yellow paper or clear his throat and tell me I should get regular exercise. I was still spending most of my time in bed and thought he must be from another planet. I do not remember what we talked about, or any insights I may have received into the causes of my depression. I finally stopped therapy when going felt worse than staying away. The depression was lifting, for its own mysterious biochemical and emotional reasons. I felt I could cope on my own and wanted to leave Dr. L's chilly care.

But perhaps I misremember. Perhaps he was a warm, kindly man and I was too depressed to notice. Perhaps we laughed occasionally. Perhaps he did lead me, or want to lead me, to painful insights that I was not ready to receive. What I do know is that I did not feel comfortable with him, and I was afraid to say so. I also know that he never suggested antidepressants, even though they were available in 1969.

I QUIT THERAPY in the spring: my depression had lifted, and I spent the extra time studying for my orals. I felt well prepared, but when I walked into Warren House and saw those three professors sitting at the long table, I got worried, particularly when the Americanist walked over to a bookcase and started to check out some dusty leather-bound volumes. The enthusiastic sort, he turned around, holding an open book, exclaiming "Wow, I didn't know we had the *complete Walter Scott* here."

Oh God, I thought. He's going to ask me about Scott. I hadn't read Scott since ninth grade, when Miss Skahan conducted a forced march through *Ivanhoe*. I vaguely remember that he wrote about knights. He was Scottish, right? Or did I just think that because of his last name?

Someone threw out the first question and I found myself talking, and maybe making sense, and I started feeling like I might get through this when the Americanist asked "What if I asked you to compare Scott and Newman?"

I didn't get smart and ask if he were really asking me to do this. I took a breath and thanked God for my father's obsession with Newman, and then there was that memory of Scott and the knights. "Well, they were both really interested in tradition and order, except in different ways," and saw the three professors nodding like I knew what I was talking about, and then I steered the conversation toward Newman and I knew I was passing my orals.

I DID WORK IN that town again. I had a fellowship that guaranteed my teaching tutorial to individual students, so in a year I decided to redeem myself by taking on what amounted to a full-time teaching load—two units of tutorial teaching at Harvard (a full load for most graduate students), and in addition two sections of expository writing at Newton College of the Sacred Heart, a nearby women's Catholic college. "Get back on the horse" was my philosophy, and even though I threw up before teaching at Newton for the first month, I walked into a class of twenty students and did okay. I made up my own reading list this time, and—just discovering the women's movement—taught what retrospectively was my first course in women's writing. We read Doris Lessing's *Martha Quest*, Mary McCarthy's *Memories of a Catholic Girlhood* (which my students loved), Sylvia Plath's *The Bell Jar*, and a collection of stories that included Lessing's "To Room Nineteen" and Susan Glaspell's "A Jury of Her Peers." My students were eager to talk about these readings, and I began to look forward to class. Concerned that I might be lapsing as a Catholic (based on my approach to McCarthy), students invited me to their guitar Mass, and I went, and even took communion, which was crusty Italian bread.

*T*HE FOLLOWING year—still not sure if Professor K had in fact blackballed me from teaching sections or courses—I applied to teach a section in English 70, Alan Heimert's American literature survey, and—along with two other graduate students who became close friends—was selected as a section leader. The three of us would meet each week to plan our sections, and I began to see that teaching need not be a lonely enterprise. At the end of the semester, Professor Heimert invited us all to lunch at Eliot House. As the four of us sat around the table drinking wine and eating pasta with scallops—I still remember that meal—he thanked us for our work and said "You guys weren't bad at all."

In my fifth year I wrote my dissertation on Willa Cather. Daniel Aaron was my adviser, and I am not sure I would have finished graduate school if I had not found him. He had high standards and encouraged me to meet them, and little by little, I did. I told Aaron stories to my parents and knew that my father approved of his methods—made clear in a poem he wrote for my twenty-seventh birthday (my father composed poems for most family occasions).

So clear your mind and hit the books:
Soon you'll be a doctored Sharon.
My advice to you is simply this:
Write, and follow Aaron.

ARVARD MIGHT have seemed a more welcoming place earlier, and my bout with depression less lonely, if I had been able to speak with my father about it.

I simply could not tell him about my depression or the precipitating cause, which shamed me even more: my resigning from my teaching fellow position and repudiation by the professor. I was afraid to seem a failure in my father's eyes. He had been thrilled that I was going to teach freshman composition, and he had written me a long letter over the summer telling me how he would go about teaching the course.

July 29, 1969
Dear Sharon:
Your description of your teacher conducting a class unlocks something in me and tempts me to pour out some idle thoughts on teaching composition that recur. If I were to teach a freshman class, and were given carte blanche, I know just how I would conduct it. I would inform the class that I had two objectives, one maximum and one minimum: the maximum, to teach them to write WELL, and the minimum, to write CLEARLY.

What was "unlocked" in my father was his own desire to teach, his road not taken. He described how he would structure the class: meetings on Tuesday and Thursday for the whole class, with his focus on clarity; Saturday classes for those few who wanted to go further and write well. *I would use no text book, just good writing, from the masters.*

Thinking about me teaching, my father had dipped back into his reading journal and found several entries on good writing and teaching. "I intend to quote from it," he wrote. "Brace yourself."

He had typed out two long quotes from Sir Arthur Quiller-Couch's *The Art of Writing*, another from a Newman scholar, and a passage from Browning. I must have skimmed these quotes at the time, thinking "Quiller-Couch? Not that old fogy again." My father had been pushing Quiller-Couch on me for years, and I thought him hopelessly old-fashioned. The first quotation from Sir Arthur attacks one of my father's favorite targets—jargon. He despised puffy, abstract, pretentious language, and one of the essays he'd introduced me to was Orwell's "Politics and the English Language." Sir Arthur's second quote and the two from the Newman scholar and Browning referred to a class of almost shamanic teachers who could be conduits of invisible mysteries, seeing "through the veil of the visible" to the "invisible that lies beyond." The Browning quote described these teacher-priests:

Through such souls alone
God, stopping, shows sufficient of his light
For us in the dark to rise by. And I rise.

My father ended his letter saying that if these ideas had "got home" to me, I should seek out such writers myself and "use them for standards. So, you see, I became both literary and philosophic, and professorial."

I simply could not tell him that I had panicked at the thought of teaching, the precipitating cause of my depression. He was the real teacher, not me: not only had I bailed out, but there was no way I could ever imagine teaching on Saturdays, let alone fulfill Browning's exalted description of the inspiring teacher. I thought that my father had such expectations of me. Now I see that he'd simply been carried away with excitement and ideas, hoping to pass on the thoughts that mattered to him.

*K*EEPING SILENT about my fears and inadequacies cut me off from the conversation we could have had. Who better than my father to understand the depression following failure at work?

Maybe we would have been having lunch at Ferdinand's, and I'd have told him how scared I'd been about teaching, and how bad I felt. Maybe he would have told me what he'd felt like, back in the 1940s, being depressed and out of work, and said something to make me feel better and give me hope. Maybe he would have quoted Newman, saying "Bear with me a little, now, I am going to become literary, but Newman has a lot to say to both of us. 'I shall console myself with the reflection that life is not long enough to do more than our best, whatever that may be . . . that they who never venture, never gain; that to be ever safe is to be ever feeble.'

"You did your best," my father says. "You ventured. You signed up to teach early. You took a risk. Even Cardinal Newman couldn't do any better."

"Newman never bailed from Expository Writing."

"Newman never signed up to teach as a second-year graduate student," he says. "Newman didn't have to deal with that so-and-so professor of yours. You just got out a little ahead of yourself, that's all. Sit back, study hard for your orals, and wait for yourself to catch up. You'll teach later, when you're ready."

"Okay."

"Good. So here's the really important problem for you to address. What do you want for dessert?"

"Coffee ice cream. How about you?"

"The same," he says, as I knew he would. We both love coffee the best.

THEN I'D walk back to Widener, thinking *maybe not being able to teach this year isn't so bad. Some day I'll be able to do it.*

You know what? I think I just got out a little ahead of myself.

Order of Dances

A lady never asks a gentleman to dance.
—EMILY POST

Dance card with tassel, 1912

THE QUINLANS left enough stories and records to fill a small historical society. The O'Briens left one half-filled box. In the box are scattered photographs of people I do not recognize, second cousins and great-aunts and uncles wearing turn-of-the-century bathing suits. They are posing on the beach in Old Orchard, Maine, the "Irish Riviera" where even working-class people could afford to go for a week in the summer. There is one letter, written by my grandfather Daniel O'Brien during a business trip to New York City in the 1890s; it is addressed to "Dear Mother," the Irish husband's way of addressing his wife.

At the bottom is my aunt Gert's scrapbook, which follows Gert up until her early twenties: then dozens of blank pages, covering most of the span of her life. Tucked in the back are the records of her death in 1965, Mass cards sent to my father from her friends in the à Kempis Circle, a Catholic women's group concerned with the missions. The blank years are when I knew her.

When I was visiting the Lowell Historical Society I had been surprised by the curator's enthusiasm for Gert's book. "These dance cards are particularly wonderful," she had said. "Quite a record of early twentieth-century Irish Catholic social life. We have so few records of women's lives—would you consider donating this to us?"

When I got back to Cambridge I looked through the scrapbook again, taking more notice of the dance cards. I teach women's studies: how could I not have noticed that my aunt's life had a story beyond my knowledge of her?

Gert kept her scrapbook from 1913 to 1920, beginning when she was fifteen and ending when she was twenty-two. She included newspaper clippings, concert programs, playbills, photographs, postcards, graduation cards, calling cards, invitations to St. Patrick's Day and Valentine's Day parties, and more than twenty dance cards. Now that a stranger had praised it, I could see a side of my aunt I had never seen before: an Irish Catholic girl coming of age in the early twentieth century. This was a lighthearted, active girl, one who liked to have a good time.

By the time I knew Gert, in the 1950s and early 1960s, she was going in and out of Bournewood Hospital in Brookline for shock treatments. This can only mean that her depression was pretty severe. We didn't speak about this but we knew it, and I wish I could say the knowledge made me look on her more charitably, but it didn't. She bugged me. She was overweight, and I didn't like that about her, and when she came to visit she would take the other twin bed in my room, and I didn't like that either. She would bring gifts of food—Brigham's ice cream, pecan rolls, Sara Lee coffee cakes. I would eat these treats grudgingly, sure that Gert wanted to lure me into the country of fat, unmarried, depressed women. Adrift in my miserable, boyfriend-less, acne-conscious adolescence, sulky and self-absorbed and dreadfully lonely, I simply could not have kind feelings for my aunt. I saw myself in her: eating was my own secret pleasure, and like most teenage girls I thought I was overweight.

"Don't you want some Sara Lee?" she would ask, cutting the coffee cake into generous slices. "No," I'd say, going to my bedroom, shutting the door,

Gertrude with friend, dressed for a dance, 1912 or 1913

knowing I would go back to the kitchen later when no one was there and eat beyond my share, wondering if she knew that too.

My sister, who did not see her own shadow in Gert, remembers her love of food differently. "It was great when she visited," Maureen says. "She took us on picnics by the Charles River, and brought those great cupcakes." Gert's cupcakes come back to my memory—lemon and raspberry, purchased at Dorothy Muriels, wearing little cakey hats sprinkled with confectioner's sugar.

EVERY SO OFTEN Gert would disappear for two or three weeks for one of her stays at Bournewood, emerging with her short-term memory in tatters. Then I was an oblivious ten-year-old; now I wonder what it must have been like for her to leave the hospital and return to her empty apartment in Lowell. She had sold the family house and moved after her brother died, so there would have been no one there to welcome her home.

Gert had been supervisor of music in the Lowell Public Schools for years, leading a busy and I think happy life as teacher, conductor, and performer— she played the piano. During the period of her shock treatments she was retired, and so she would have returned not to work but to the bits and pieces of her quieter life—the private piano students, the meetings of the Catholic Ladies' Sodality, the à Kempis Circle, the lunches at Schrafft's. She had a grand piano in her apartment, and she would have found some comfort there. I remember her playing—she had lovely hands with pearly, polished nails, and they ranged over the keys like they were at home there. The piano stool was her seat of power, and when she was visiting the bars of Rachmaninoff, Chopin, or Mozart would thunder through the house.

Gert would have returned from the hospital without the safety nets I now take for granted—therapy, medication, support groups. It's hard enough with all these aids; I don't know how I would have managed to bear the isolation she confronted. She took sleeping pills, prescribed by some doctor whom I imagined giving tranquilizers to dozens of depressed women without asking to hear their stories. Her restored tranquility would not last, and she'd go back to the hospital.

*W*HEN I BEGAN reading Gert's scrapbook, I knew the sad last period of her life, and I thought I might find some clues about the sources of her depression in the record of her younger years. What I found was a lively young woman who seemed to have only a bright future ahead of her. One of her early entries is a clipping from the *Lowell Sun* reporting the graduation ceremonies at Notre Dame Academy, the convent school she attended until 1913. The Reverend Francis J. Mullen, graduation speaker, warned the young women before him that in leaving Catholic school for the secular world they were facing the pernicious influence of divorce, socialism, anarchy, and materialism. By all means they must avoid "sensual pleasure," he warned, because the "eat, drink, and be merry" philosophy would lead their immortal souls to destruction.

Did Gert roll her eyes at one of her girlfriends while Father Mullin was talking? I think so. The rest of her album is studded with dance cards, postcards from Old Orchard Beach, invitations to socials and "gatherings." And, daringly, there's a cigarette pasted on one page, with the caption "Oh, no, this wasn't a party favor!"

The dance cards record her experiences at the parties held by the local Catholic groups—the Holy Name Society, the Ladies' Aid Society of St. Patrick's Church, the Knights of Columbus, St. Margaret's Parish. I did not grow up with dance cards, and they look terrifying. Each one has the title Order of Dances, and below a list of twelve, sixteen, or eighteen dances, all numbered and described (waltz, two-step, fox trot, one-step, schottische, quadrille). Next to each dance is a line where the young man signs his initial, claiming his partner. The first and the last dances are always waltzes.

Gert's dance cards usually weren't completely filled, and the first and last waltz are frequently vacant, as are most of the waltzes. She must not have been one of the popular girls. The young woman was supposed to share the first and last waltz with the same person, the boyfriend or suitor who brought her to the dance, or the young man who decided to court her. The waltz had been scandalous in the nineteenth century, but by the early twentieth century it would have been accepted and considered the most romantic and intimate dance. The blank lines by the waltzes say that no one was singling her out.

I can remember how painful it was to be on the sidelines at a dance, waiting to be asked and not being chosen. A boy is striding across the room—

Dance card, 1913

could it be my turn?—and I'm sweating inside my cotton gloves, and then I see he's heading for the shorter, prettier girl next to me, and now I have the worst problem, figuring out what to do while others are dancing. I wonder how Gert handled herself while those waltzes were playing and couples were swooping around the floor. Did she chat animatedly with the other wallflowers, pretending that it didn't matter? Did she walk over to the piano and turn the pages for the player, giving herself a job? Did she drink lemonade and talk with the mothers? Whatever she chose to do, she was marking time, waiting for the order of dances to proceed.

The penciled comments she wrote on the dance cards remind me that Gert had no choice but to accept a social world in which women waited for men to choose them—to dance, to marry. In turn-of-the-century Irish Lowell, that was the order of things. "Very nice," she wrote after one dance. "Good time? Best ever," after another. She wrote the most comments on the Holy Name dance of 1916, when she was chosen for both the first and the last waltz by "S.W.H.," the only time her dance card was filled. "Oh no, I didn't have a good time at all. Sarcasm? Well, a little. . . . Some dances were better than others. Which ones? Don't ask such a personal question." After that dance S.W.H. disappears from the record and the waltzes go blank.

The last waltz was not, I discover, the last moment of male choice at a dancing party. There were the "Extras." Nice boys, the ones whose mothers told them to dance with the wallflowers, would dutifully sign up for regulation dances, but "Extras" were the field of free choice—for the men. Gert, like the other young women, would have waited to be chosen during the extras, and she rarely was. Born in 1898, Gert entered a culture that expected her to marry. The dances she attended were about pairing up with someone from the same ethnic group. Whether there were fourteen or eighteen dances—so many times to be chosen or not chosen!—the order of dances led inevitably to the last waltz and the extras, just as the world of the dance was supposed to lead to engagement and marriage.

I wonder if Gert had wanted to marry, and continued to feel the loss even as she led a happy and useful life as a music teacher. But marriage is no cure for loneliness or depression, and singleness no cause. ("I used to live alone, and then I got divorced" reads a bumper sticker I saw the other day.) It would be a mistake to read the source of my aunt's depressions in those crossed-off waltzes and blank "Extras": had she married S.W.H., she could have ended up in the same hospital.

Gert's life partner was her brother Ray. The two of them stayed together in the family house. She and Ray spent holidays and some weekends with us, always coming and going together. At Christmas Ray might also bring his patient girlfriend Lorinda to visit us: the two had been "seeing each other" for more than twenty years, but Ray continued to live with Gert and never married. When he died in 1952 the loss must have been terrible for Gert— much more so than for Lorinda, who picked herself up pretty quickly and got married. Gert would have lost the person she shared daily life with, and probably the person she shopped and cooked for, the person she traded stories with at the end of the day. She had retired by then, and must have been dreadfully lonely. It was that blank space, I think, not the missing dances or marriage, that sparked her depression.

As I pore through Gert's album book, I find she had an adventurous, even zippy side I had never suspected, a part of her personality that diminished over the years and vanished into her depressions. According to her obituary in the *Lowell Sun,* one of her hobbies was driving. In her scrapbook I find this confirmed: the young woman left a colorful set of notes on cars she was considering buying. The language is spiky and authoritative.

WINTON: Looks big, wears well, rides easy. Very rare.

SCRIPPS BOOTH: Sporty model. All on the outside, showy. Poor motor power.

DODGE: Inoffensive. Sufferable.

BUICK: Make a lot of noise. Wear poorly. Cheap. Common. Popular with those who aren't fussy.

FORD: Slow and dependable. Not much on looks. Always around.

The young woman who made those notes knows what's what. She doesn't want a car that's boring or common or showy—she wants one she can drive, one with "motor power." She wants to get on the road, go fast, make choices; she doesn't want to have to stand there in the dance hall, motionless, while somebody decides whether or not he's going to waltz with her. She'd be off in a shiny new roadster at a moment's notice, smoking a cigarette, humming an aria, the wind blowing her hair back, showing the young man in the passenger's seat how slickly she can corner. There'd be no order of dances, no male-chosen measures of feminine power. Behind the wheel, glorying in her motor power, Gert could make up her own order, her order of cars.

"I don't think you should buy the Buick," she'd say to S.W.H., who's a little nervous because she drives fast. "It's noisy and common, only suited for people who aren't fussy about cars. And the Scripps Booth is showy but slow. Fords are everywhere these days, not distinctive enough. You can do better than that."

"Oh," he says, impressed. "What do you recommend?"

Wash Your Way Out

We leave you sparkling!
—slogan of Restoration, Inc.

AFTER MONTHS OF LETTING friends cook for me, I'm ready to give a dinner party. I've invited Cathy, Jeannie, and Kate, my buddies who've taken care of me this year, and I'm looking forward to being a hostess. I'm making pasta with pine nuts, artichokes, and tomatoes.

My friends arrive, armed with crusty Italian bread, soft blue cheeses, and cold white wine. I put out grapes and cheese, open the wine, put the bread in the oven, and we settle into the living room. My living room. We laugh and talk and sip our wine and I am happy.

"What's that funny smell coming from the kitchen?" Cathy asks all of a sudden, and we rush out there. The stove is on fire. The gas stove. I can see the fire finding the gas main and the whole house blowing up. I've had two small house fires before and I know what to do. I grab the cat and cell phone and push everyone outside the house while I dial 911. I'm shaking but calm: I give perfect directions and we hear the sirens almost as soon as I hang up. The fire station is on Garden Street, about three blocks away.

"Here, let me hold the cat," Jeannie says, "you have to deal with the firemen," and I hand Megan over.

The firemen rush in with hoses and axes and by now all the neighbors have gathered. "Whose house is it?" someone asks, and I have to say "mine." My landlady is out of town. I imagine her returning to a charred hole where her house used to be. I imagine the conversation we'll have.

"It's undah control now," a fireman tells me. "Fiyah started in the broilah, a plastic lid caught on fiyah." Oh God, the bread. That's what did it. I had thought that lower drawer was for storage, the way it is in my stove. I had put a lasagna pan with a plastic lid in the broiler.

"Can I sleep here tonight?"

"No problem," he says. "It's a little smoky, but the fiyah's out."

My friends come inside with me. The apartment is a mess. The walls are covered with soot and the wood floors with water. The stove is pulled out from the wall, marked with a red tag that says in big black letters, "Condemned. City of Cambridge."

We mop the floors and try to clean the walls, but the soot smears and the walls get even blacker. I find out later that plastic fires are the worst: you can't use water to clean with.

"Let's eat," I say. "This cleanup thing isn't working."

"Really?" they ask. "We should probably leave."

"No, stay. We're hungry. The salad's fine and the microwave still works. We can heat up the pasta."

We set the dining room table, and I turn off the overhead and light candles so the fire damage won't be so noticeable.

"We'd better keep an eye on those candles," Kate says, "we don't want those firemen back here tonight."

"I don't know," Cathy says, "one of them looked really cute in that yellow rubber outfit," and we laugh and eat and talk.

After they leave, I walk through each room, looking at the blackened walls. Soot is everywhere, even in the front hall.

*L*ATE THE NEXT afternoon Joe and Cindy arrive. They're a husband-and-wife cleaning team from Brockton. They work for my landlady's insurance company, but have their own business.

Joe and Cindy are dressed in sneakers, blue jeans, and identical navy blue T-shirts saying "Restoration, Inc." They walk through the rooms with me, surveying the blackened walls and light fixtures and baseboards with professional interest.

"It's really bad, isn't it."

"Not too bad," Cindy says. "We've seen worse, haven't we Joe?"

"Oh God yes," he says. "Much worse. We've had jobs that have taken us three weeks. This is probably a five-day job, wouldn't you say Cindy?" and she nods.

"Really?" Five days sounds quite long to me.

"No, really," Cindy says, not getting my tone. "This won't take too long. About a day a room, I'd say, right Joe?" and he nods.

"How do you go about a job like this?" I'm beginning to get interested in their methods.

"We'll start in the room farthest away, " Cindy says, "the kitchen in your case, and that's handy because that's where most of the damage is."

Joe nods: Cindy has had a good insight.

"Then, after we're done with the kitchen," she continues, "we move room by room to the front. That's how we do it, we wash our way out."

"You've really had worse jobs than this? What were some of your worst fires?"

Cindy starts to reminisce, making me feel better as she describes the memorable cleanups they've had—the fourteen-room mansion in Belmont where the lady followed them around all day to be sure they didn't steal anything, the grocery store where they had to take everything off the shelves.

"Remember the catfish fire, Joe?"

"Oh God yes," he says. "How could I forget? My nose can't forget."

"Catfish fire?" I ask.

"Man in Randolph," she says, "cooking catfish on a gas grille in the breezeway, must have been enough catfish for an army, right Joe? Grill catches on fire and starts things off, the whole place stunk for weeks. When Joe and I would get home we'd smell like burnt catfish and have to shower and wash our clothes, remember Joe?"

"Oh God yes," he says. "We stank. Driving home was no treat, I can tell you that."

"So your place isn't so bad," Cindy says kindly. "No catfish stink, anyway."

"Right," I say, feeling obscurely better.

"But of course we draw the line somewhere," she says.

I look at her inquiringly.

"We don't do suicides," she says.

"Oh," I say. "Of course. Somebody has to clean up afterwards, don't they?"

"Yeah, but not us," she says, "there's a limit, isn't there Joe?" and he nods, but by now he's hunkered down wiping off a baseboard with a special sponge they use for plastic fires, too absorbed in his work to speak.

I TAKE MY RUGS to the dry cleaner and pack up all my books and papers so Joe and Cindy can get at the bookcases. I offer to help with the cleanup but they turn me down. I go out to Bedford and stay with Jeannie while they work. When I get back home and open the door, I see white walls and gleaming wood floors. Joe and Cindy have washed their way out, and I walk into my shining house.

The Bookmark or the Rose

The books we read when we were children shaped our imaginings, and it is through our imaginings that we live.
—WILLA CATHER

IT'S A COLD, BLOWY MARCH DAY in Cambridge. I'm finding it hard to shake midwinter depression. My light box isn't doing any good, even though I bathe myself faithfully in its techno-cool white light every morning.

I hadn't wanted to have to find a therapist in Cambridge. The thought of telling my story to a new person is exhausting, and besides, I think the problem now is really with my meds. But you can never be sure. I decide to call up my friends and get some recommendations. It's a way to act.

I'M IN WILL's office in Somerville. The walls are lined with books on meditation, Buddhism, and Eastern religions, and there's a statue of a sitting Buddha in the back, surrounded by a half-circle of meditation cushions. I'm sitting on a plush Victorian couch, slightly shabby, the kind you'd pick up at a Cambridge yard sale. Will sits about ten feet away from me in a high-backed chair. It's not your typical psychiatrist's chair, the leather kind that gives off the aura of burnished authority and a six-figure income. His chair has knobby wooden legs and is upholstered in purple-red velvet, rubbed shiny in places from use. It suggests fading royalty and may be ironic.

I found Will through a mutual friend: she told me that he took a spiritual approach to therapy—he's a Jungian—and that drew me in. I like Jung's way of thinking about the second half of life.

Will is a large, pear-shaped man who rubs the side of his nose when I talk. He has a gentle, placid voice that packs each sentence in bubble wrap, as if it were about to take a long trip. He tells me that "therapy is a spiritual journey that you and I take together." I've only read about thirty pages of Jung, but Will is the real McCoy, and he gives me the story of depression I have come to like. "You're in the alchemic state of *dissolutio*," he says, "when all the structures defining you have dissolved and everything is poised, waiting for a new integration and birth." I'm not sure about the alchemy but I like the metaphor. Yes, I think, this has been my year of dissolving. The new birth is just taking longer than I thought, but Will is going to help me through.

I tell him I've been wanting to write about depression, but now I'm stuck in the depression I'm supposed to be writing about and can't write. He nods, as if this is a very good sign, and tells me our therapy will get me unstuck because we'll be doing "deep work." "I'm always glad to find someone who's ready for deep work," he tells me, and I feel pleased with my progress. I'm not a depressed schlump who can't get out of bed: I'm a spiritual journeyer who's gone further than many mortals.

I tell Will about my mother's throwing my sister out of the family, and how my fear of abandonment caused me, time and again, to cave in. I move through this quickly, feeling—could this be true?—*bored* with the whole story, but Will is giving me his eager attention, nodding enthusiastically every time I use the word "abandoned."

I sketch in the parents of my childhood—intense, scary mother; calm, bookish father—and tell him about my miserable teenage years.

Will leans forward in his velvet chair.

"Have you grieved for yourself?" he asks.

I always hate that question. "Probably not enough," I say dutifully.

"That will be part of your work," he observes, and I nod, a good pupil. Assignment: *Grieve for myself.*

"Do you want a long-term relationship with a man?" he asks.

"Not right now," I say. "Maybe someone to go out with, dinner and the movies, but really all I want is to get through this depression." He raises an eyebrow. I gave the wrong answer. "Eventually, of course, I'd like that," I add.

"Your mother was the witch," he observes.

"The witch?"

"One of Jung's archetypes. The bad mother, the witch who needs to destroy her children's sexuality. She has to kill the drive that breaks up the family of origin and brings in strangers. Now you have to kill off the witch."

"Oh," I say. "Kill off the witch." Oh God, another thing I have to do. But he's probably right. Assignment: *kill the witch.*

"Neither parent helped you become a woman," he adds. "Your father didn't give you the rose."

"The rose?"

"It's the sign in the fairy tale that the father's helping the daughter become a woman. He's mirroring her sexuality. But your father gave you a bookmark."

This is sad and devastating. No wonder I'm not married. I got a bookmark from my father instead of a rose. Assignment: *get the rose.*

"This is why your relationships with men have failed," he says, leaning back in his chair, glancing at his watch. Did I really tell him this? "Your journey is to reclaim your sexuality and your femininity, the gifts your parents stole from you." He pauses. "Well," he says, "I guess time's up. I'm really looking forward to working with you. I feel we've really established a bond today."

"Right," I say as I write out a check.

J HAD JUST WANTED someone to help me through this depression, but now it seems that my depression won't lift until I kill the witch, get the rose, and reclaim my femininity. This could take a long time, and my sabbatical is over in August.

On the way home I realize I didn't like Will's using the word "fail" to describe my relationships with men. They didn't fail: they just were what they were. And what does he mean, "reclaim my sexuality and femininity?" I'm in the midst of a clinical depression, that's what's turned my libido into a shriveled pea and made me think that jeans and a grungy sweatshirt is a good outfit to wear to your shrink's office.

A half hour later I am really pissed. I know enough from past therapy to understand what my real assignment is. At our next session I have to tell how I feel.

J WAS ANGRY WHEN you said my relationships with men had failed," I tell him a week later.

Like many of us who've been part of therapeutic America during the last decade I know I should use the infamous "I statements" and tell Will how he made me feel rather than say "You know, you were really narrow-minded and judgmental last time." It's really easy to make fun of the psychotrendiness of I-statements ("When you say that you want to break up with me it makes me feel that you are an asshole"), but it's hard to object to the idea of taking responsibility for your own feelings.

"Really?" Will asks. "Tell me about it."

While I tell him about it he nods encouragingly from his place on the other side of some emotional finish line, as if saying, "Come on, come on, I know you can do it."

"I appreciate your honesty," he says when I'm done, and it's not until I'm driving home that I realize he never admitted he made a mistake.

I see Will two more times. I keep going because first of all, I feel lousy, and second of all, I think we share the same story: the story that midlife is the time to take the spiritual journey of integrating the self. During our fourth session it becomes clear that I don't want Will as my fellow traveler. He spent most of the session telling me his personal theory of the inner child. How there were four different types of inner child. (Silently I think, "you really should be saying inner children.") How Fellini understood this (Fellini?), and made "Juliet of the Spirits" to explore the inner child. How the notion of the inner child has been corrupted by popularizers like Bradshaw and weekend workshops promising to "get you in touch" with your inner child. "That's absurd," Will said, "you don't get in touch with your inner child: *your inner child gets in touch with you.*" He talked and talked and talked. After a while I realized that this was a lecture that had nothing to do with me. Doesn't he notice that he's losing me?

While he's talking I'm aware that this is a bad session. On the way home I realize this is such a bad session I'll have to tell him about it next time. Once I'm home I realize—triumphantly!—that there doesn't have to be a next time. I leave Will a message on his answering machine, canceling our next appointment and terminating therapy. "Things just aren't working out," I say, trying to be firm but tactful. "This therapy doesn't feel useful."

I feel relieved. My pattern has been to stay with men who are not good for me months, years too long, using all my creative energy to turn not okay into okay. Saying good-bye after four weeks is progress.

I'M NOT SURPRISED when Will calls me back. Therapists are very insistent that you handle what they call "termination" properly. "I'd like to see you to talk this over," he says. "You won't have to pay, but I'd like to understand what's going on."

It's still March, I'm still feeling shitty, and the last thing I want to do is drive over to Somerville and tell Will why I don't want to see him anymore. But ducking this kind of confrontation is one of those weasely little acts of avoidance that add to depression.

I'm not looking forward to our conversation because I know how easily therapists can fit anything into their system. You want to leave therapy, and say it's because I'm not the right therapist for you? *Obviously you're avoiding something and should stay until we find out what issues you want to run away from.*

Will doesn't make that easy maneuver. He listens respectfully while I tell him that I feel emotionally cut off from myself in his presence and I don't think we're having a conversation, I think he's talking at me.

"You seem to have thought this through carefully. I was wondering if you might be avoiding something that had come up in therapy, but I don't think you are. You seem grounded and convincing."

Maybe he listens better than I thought.

"But I still think we should work together," he says.

It's like trying to get rid of a bad date. He hasn't heard anything I've said.

I start my story all over again, but Will interrupts me after a few minutes. This time he gets it. He's pissed.

"Well," he says, putting his notepad down, "I guess we've processed this as much as we need to."

"I think it's time to say good-bye," I say, as we wrestle over who's going to define what's happening. We shake hands and I leave.

I WALK OUT INTO Davis Square and decide to go over to Au Bon Pain. I feel like celebrating. Assignment: *order a cafe latte.*

I start thinking about my conversations with Will and I start to wonder: who says that a bookmark is such a bad thing to get? You can connect to your father through books, you can flirt, you can develop your femininity and sexuality through reading.

*W*HEN I WAS a kid, orbiting around my father like a devoted small planet, I did not experience him as remote or unavailable. He was away maybe a week a month on a business trip, but that absence only made his return more thrilling. On the day of his return my mother would start hovering by the living room windows an hour or so before his expected arrival time, "just in case he's early," brushing back the gauzy curtains and peering out at every pair of headlights that swept up the street, turning back to her book or her puzzle when the headlights did not turn in at our driveway.

When we heard the reassuring throaty rumble of my father's Pontiac heading toward the garage we went to the kitchen to greet him. He'd come in the back door, wearing his fedora and grey overcoat and carrying his briefcase, his clothes chilly in winter. When he would hug me his cheek felt cold against mine, and somehow that was thrilling, as if he had brought into our house all the drama and the life the outside world had to offer.

After supper I might pester him to let me help him with filing, or to go over my homework with me. School was our bond, and he always said yes. Often he'd suggest books for me to read, and we'd have a private tutorial. When I was nine or ten he started me on Dickens, his favorite novelist. We began with *David Copperfield* and went on to *Oliver Twist, A Tale of Two Cities, Hard Times,* and *Dombey and Son.* My father had a complete set of Dickens from his Harvard days, one of his few prized possessions, and he would let me use these editions. He'd tell me what some of his favorite lines were—he knew them by heart—and then I'd memorize them too, like those stirring words of Sydney Carton, about to go to the guillotine in his friend's place: "It is a far, far better thing I do than I have ever done, and a far, far better rest I go to than I have ever known." What sacrifice! What honor! What poetry! Or how about the beginning to *A Tale of Two Cities*, filled with those wonderful phrases my father said were paradoxes: "It was the best of times, it was the worst of times."

The names and quirks of Dickens's characters became part of my childhood repertoire, my way of seeing the world, inherited from my father: there was the always hopeful and engagingly irresponsible Mr. Micawber, sponging off David while chanting his "Something will turn up" mantra; there was the obsequious, hand-wringing Uriah Heep, that hideous snake; the mysterious convict Magwitch, who scared me until my father, reassuringly, told me "He just wants to make amends for a great wrong, he's really very human." I never read *Bleak House* in childhood—perhaps my father thought it was too long, or too sad—I'd wait until college to discover that great novel where the fog rolls through London, separating people from each other and hiding the past.

My father also introduced me to stirring romantic tales of derring-do— *The Count of Monte Cristo, The Thirty-Nine Steps, The Prisoner of Zenda*— and I liked nothing better than to settle down with a six-hundred-page romance, eager to enter the world of suffering and triumphant heroes, evil villains, and exalted love.

When I was ten I received *The Complete Sherlock Holmes* for Christmas, and, as with all books, it somehow wasn't complete until I shared it with my father. I loved Conan Doyle even more than Dickens and read and reread his works obsessively for the next two or three years. I loved the language and I loved the reassuring formula of each story—in the beginning, all was chaos and confusion, but when Holmes applied his superior intellect, discovering and unraveling clues others had missed, the truth would be revealed. And throughout each story was this forward-going energy, what Holmes called "the pleasures of the chase"—what could be more exciting than being on the track of something, moving closer and closer to a revelation?

After several readings I developed a game I played with my father. He would read me one sentence from the twelve-hundred-page collection ("Just one, Dad, I know I can do this") and I would tell him exactly what story it came from. We would play this game in the living room, now a playroom as he sat gravely in his chair, adjusting his glasses and opening my copy of *The Complete Sherlock Holmes* while I hopped excitedly about the room, as full of beans as a show-offy four-year-old.

" 'Of all these varied cases, however, I cannot recall any which presented more singular features than that which was associated with the well-known Surrey family of the Roylotts of Stoke Moran,' " he would read.

"Come on, Dad, that's too easy, don't read me anything with a name in it. 'The Adventure of the Speckled Band,' of course."

"All right, young lady, you asked for it. How about 'I don't know what there was about that face, Mr. Holmes, but it seemed to send a chill right down my back.' "

" 'The Yellow Face.' Still too easy! Another one!"

" 'His head was horribly mutilated by an expanding revolver bullet, but no weapon of any sort was to be found in the room.' "

" 'The Adventure of the Empty House!' "

"Right," he'd say, impressed, I used to think, in spite of himself. Occasionally he'd throw in a real stinker, just to give me my comeuppance:

" 'It was indeed like old times when, at that hour, I found myself seated beside him in a hansom, my revolver in my pocket, and the thrill of adventure in my heart.' "

"No fair, Dad, that could be from any story at all."

"I thought you were supposed to be the expert," he said, peering over his glasses, a smile around his eyes.

"Come on. Play fair."

"One more. 'I think that I am as strong-nerved as my neighbors, but I was shaken by what I saw.'"

"'The Adventure of the Creeping Man.' Another!"

"That's it for today," he said, handing me back the book, and I took it off to my room to savor and reread.

Yes, it's true that my father was not able to "mirror" my developing sexuality. I doubt that many Irish Catholic men in the 1950s could have done so very well. He barely looked at me when I was primping in front of him for my first dance at Mr. Anderson's ballroom dancing school, wearing a scratchy new petticoat, a black taffeta skirt, a ruffly blouse, and my first stockings, held up by my first garter belt. "Take a look, Norb," my mother said, standing behind me in the bedroom, while my father worked at his card table. I waited, breathless. Would he say I looked pretty? My father glanced at me. "Isn't she a little young to be wearing stockings?" he asked.

But there's the contradictory evidence of the books. Tell me that *A Tale of Two Cities* isn't sexy! I used to daydream about Sidney Carton. Sometimes I'd be the hero in my daydreams, wielding the sword, but sometimes I'd be the heroine, and the hero would kneel at my feet, overwhelmed with desire. And the Sherlock Holmes game we developed—which took me out of the book and into the world in another way—allowed me to play with my book-loving father, and to flirt with him as well. I got to prance and crow and have his undivided attention, always possible when a book was the medium of exchange.

And who says that fathers have to give you everything? Some things you have to give to yourself.

$\mathcal{W}$HILE I'M WALKING to the car I keep thinking about the sexiness of books and reading. And even more, what about the incredible eroticism of the bookmark! What is it for, but to mark your place when you put the book down, as you would when you're about to make love? One of the most passionate moments in literature occurs in Dante's *Inferno*, when we hear the story of the adulterous lovers Paolo and Francesca. Paolo tells Dante that they were reading together in the garden when they looked into each other's eyes and . . . then that great understated line,

And that day we read no further.

I'm sure Paolo and Francesca used a bookmark—probably an ornate leather one embroidered with roses.

THE BOOKMARK or the rose? A false dichotomy. There's no reason why a girl can't have both.

Reading Dickens to My Father

It is not difference that separates us so much as silence.
— AUDRE LORDE, *The Cancer Journals*

MY FATHER DIED WHEN I WAS THIRTY—old enough to have been an adult, but still, in relation to him, a child.

I hadn't thought that parents could really die. None of my friends' parents had; I was the first to lose one (an odd verb, "lose," as if I had been careless). Certainly my father could not die; in his quiet way, he held the family together, the one who tried to repair and reweave the ruptures my mother's fears and anger caused, as when he brought my brother-in-law Warren into the family. And as when he wrote me during my year in England when my mother was silent.

It was my father who took on Quinlan family responsibilities, executor of the wills of my mother's sisters Geraldine and Marion, sitting at his card table in the evenings pecking out dozens, hundreds of letters to funeral homes and Medicare and creditors, trying to tidy things up, sending more letters (putting in four sheets of carbon paper) to the surviving Quinlan sisters (suspiciously peering over his shoulder from California and New Jersey and Washington), keeping Margaret and Dorothy and Ruth apprised of financial matters, working hard, against tremendous odds, to keep harmony in the Quinlan family too.

He was the stable center of the family, the one we could count on, the one the three of us turned to when we had something difficult to discuss. He had never had a serious physical illness. He was sixty-nine, but he had black hair still and played golf and did not seem old. I thought he was immortal.

THROUGHOUT THE early spring of 1976 he had been complaining of weakness and shortness of breath, and early in April was hospitalized for tests and X-rays. I drove up for the weekend to visit my father at Sancta Maria,

Belmont's small hospital, and I was relieved to find that the doctors had uncovered nothing. "What a way to get me up here for my birthday," I teased
him, and he smiled and said maybe it was a little extreme, but hadn't it
worked?

There was fluid in his chest, which they had drained, but no apparent
source. He went home and began his own regime of recovery, walking every
day to regain his strength. He would walk back and forth in our small back
yard, a hundred, two hundred times, traversing and re-traversing the same
thirty feet. "Why doesn't he go for a walk?" I asked my mother, looking
out the kitchen window at my pacing father, obscurely angry at him for
subjecting me to this view of his frailty.

"I don't know," she said, "he just prefers to be here."

I was in my first year of teaching at Dickinson, just having made the
break from home. I had wept all the way from Boston to Poughkeepsie when
I moved to Carlisle over the summer, but once there, I adjusted quickly,
throwing myself into the small-town scene—going to auctions, taking
square dance lessons, having breakfast at Fay's Country Kitchen. A new
life was beginning for me, and I gave my father's health little thought, once
I returned to Carlisle.

One Sunday afternoon in May the phone rang. It was my father calling
me, and I was alarmed. My father never originated phone calls—letters were
his form of communication to me. Did he have bad news? Had his condition
worsened?

"Dad, is something wrong?"

I remember very little of this phone call. "I'm just calling to get you
up to date," I think he said. "Nothing's wrong." He told me about his exercise plan—he thought he might leave his rounds in the back yard and
start walking up to church and back—and he said he'd be seeing the doctor
again on Wednesday. "I think the walking is helping," he said. "I feel a little
stronger."

I kept feeling that he wanted me to ask him something: he was looking
for a sign from me that I was ready to take the conversation deeper. To give
him room to speak some truth I didn't want—or wasn't ready—to hear. Any
opening he gave me—even a tiny crack—I puttied and plastered up so fast
that the wall between me and his death stayed thick and strong.

"Your mother is a little worried," he might have said. "Well, you know
how she is," I would have said, "always making mountains out of molehills."
The simple question "Are you worried too?" was years beyond my reach.

If his dying had been different, I wouldn't be looking back at this phone call, thinking that I failed him, wishing I'd been braver. That's what dying can do to a life—it gives an end, and then it's very hard to not read the whole life in terms of the way it ended. Every form of communication we had was about to break down, and I can't help reading that Sunday call in light of what happened later.

TWO WEEKS LATER, his doctor had checked him into Mass General for exploratory surgery. There was fluid in his chest, but no apparent cause. My classes were just over and I was preparing for a visit from a friend from England. "You don't have to come up," my mother said, "it's probably nothing, you were just up here in April," and I seized this reprieve. I would stay in Carlisle, host my friend, and wait for word.

Driving to Harrisburg the night before his surgery to pick up Judith, I mustered up my courage to call him at the hospital—I'd been postponing it all day. It was eight-thirty or so, and I called from the pay phone outside the train station. A nurse answered. I wanted to speak to my father, I said. The phones were turned off, she said. I wouldn't be able to reach him before his surgery.

I had no idea that hospitals turned phones off in patients' rooms. "I really need to talk to him," I said.

"You can call tomorrow night," she said. "I'm sure he'll be glad to talk with you then."

When I called the next day, I could only talk with my mother. My father was not able to speak.

When I saw him two days later in the Intensive Care Unit at Mass General, entwined with tubes and surrounded by blinking machines, a tube entering his throat from a machine that did his breathing for him, I had knowledge that had been withheld from him because of my mother's wishes: I knew that the surgeon had discovered terminal lung cancer and that if he recovered from surgery, he had less than six months to live. "We won't tell him this," my mother said, "we just need to tell him that he's going to get better."

I took his hand. "Dad, I just want you to know how much I love you," I managed, and he nodded a little and squeezed my hand back. "I'm sorry it took me so long to get here," I said, and he shook his head, as if to say that I was here now, and that was all that mattered.

"Guess who's ahead in the Masters, Norb," my mother said. The whole family, except for me, were rabid golfers. He looked inquiringly. "Fuzzy!" she said. "Your favorite dark horse," and he nodded again, and listened to my mother, brother, and sister talk about golf. I could tell he wanted to throw something in, but he couldn't—they'd given him a tracheotomy so the oxygen could go right into his remaining lung, and that cut off his voice.

I OFTEN ASK myself just what it was about his dying that was so terrible, trying to put the feelings I couldn't name then into words. What was it that stunned all of us so that it took my mother ten years to put up a headstone, and thirteen years for me to begin to grieve?

I think it was the combination of silence and avoidance, even more than his physical suffering and the pain of our loss. We had to play a charade in front of him—our mother wanted this, and we deferred to her. More than once I thought of mutiny: I would come into the ICU by myself and say, "Dad, everybody's lying to you." But part of me also wanted to pretend that he was going to get better, come home, be well again. My father, who I'm sure ultimately knew the truth, could not interrupt because he could not speak, and was too weak, or drugged, or disoriented, to write. Or perhaps he could not interrupt because we were not inventive or attentive enough to imagine ways for a dying, voiceless man to communicate—a board with magnetic letters? a code, with nods and blinks to signify letters? Recently I read a memoir called *The Diving Bell and the Butterfly* that was blinked out, coded letter by letter, by a narrator paralyzed except for one eyelid, his urge for expression was that strong. We probably could have done more, had we not been afraid of what he might ask or say.

When we visited my father I knew that he had hundreds and thousands of words imprisoned inside him, wanting to get out, but we couldn't, together, find the way to pick the lock. And then after a while, he withdrew into himself. *What was the point?* he must have thought.

I MOVED BACK to Boston for the summer, back to my childhood bedroom with the green wallpaper, and I used my father's Pontiac to drive my mother back and forth to Mass General every day. Often my brother and sister would meet us there; sometimes it would be just the two of us. In those days—long before hospice and palliative care—the ICU had strict visiting rules. You could visit for ten minutes on the hour, and then you had to leave; you could wait for fifty minutes and come in again for another ten, and so forth, all day, if you wished. But only ten minutes at a time: then the nurses would shoo you out, and you'd sit on the long wooden benches outside the unit, watching the wall clock until it was time to go in again.

ICUs are terrible environments, and people are only supposed to spend a few days there. After my father had been there for three weeks, getting weaker from infections and finally kidney failure and then the daily strain of dialysis, he seemed to withdraw more and more into himself, to be less and less able to interact with us with his nods and smiles and attempts at handwritten notes. "Sometimes people become psychotic when they stay in ICUs too long," a doctor friend told me a few years ago. "How long is too long?" I asked. "Anything over two weeks." That didn't happen to my father, but I'm sure that as we moved into week four and five in the ICU my father, knowing he was dying but unable to speak, became very depressed. Meanwhile we kept telling him he'd be coming home soon, putting on our act.

ONE DAY IN mid-June, his fifth week in the ICU, I discovered it was possible to break the visiting rules. It was a Friday morning, and I was stopping by MGH on my way to Washington, to spend a weekend with my new and luscious boyfriend. This was the first time I'd been alone with my father, and I was a little scared. I sat by his bed and asked if he wanted to listen to the portable radio my mother had brought him. He didn't respond, and so I turned it on to WCRB, the classical station. All of a sudden his arm, swathed in IVs, arose and sent the radio smashing to the floor. The plastic case broke and batteries rolled in all directions.

I had never in my life seen my father angry. He was the one who calmed my mother down; it was scary to witness this mute eloquent action.

When my father had tried to communicate in writing it was often hard to read his handwriting—he could barely hold a pencil, and his hand shook with effort so the letters didn't make sense. Often we couldn't translate, leaving him frustrated and then resigned.

Smashing the radio meant *This is bullshit. I'm dying and you want me to listen to the radio? I don't care what's on the radio.*

"Try to write, Dad," I said, giving him a pencil and holding the clipboard out toward him. He took the pencil and labored, it seemed, for minutes, then fell back exhausted. I looked at the clipboard. Written there in large, shaky letters was only one word I had no trouble reading.

"I know, Dad, you want to go home."

He nodded and closed his eyes. I could see what he was seeing: he'd be in his hospital bed at 28 Lewis Road—it would be in the living room, I could see that—and we'd be around him, the sun coming in the front windows, a nurse hovering in the background just in case, and he'd still be sick and dying but he'd be content and we would all feel safe.

It seemed like such a simple request, for a dying man to go home, to be surrounded with his family and familiar things. But in 1976 there was no way for him to go home.

I felt this was a plea just from him to me: he wanted me to help him go home, and there was nothing I could do. He was too sick to go home: they wouldn't release him, we'd already asked. I wanted to rescue him, and I couldn't.

"I want you to come home too, Dad." I didn't want to say anything that wasn't true. "I wish I could get you out of here." He looked at me, acknowledging the desire, the impossibility.

Then I looked at the clock. It was 10:25. My ten minutes had been up at 10:10. "I guess they're not kicking me out today, Dad." He raised his hand and gestured toward the night stand. The two books he'd brought to the hospital were lying there, *The Imitation of Christ* and *Bleak House*. Later I'd understand why this odd pairing: both were stories about giving meaning to suffering and offering, after great pain, the promise of redemption.

"You want me to read to you, Dad?"

Another nod. I picked up *Bleak House*. "Remember when we used to read Dickens together, Dad? . . . *It is a far, far better thing I do than I have ever done. . . . It is a far, far better death I go to than I have ever known.*"

He looked at me, little shake of his head.

Oh. "*It is a far, far better rest I go to than I have ever known.*"

A nod. Maybe a little smile, acknowledging my slip.

𝓘 SAT BY HIS bed and read *Bleak House* for a long time. Nurses would stop by, take his vital signs, and leave. Once the attending physician came by and talked with him respectfully, telling him it would be time for dialysis in a while and calling him "Mr. O'Brien," which pleased me. Minutes went by, and I saw that the whole ICU staff had put me and my father in a separate category. They were shooing other visitors out after their ten minutes, but for us they were throwing that ten-minute rule out the window. They knew how sick and alone he was and that he did not have long to live and they wanted me to stay.

When the orderlies came to wheel him away for his dialysis, they told me I could stay with him if I wanted to, and so I did. After an hour we came back to the ICU, and he slept awhile and I went off to get lunch at the cafeteria and got ready to say good-bye. It was 1:30 by then, and I needed to get on the road.

Part of me wanted to stay. This time with my father was getting to seem almost normal; I was getting used to the IVs and the machines, and even to the sight of the metal tracheotomy fastener attached to his throat and the purplish bruises on his arms and legs where the nurses had hunted for veins. I'd read a little, then he'd doze and I'd hold his hand, and then he'd wake up and I'd read some more. I felt, for the first time since he entered the hospital, that he was my father again.

The only thing was, I had this boyfriend waiting for me in Washington, and it was a nine-hour drive. I felt ashamed of how much I wanted to leave the hospital and my dying father, even in the midst of this island of attachment we had made.

Several times that afternoon I told him that I'd be leaving soon, I had a long drive ahead, and start to say good-bye. And he would shake his head and grip my hand as hard as he could and then I would sit down and tell him okay, I didn't have to leave just yet, and he would lie back and I would pick up *Bleak House,* that novel of family connection lost for so long in the fog, but finally remade. I stayed all through the afternoon and into the evening, even though it was hard to tell what time it was because we were curtained off and away from the light. I read through a change of shift and several cycles of other visitors, holding my father's hand while he slept, feeling privileged to be there and impatient to leave. I stayed until 8:00 and all visiting hours were over for the night, and the nurses finally came by to tell me I'd have to leave.

I kissed my father good-bye and drove through the night, down 95 to Washington, pulling in around five in the morning. I got into bed with my sleepy boyfriend and tried to forget where I had come from.

WHEN I GOT back I didn't tell my mother about my discovery that you could break the ICU rules and stay all day—I couldn't bear to do it again. So we resumed our ten minutes on, fifty minutes off, until one day—in the middle of his sixth week in the ICU—doctors blessedly made a decision for us and took him off dialysis and put him in a private room, where he would die within a few days.

My mother got in touch with her estranged sister Ruth, who came for the weekend with my uncle Norman, and I remember us all crowding into my father's room—my mother, Kevin, Maureen, Ruth, Norman, and me. All the words of good-bye were unsaid, except this time things felt different; I remember a kind of lightness in the air, which came from my father. He wasn't angry, he wasn't depressed. He was nodding and smiling and responding to everyone in the room. No matter what we said, he'd give each one of us an understanding and peaceful look, as if he knew all the words that were below the surface, the ones we couldn't say, and he forgave us for not being able to say them, he forgave us all.

At four o'clock in the morning we got the call from the hospital. The next time we saw my father he was lying in a coffin at the funeral home, rosary beads entwined in his hands. All the folks from Our Lady of Mercy were saying what a good job the funeral director had done, and how life-like Norb looked, because that's what the Irish always say at wakes. I was wearing a black dress I had just bought at Filene's, and the only thing I remember is that I couldn't cry. Not during the wake, or the funeral, or the next thirteen years.

I went back to Carlisle in August and told everyone I was fine. I didn't think about my father at all, except fleeting memories that I chased away, because I couldn't see his life anymore: all I could see was his dying, and the dreadful silence, and if I thought about it too much the guilt for abandoning him welled up and I couldn't bear it. *One day, that's all you gave him out of six weeks. One day. And even then you kept wanting to leave.*

I THINK ALL four of us, in different ways, couldn't bear thinking about what happened; that was why we didn't talk about my father much, and why it took my mother almost ten years to put up the headstone. I was just as glad it took her that long, because then I didn't have to remember. When my brother would mention my father when saying Grace on holidays, I'd get impatient. "And we all miss Dad," Kevin would say, "and wish he could be here with us," and I'd be thinking *Hurry up, just get through this please, I don't want to feel anything.*

*A*FTER MY MOTHER put up the headstone, with her name engraved below my father's, I avoided visiting the cemetery for three years. It wasn't until I was about to fly off to Ireland for the year that I could bring myself to visit the grave and tell my father how sorry I was for abandoning him, and how much I missed him, and let myself begin to cry.

It shouldn't be the case that someone's dying can wipe out the memory of their life, but that, for the longest time, was what happened, and so I lost my father twice. If we could have spoken and said good-bye, I think things would have been different—but his silence made his suffering seem immense and unimaginable, and since I couldn't stop thinking about it once I started, I didn't let myself start.

I made a pledge to him, years later, that I would never again abandon the people I loved if they were sick or dying because I was afraid, and I could see him nodding and believing me, and both of us thinking that well, then, his dying had been of some use, because it had changed the way I would be next time.

Family Gathering

MY SISTER MAUREEN CALLS ME early one weekday morning. "Sharon," she says, her voice tired and anxious, "could you come and stay with me? I'm not doing too well."

"What's wrong?"

"I've been waking up with panic the last three nights. I've been trying to go down in my meds again. Big mistake. I'd rather not be alone right now."

"Of course I'll come."

WHEN I GET there, Maureen is lying on the couch, her face thin and drawn, wrapped in her favorite blanket.

"I'm having nausea and my blood pressure is way high," she says. "Of course, I go right to the brain tumor. The MRI. The tube. They are going to have to kill me to get me in the tube. Deep breathing? For*get* it."

"Maureen, no one is talking about the tube. The brain tumor—that's jumping the gun."

"Sharon," she says, "I'm afraid you're looking at your *mother*."

"We're lucky we only have chronic anxiety and depression," I tell Maureen. "We could have ended up in the mental hospital."

"The back ward." The back ward is my sister's mental-health equivalent of the MRI.

I'm lying on the other couch, beginning to savor the irony. The little sister has recovered enough from the panic her move to Boston has caused to take care of her big sister. The blind leading the blind.

Maureen has all her health aids spread out on the coffee table—her Prozac, her Zantac (she has the family curse of Irritable Bowel), her Pepsi,

313

her Tums. She's clutching a heating pad (for the IB) and has the TV clicker close by.

By now I've set up shop too. My light box is in the kitchen, and I've got my own blanket, pillow, and the Sunday *Times* crossword puzzle, along with a batch of videos (all comedies). No Zantac: so far I've escaped the Curse.

"Did Kevin call?" I ask.

"He just checked in an hour ago, wanted to see how we were doing, wanted to know if we needed takeout. He'll stop by later."

"How about some tea and an English muffin for right now?" I ask her. "With honey?"

"Perfecto mundo," she says, and I go off to make tea.

The outside door opens and my nephew David comes into the room, carrying wood for the fire.

"So Sharon, are you babysitting my mom?" he asks.

David is my sister's oldest son. He has suffered from schizophrenia since he was a teenager. He's been hospitalized several times and is, like us, just beginning to accept his need to take medication.

"Just taking over from you," I say. David has slept at my sister's for two nights, to keep her company. He puts the wood on the fire and the flames revive.

"How's your book on depression going?" David asks.

"Not too bad," I say. "I keep getting new material, though."

"This family is good for that," he says.

"Want some tea?" I ask.

"Okay."

SOON WE'RE ALL sitting in the living room, watching the fire, sipping our tea and eating our muffins, comfortably quiet. Maureen pulls the blanket up around her and snuggles back into the couch. The fire crackles, and David gets up to put on another log.

"You know what?" my sister says. "At a time like this, it's great to have family around for support."

Somehow that seems like just the right thing to say.

Elephant Skin

YESTERDAY AFTERNOON THE PHONE RANG around four. "Sharon?" a man's voice asked. "This is Lou."

Lou had put a personal ad in the *Globe* and I had answered it. It's early May, the days are lengthening, the dogwoods and magnolias blooming, and I'm cheering up. I'm feeling more presentable, and I started to think it might be fun to have a boyfriend. (An odd word for a woman in her fifties to be using, but there's really no other. "Lover" sounds too strenuous and vaguely French.) I liked Lou's self-description—late forties, humor is essential in a relationship, loves the outdoors, exploring spiritual matters, has a sailboat. He had called me right away, so I knew he was interested.

We talk, and it's a little awkward at first, but I'm good at putting people at ease and soon things are flowing. Pretty soon I can see us together on the sailboat some weekend soon. I don't need to fall in love with this man: I'm leaving Boston this summer anyway, which actually made it easier for me to call him up. It removed that pathetic feeling of "please pick me!" This way, maybe we can just have a good time. And if things develop? Carlisle isn't *that* far away.

"So I'm off to play tennis in a few minutes," I tell Lou.

"Tennis, I used to play tennis," he says, "but I've got this arthritis in my elbow so I gave it up."

"Well, that's happening to all of us now. It's where we are in our lives." I want Lou to feel better about getting older.

There's a silence.

"How old are you?" Lou asks abruptly. Something's happened to his tone. It's not expansive anymore. His words are no longer floating on a stream toward the weekend and the sailboat. His words are clipped, and there are tiny spaces in between the monosyllables.

We're not in a conversation anymore. We're in an interview. He's interviewing me for a date.

How old are you? There are only three options for an answer: tell the truth, lie, or throw up a cloud cover, like "hey, we've made it through the word *arthritis*, let's congratulate ourselves and move on," or "I want you to guess when you see me, no one ever gets it right." But there's only one option that won't make me ashamed.

"I'm fifty-two." Silence.

"Oh," he says, and now his tone is shocked, laced with embarrassment, as if I've revealed some disgusting personal fact about myself that I should have kept silent. "Oh, really?"

"Do you have problems with that?"

"Well, I don't know. . . . I guess, I don't know."

The man has problems with it. The interview is over. He continues to speak, but he isn't there anymore.

"Well," he says, "I know you have to go to tennis. . . . So, it's been nice talking to you. You have my number, so call me if you want to, or vice versa."

"Good-bye, Lou," I say. At least I don't say "Sure," or "Good talking to you," something nice, something to let him off the hook. Later I'll wish I said "Lou, there's no way I'm calling a man who checked out as soon as he heard the words 'fifty-two,'" or "Lou, you really need therapy," but I never say things like that.

He never calls back.

*H*E WAS AN asshole," my friend Cathy says. "You wouldn't want to be with him anyway."

Right, but that's not the loss. Yes, he may be an asshole, and he may just be a guy getting through midlife the only way he knows how, looking for a younger woman because he's afraid of what's up ahead. His ad said he was forty-eight, and when I checked it again I noticed that he'd said he was only interested in women "up to forty-two." I can get angry all I want at men who write off women who are over forty, or forty-five, or fifty, whatever the cutoff point is, at all the men in their forties and fifties and sixties who think they need women who are five, ten, fifteen years younger than they are. I can think "if they only could see me, they'd change their minds." But the fact is they can't see me. I've reached the age where I seem to be invisible to men, the time when the words "fifty-two" call up their images of their mothers, and of their own deaths.

It's not the loss of Lou and his sailboat. It's the loss his silence reveals. It's the loss of my younger self.

*Y*ES, I KNOW this is cultural, and my response not appropriately feminist, but that doesn't change the way I feel. What makes it worse is feeling it's politically and spiritually incorrect to hate getting older. But I do hate it—the physical part, that is, and the way our culture makes women feel about aging.

I don't think that getting older bothered my father all that much—men do have it easier—but I know my mother hated it too, and mourned the loss of her younger beauty. When I was keeping her company during her dying, she brought out a crumpled, much-handled photograph taken when she was sixty-six, right after my Dad died. The family had gone to Florida and in the photo she's standing in the sun, wearing a pink golf skirt, her face glowing with what she called "a little color." "I looked so *young*," she said, fingering the photograph, "so young." Yes, it's all relative. I know some day I'll be looking back at photographs of me in my fifties and missing my lost youth.

It's not just aging that bothers me. I hate all the nice, euphemistic words we've invented so that the baby-boomers won't feel so bad when they hit sixty. "Older person." "Senior citizen." If anybody ever tells me I'm on an eldering journey, I'll punch them in the stomach. I even hate the words the goddess branch of the women's movement has given my generation. *Wise wommon. Crone.* I don't want to be a wommon or crone or to have a croning ceremony and I know the goddess people mean well but I can't help wishing they'd use standard spelling. A croning ceremony . . . I'd rather sit around with a group of women and trade tips on skin creams and hair coloring.

Sometimes I look in the mirror and pull the skin back behind my ears, seeing how young I look when it's tightened, wondering if I'll have a face lift and knowing I won't unless I can be sure no one will ever know and there will be no side effects, like muscle paralysis so I end up with a drooping smile, or nerve damage that will give me a facial tic. Do lapsed Irish Catholic women get punished for having plastic surgery? I think so. Then I let the skin go and the little hollows in my cheeks return.

317

When I'm doing the plow position in yoga, when you lie on your back and tip your legs up in the air and then back down over your head, I see little folds of loose skin. I'm seeing the future, the way my legs will look someday. An old woman's legs. Like my mother's legs I could see when she wore bathing suits, and later, hospital gowns. Wrinkled, drooping skin. "Elephant skin," we call it in my family, passed down the maternal line. My sister has it and now I'm getting it too. I've always been the baby of the family and I never imagined this could happen to me.

For the last year or two I've been obsessively noticing other women's legs. Who has better skin, who has worse. Then I check their faces. My face looks a lot younger than my legs, so this makes me feel better.

This year my sister turned sixty. It used to make me feel better that she was always eight years ahead of me, but now it doesn't. How can she be sixty, Kevin fifty-seven, me fifty-two? We're the kids!

In eight years I'll be sixty and then, I imagine, it's all over. Death is so much closer than it used to be: now I can see the horizon and it scares me. Because I don't have children I always imagine myself dying alone, trapped in a hospital or a nursing home, no one around who knows my story.

Once I took my freshman seminar to a nursing home—the students were going to do oral histories—and was greeted by the activities director wearing a Mickey Mouse T-shirt. "You came on a good day!" he said. "This is Mickey's birthday, and the residents are very excited. We're having a party for him at eleven, and hope you can stay." Everywhere people in wheelchairs are staring into space, wearing mouse ears. "Happy Birthday Mickey!" balloons are tied to their armrests. Is this my future? A Carlisle nursing home where I'm wheeled out to celebrate Mickey Mouse's birthday, trapped in my body and my life?

"Look," I said to my freshmen when I was driving them back in the van, "If you come back to your twenty-fifth reunion and find out I'm in Thornwald dressed like a Disney character, just come over and shoot me, okay?" They promise they will.

Last week the Supreme Court ruled that assisted suicide was unconstitutional, and I was really upset. I want to be able to get out if I need to.

I GO TO MY tennis lesson.
"Don't tense up," my teacher says. "Relax your arm."

I will relax my arm. I'll relax it brilliantly. I'll give her the most relaxed arm she's ever seen.

"You call that relaxed?" she asks. "Stop looking where the ball's going. I forbid you to look at the net."

I relax my arm. I look at the ball and not at the net. "That's it," she says.

Now that I've succeeded once I'm afraid I can't do it again. It was sheer luck. I apply myself.

"What's the hurry? Slow down. You have all the time in the world."

I don't have all the time in the world, I want to snap, but I know she is right. I have to imagine I have all the time in the world because if I rush, there's no way I can be where I am. And depression always comes when I want to be elsewhere.

I have to be here, living in this fifty-two-year-old body (looks fifty-one!), with c my wrinkling skin and my tennis elbow and my bad serve and my chemically dependent hair. Because if I'm not, I'll be invisible to myself, and that'll *really* make me depressed.

"Put ice on the elbow when you go home," my teacher says.

𝒲HEN I GET home I put ice on my elbow and call up Maureen. We plan a middle-aged sisters' evening—a bite to eat, as my mother would say, a video, early bedtime, me snuggled with a good book and my cat, who by now has forgiven me for moving to Cambridge.

I'm looking forward to it.

Class of 1927

IT'S EARLY JUNE and the world is beginning to stir into life after a cold and rainy spring. The flowers are all two weeks late, but now they're making up for lost time. The locust trees on my street are dripping their white blossoms like confetti, and the days are getting longer and longer. Twilight now lasts until eight-thirty: we're edging toward the summer solstice.

I'm preparing to move back to Carlisle—gathering boxes, hiring movers (no U-Haul this time), getting the gas turned off and the lights turned on.

I used to think that there was something wrong with having the same job at the same small college in the same small town for thirty or forty years, something vaguely . . . embarrassing? A little too "Good-bye, Ms. Chips"? Now I'm telling myself a new story, that it's not a bad thing, when you retire, to have friends and colleagues who've known you for decades applauding while you try not to cry at the last faculty meeting you'll ever attend. It's a *good* thing.

I'm not going to escape aging and death by moving, although I don't need to take up the Cumberland Valley Memorial Gardens on their offer either. My sister and I have made a pact—probably cremation, and the same memorial site to make it easier for our family to find us; we'll invite Kevin to come with us.

As the early summer light has increased my spirits have lightened as well. I've stopped thinking about "cures" for depression; I'm managing it better, and I'm grateful, as I've told my friends in Wellness, that—at the moment—I'm doing okay. I've grown attached to my shiny bright Cambridge apartment; my walk into Harvard Square has become familiar, and it's great to call up my friends and family without having to use the 617 area code, the way I do when I'm in Carlisle. I've stuck it out and I've become comfortable here, and some day, if the time is right, I could make a home here. But right now my home is back in central Pennsylvania, right next to those comforting four-way stop signs. It won't be hard to get there—take Concord Ave to the Fresh Pond rotary, spin off to Route 2, then 128, then the Mass Pike to 84 (try to avoid Hartford at rush hour), then pick up 81.

Before I leave Cambridge, though, there's something I have to do: attend my father's seventieth Harvard reunion. Normally the last official reunion is the sixty-fifth, but the thirty or so feisty remaining members of the class of '27 said they wanted a seventieth. Nineteen of them will be attending. I'm going in my father's place.

THE DAY STARTS with lunch at the Faculty Club. I'm surprised by the number of people here: there must be fifty or sixty, half of them '27 alumni, the rest wives and widows and children and grandchildren. Most men arrive in wheelchairs and walkers and on the arms of their children. Others walk in under their own steam, slowly but steadily.

I'm seated next to Guernsey Camp, a courtly man with a crisp white beard, wearing an immaculate tan linen suit, starched blue shirt, and maroon Harvard tie dotted with little *Veritas* emblems. On his other side is another '27 daughter.

"A thorn between two roses," Guernsey says. "Would you like some Chardonnay, my dears?" he asks, pointing to the open bar.

"Let me get them," I say.

"No, absolutely not, allow me."

Guernsey gets up and walks slowly to the bar, coming back balancing two glasses of yellow-gold wine. He sets them down in front of us and we clink glasses all around the table.

"To the members of the class who are not here," he says, and we drink to them, and then a stylish elderly lady with blonde tinted hair wearing perfect makeup and a brave pink suit adds another toast, "And to those who are here," and someone's child says "Hear, hear!" and we then drink to the living. "And to our table in particular!" I offer, holding up my glass, and we all clink again.

The university chaplain gives the blessing before we eat, including the "living and the dead" in his prayer. I'm pleased he uses the word "dead" instead of "those who have passed on" or some other euphemism. "And yet," he goes on, "as long as even one of you is living, the whole class of 1927 is alive in memory." The chaplain pauses and the room is quiet.

"To what do the nineteen of you owe your longevity?" the chaplain asks.

"Time," somebody says.

*L*ATER THAT DAY we're in a Harvard classroom watching a 16-millimeter film some classmate made at the 1937 reunion, sixty years ago. I stand behind the viewers watching turtle-backed elderly men watch their young selves on the flickering screen, imagining the tears in their eyes as they see themselves raising beer glasses to the camera.

"Who are those men?" asks the pink-suited lady, pointing toward a carousing group of thirty-odds on the old black-and-white film.

"Damned if I know," answers a crackly voice. "Never seen 'em before in my life."

*T*HE NEXT DAY we go on a bus trip to Salem and Marblehead. I'm sitting with Guernsey Camp, now my escort. He's great company. Across the aisle is the pink-suited lady, today wearing turquoise linen. She's holding the blue-veined hand of a '27 alum. They got married three years ago, she tells me, when she was eighty-seven and he was ninety. "It's never too late!" she says, looking at my ringless left hand. They've smuggled a bottle of champagne and some plastic glasses onto the bus. At the first rest stop they give glasses to Guernsey and me and pour the champagne. The turquoise lady raises her glass in one hand, still holding her husband's hand in the other. We raise our glasses.

"To our next reunion," she says. "To the seventy-fifth!"

"To the seventy-fifth!" we echo.

PART THREE *The Emigrant Irish*

Like oil lamps, we put them out the back—

of our houses, of our minds. We had lights
better than, newer than and then

a time came, this time and now
we need them. Their dread, makeshift example:

they would have thrived on our necessities.
What they survived we could not even live.
By their lights now it is time to
imagine how they stood there, what they stood with,
that their possessions may become our power:

Cardboard. Iron. Their hardships parceled in them.
Patience. Fortitude. Long-suffering
in the bruise-colored dusk of the New World.

And all the old songs. And nothing to lose.

— EAVAN BOLAND, "The Emigrant Irish"

Remember Skibbereen

Oh! father dear, the day may come when in answer to the call,
Each Irishman, with feeling stern, will rally one and all,
I'll be the man to lead the van beneath the flag of green,
When loud and high we'll raise the cry—"Remember Skibbereen."
—"Dear Old Skibbereen"

DRIVING IN IRELAND is much worse than I remembered it. It's not the driving on the left—I got used to that driving a car here for a year, and even the roundabouts non-Irish drivers dread aren't too scary since I've been retrained as a Boston driver. It's the combination of too many new cars on roads that won't hold them and the Irish driver's fondness for risk, passing on two-lane roads in heavy traffic and speeding on small country roads that barely hold two cars. It's the Celtic Tiger superimposed on nineteenth-century Ireland—hundreds of thousands of new cars, Peugeots and Mercedes and bulky Lexus SUVs, churning down roads made by cattle, filled with impatient drivers who seem to want, in the American sense, to "make time."

By the time I pick up my car at Cork Airport I'm really dragging. It's four in the afternoon and I haven't slept in more than twenty-four hours. Aer Lingus has lifted me over five time zones and I've lost the five hours I won't get back until my return flight, which will leave Dublin around 1:00 and send me westward into an endless afternoon.

The main road takes me through a succession of West Cork towns—Bandon, Clonakilty, Ross Carbery, Leap. I'm headed for Skibbereen.

I LEFT THE States on August 15, 2001, four years almost to the day after I returned to Carlisle from Boston. I chose the Feast of the Assumption for departure because it's the Holy Day of Obligation when Mary ascended into heaven, a good day for flying. I called my friends Niall and Mary, setting up a plan to meet them in Dublin; reserved a bed and breakfast in Skibbereen, called the cat-sitter, packed my bag, and set off for the airport, thinking all the time *if I were depressed I'd never be doing this, not in a million years.*

*T*HIS IS MY FIRST big trip in a long time. I've been spending the last four years settling in to my life again, staying close to home except for visits to family and friends. I no longer think about "recovery" from depression, but I've been, for the most part, in remission, so I've picked up the courage to take the trip back to Ireland I've been wanting to make for a long time. I'm returning to Skibbereen, the village in Cork where my great-grandfather Patrick O'Brien was from. No one in my family has been back here, and I want to see where we came from. I doubt that I'll be able to trace my ancestors (every third person here seems to be an O'Brien), but that doesn't really matter.

*D*URING THE FLIGHT over I got to know my seatmate, Mr. O'Donnell, a man in his eighties traveling with a knapsack full of medicines. He was born in Cobh, Cork city's harbor, "where the *Titanic* left from," he told me proudly. His boyhood bedroom was on the second floor, his parents' house on a hill, and his window "looked right out at the mooring of the *Titanic.*" He mentioned this several times during our half-hour conversation, reminding me of the half-starved Irish, boys and girls, really, who boarded the vessel, off to work in America. He lives in the States now, but was traveling back for a family reunion and wants to take his grandchildren back to Cobh and the family home. Talking to me set him traveling back in time, too, and as he spoke I could see his house and room, the boy peering out the window at the doomed ship and the sons and daughters of poor families from the west of Ireland crowding to get into steerage.

Later I realized he was not old enough to have seen the ship—he could only have viewed the empty dock slip. His parents had told him the story and now it has become his own. "You could see the *Titanic* right from your own bedroom window," his father would have said. "All those poor lads and lasses, not much older than you, heading off for America, God rest their souls."

"My father fought with Michael Collins," Mr. O'Donnell informed me, proud to be giving me history. He wanted me to visit the marker where Collins was shot. "It's not too far from Skibbereen, where you're going."

"I will go," I told him, and he settled back in his seat for a nap, mission accomplished.

*A*FTER I GET settled at my B&B I walk through Skibbereen and I'm surprised by its beauty. I don't know what I expected to find—maybe a grim nineteenth-century famine town—but Skibbereen is a prosperous, bustling town in one of the most visited parts of Ireland, West Cork, home to farms and fishing villages and, I discover, painters and artists and writers and health food stores. In addition to a slew of pubs, Skibbereen has two upscale restaurants, a pricey fish restaurant and a bistro. My first night in town I have grilled brill with sun-dried tomato vinaigrette, asparagus, and potatoes roasted in olive oil and rosemary in Kalbo's Bistro, which also has a takeout gourmet shop. When times were good, nineteenth-century Irish laborers and farmers ate up to thirty pounds of potatoes a day, all boiled in the one pot the family owned. No fruits, other vegetables, meat. No olive oil and rosemary on the potatoes. My potato helping seems huge and my appetite, never large, is screwed up with jet lag, but I eat past hunger; I don't want to be sending any potatoes back to the kitchen and the trash can.

*T*HE NEXT DAY I walk through town on my way to the Heritage Center where there's a famine exhibit. I'm going there first because I'm not ready, yet, to visit the famine graveyard where ten thousand bodies were thrown into an open pit. No funerals, no grieving, no coffins, no markers. I don't want to think about that so I worry about how I'm going to do as a famine pilgrim. Should I buy the candles they sell in the Heritage Center to honor the dead, or is the one candle I've brought from the States okay? Should I have consulted some appropriate book, perhaps in the spirituality section of a bookstore, to create a ritual to honor the dead, or have asked a friend who's a healer to help me create one?

It's strange to think about all the starved skeletons buried in Skibbereen famine graves and the mysterious Patrick O'Brien, the ancestor I never knew, and then to think about my great-niece and nephews, Dylan and Zain and Amar and Jahan, beautiful and thriving children, the Irishness watered down to one-quarter but still leading straight back here to Skibbereen. Patrick's great-great-great grandchildren are five generations away from the ten-year-old boy who left his starving country for a job in Lowell's textile mills, and because he survived the Atlantic crossing on the famine ship and lived in exile my family now has children who celebrate Chanukah and Ramadan and do not go hungry.

Remember Skibbereen. How can I remember something I never knew about? No matter how many famine accounts I read or heritage centers I visit I'll never understand what it was like to have suffered starvation or, for the lucky ones, emigration, although "emigration" itself is a kind of sanitizing word, covering up the coffin ships where one out of four would die, sometimes starving or dying of fever before even catching sight of the new world.

I can't remember this: my family and my culture gave me no stories— but I can be mindful, and maybe that's all my ancestors hope for, that I be mindful, and maybe they don't give a damn what kind of candle I brought or even if I light it. "Waste of a good candle," they might be saying to each other, "let her save it for a dark night when the lights go out in the storm." I've been a little afraid of these famine ancestors, afraid of their suffering and afraid they'll judge me harshly, me with my soft American life. As I walk through Skibbereen that all starts to drop away and what begins to take the place of the dreary guilt and narcissism is the simple feeling that I'm in the right place.

O N MY THIRD day I go to the health food store for lunch. I eat my cauliflower and kale soup in the small back room; it's quiet, because I'm early. The room starts to fill up and I realize I'm being unwelcoming, having heaped my knapsack on the other chair. I stow it under the table to make it easier for someone to sit down, aware, as I'm doing so, that if I were depressed I'd not be so welcoming: it would be too hard to talk to anyone.

"Do you mind?" A young woman approaches with her tray. She's dressed in black—jeans, sweater, coat, lipstick.

"It's for you. I just cleared it off."

She smiles and sits down and I have another moment of thankfulness that I'm not depressed: that would have made this brief encounter a torture.

Her name is Valerie. She's seventeen and she's just done her Leaving Certs—the subject exams that solely determine students' placements in third-level education (universities and technical schools). Valerie's done well on her Certs and thinks she has enough points to get the course she wants. "Kids are under a lot of pressure now," she tells me. "You can feel like you're supposed to go to university. You have to do well on the Certs. Your parents expect it."

"What if you don't do well?"

"If your parents have money you go someplace like Bruce College for a year, they get you ready for the exam and you take it again. They guarantee to raise your points but I've heard it's like jail."

After she leaves I finish reading the *Irish Times* and see an ad for Bruce College. The Leaving Certs course results were released the day I arrived, and the paper is full of articles and ads. "Maximize your academic potential." "I increased my Leaving Certs by 200 points after only a year at Bruce College!" There's even a Leaving Certs advice column, addressed to parents who want to shepherd their kids into better academic homes.

$\mathcal{F}$OR THE NEXT ten days I will hear about the Leaving Certs in one way or another almost every day. "And who spoke to you about the Leaving Certs today?" my friend Niall will ask. People are preoccupied, even obsessed, with this exam, and it's understandable—performance on the Certs is all that counts for entrance to university. No attention is paid to course grades or class rank; there are no teachers' recommendations, no essay on "turning points in my life" like those beloved of American colleges. "Let's do the numbers," they say on NPR's *Marketplace*, and that's always been the case in Irish higher education: it's just that now that Ireland's capitalist marketplace is humming, the pressure to achieve—and to accumulate points—is higher than it's ever been. Before I left the United States I'd been wondering if rates of depression in Ireland might be rising along with the strengthening economy—this is a communal society that's rapidly becoming more individualistic, and the possibility of economic success could be translated, as I think it has been in the States, into a requirement for children of the middle and upper middle class—one of the breeding grounds for depression.

I find out, over the next few days, that rates of suicide are rising among young men, that "stress" workshops are being offered all over the country, and that a new organization—Aware—has been created to provide information about depression, support, counseling, and a hotline. In the Skibbereen public library I see a poster announcing a one-day conference in Cork on "Stress and the Celtic Tiger," and I wonder what my ancestors are thinking. "No workshops on 'Stress and the Famine,'" I imagine them saying, "no depression counselors when we were starving in the back lanes, no hotlines for us on the famine ships, now we're having an economic miracle and people are not content—what is this country coming to?"

A͟FTER LUNCH I go to the West Cork Arts Center. There's an exhibit of lo-cal artists, landscapes and horses and lighthouses, a few nudes, a porce-lain Christ on the cross, and an all-black oil painting, four feet by three, with the words *Crying crying crying crying* in red covering the top half, and down near the bottom, in larger script, *Stop Fucking Crying*. Over in the corner is a portrait of Mother Theresa alarmingly near a larger abstract painting from which a wooden phallus leaps.

I strike up a conversation with Teresa, who's in charge of the museum shop, and George, who hung the show. George is irate that when people buy a painting they get to take it away immediately. No red dots signifying "purchased," just an empty space he has to fill with a backup canvas. "It's outrageous," he says. "This wouldn't happen at a proper gallery show—it's you Americans, you're on tour, in Skibbereen for an afternoon, and you have to take your painting *now*."

"Shocking," I agree. "We should make the Americans pay shipping char-ges, tell them they'll get their painting when the show is over—surface or air, it's up to them." It's happening again—in Ireland I slip into viewing Americans as "them."

George and Teresa don't notice my slip; they're too enthused with the idea and start looking up shipping charges. "Not too bad," Teresa concludes, "about thirty pounds surface, eighty pounds air."

"It might cost more to ship that painting with the penis," I point out. "You'd need a bigger crate."

"Oh God, that painting, don't get me started," George says. "I was bending down to read the title, coming up I got hit on the head with the fuckin' penis, almost knocked me out."

"It's a danger," Teresa agrees.

George goes off to fill the latest blank space created by American tourists and Teresa and I start talking. "How long have you been in Skibbereen?" she asks, and when I say "three days," already six times longer than the average American tourist, she knows there's a story. I tell her about my attempts, so far fruitless, to locate family records. She becomes invested in my search and gives me a few tips. "Good luck," she says. "Come back and tell us how you make out."

I͟'M SITTING ON A bench looking out over Schull harbor, dotted with sail-boats and yachts. I have the *Irish Times* beside me but I'm content just to sit and look around me. I see an elderly couple looking for a place to sit—

there's another bench down the way, but mine is closer and I invite them over. If I were depressed this would never have happened; I'd have looked away and prayed for them to take the other bench, knowing I couldn't bear to talk.

I'd thought they were a married couple but find out they are friends, and probably twenty-five years apart. Charles is in his mid- to late nineties, and Anne around seventy. "I was a child in the second World War," she tells me, "and Charles in the first." Charles—a delicate, courtly man with spidery red veins on his cheeks—is, then, my father's age, had he lived. Charles is English but has lived in Schull for fifty years, a widower for the last twenty.

Charles is a little hard of hearing and so talks a good bit. He wants to tell me about Irish history, beginning with the sources of The Troubles in the emigration to Ulster from Scotland, then European history. His life spans the twentieth century and he's aware of that. "It was a terrible century," he says. "People now don't realize how privileged they are, not to be at war. World War One devastated Europe, and then no sooner were we beginning to recover than World War Two comes along. You're lucky," he says to me, not accusingly but observingly, "to have been spared famine and war, to be born in America when you were."

"I know," I say, "I'm grateful."

As we continue to talk Charles drifts further back in time, sparked by our conversation about Fastnet Lighthouse—in operation for more than a hundred and fifty years, a few miles west of Schull Harbor on a rocky outcropping in the Atlantic. "That's a lovely trip if you can take it," Anne tells me. "Charles and I have. It's called the Teardrop, did you know why? Charles, tell her the story." Anne is definitely a big fan of Charles.

Charles hasn't heard so Anne leans closer to his hearing aid. "Tell Sharon the story of the Fastnet Lighthouse, why it's called Ireland's Teardrop."

"Oh," he says, straightening up, "because it's the last bit of Ireland the emigrants would see before going to America. They would all be gazing at it until they couldn't see it anymore, they knew they'd probably never come back."

"And the Irish name means something too, doesn't it Charles? Tell her about that."

"Carraig Aonar. The Lonely One."

CHARLES HAS DRIFTED far back in his memory, back to the 1920s when he was a young man working on the Cunard Line. The ships would leave

Liverpool, stop in Cobh to pick up the Irish steerage passengers, following the route of the *Titanic*. "Girls they were," Charles says, "sixteen years old, hundreds of them, weeping their eyes out, hugging their parents, so sad they were to leave home, they knew they wouldn't be back—going to be domestics in an American family. Some American families employed Blacks but if they wanted to be up a notch they'd hire white Irish girls off the boat."

"Do you remember the crossings?"

"They were terrible for those girls. Four to a little room, they could scarcely move, and way below deck—no windows or fresh air, just a duct that went up, and they'd get sick. No one to clean it, those poor girls lying in that room with their sick on the floor. Then at Ellis Island they'd turn the sick ones back after all that."

Charles is still sad for those girls, who are now, if they've lived, in their mid-eighties, and I'm thinking *he's talking about the 1920s*, when my father is going to Harvard and my mother is having fun with her chums in Elmira, not the 1850s: these terrible partings and voyages kept on going long after the Famine.

We sit in silence for a while, looking out at the harbor. It's a sunny, breezy day and everything looks washed clean. "A beautiful day," Anne says, and we all agree on that. "I must go," Charles says, "I'm a little tired now," and Anne helps him to stand up. We say good-bye and I watch them walk slowly off toward the main street, arm in arm.

I KNOW THE FAMINE is still affecting us, even if we don't know it," a woman who's staying at my B&B said this morning. "How?" I asked. "The fear of poverty. We can't get away from it." Of course: that's the phrase I need to add to my family history, *the fear of poverty*. It wasn't just ambition and upward mobility, the desire for more, that were fueling their need to rise, it was also the fear of what lay below.

I've come across a pamphlet put together by the Famine Committee, *Dear Old Skibbereen: A Glimpse of Conditions in This Town during the Great Irish Famine*. In reading it I've been able to move beyond my generalized knowledge of the Famine—the population dropping from 8 to 5 million within a few years, Irish people starving while corn was being shipped back to England—to the local story, learning what my ancestors must have experienced here, in this place.

Skibbereen was one of the hardest hit parts of Ireland. The town drew several English and American observers who wanted to view famine conditions, so it may be the most written about famine town in Ireland. The pamphlets describe scenes the unknown O'Briens must have witnessed.

> Almost the first thing we saw on entering the town were the coffins. . . .
> Round the inn door were crowded numbers of the most wretched beings one
> had ever beheld, not so much as clamouring for alms, as looking on in list-
> less inactivity. . . . The poor had pawned nearly every article. . . . Many have
> parted with the means of future subsistence, as in the case of some fishermen
> who have pawned their boats and nets. . . . Every day the dismal visits of the
> funeral cart, the call to the inmates to bring forth their dead. . . . The bodies
> had been thrown daily in, one over the other. The local Committee estimates
> the number of deaths every day at from 35 to 40, exclusive of those in the
> Workhouse.
> The Churchyard of Abbeystrowry was the spot in which a generation
> of Skibbereen people was buried in a year and a half. Immediately inside
> the gate, a little to the right, are those monster graves called by the people
> "the pits" into which the dead were thrown coffinless in hundreds, without
> mourning or ceremony, hurried away by stealth, frequently at the dead of
> night. . . . A little saw dust was sprinkled over each corpse, on being laid in
> the pit, which was thus kept open until it had received its full complement of
> tenants. . . . Many burials took place at night, with many burying their dead
> in secret, too ashamed to be seen doing so without a coffin or shroud, or too
> afraid to have it known that fever had entered their dwelling. . . .
> How scared, terrified and secretive the scourged people were. To make
> it known that famine fever had visited your house was to put a ring of fire
> around it . . . people tried to conceal the fact that they were victims.

$\mathcal{A}$s I walk through the gates of Abbeystrowry cemetery, I see that the famine pit is now a fresh green expanse of newly mown lawn, signaled by a marker put up by the Famine Committee in 1997. "In Memory of the Victims of the Famine whose Coffinless Bodies Were Buried in This Plot." The cemetery stretches up the hill, scattered with the gravestones and markers of those who survived the Famine and their descendants. "You could break your ankle in that cemetery," Teresa had warned me, and now I see why: except for the famine plot, the cemetery has not been tended in years. The grass is waist-high around the graves and the underbrush has filled in the empty spaces.

Abbeystrowry Cemetery, Skibbereen, County Cork

In front of me, under the freshly mowed grass, lie between eight and ten thousand people, some of them my relatives. I left my candle in the car, and I've invented no ceremonies or rituals. I've realized that my ancestors don't think it's important to do anything fancy: what's important is just to show up.

They don't care about how well I've done in school, or how many books I've published, or how clean my house is. They're just glad that I've made it back to this little town in West Cork and to this graveyard.

I say the Lord's Prayer, but that doesn't seem enough, so I start to tell them about the family. "So Patrick made it to America all right, and then his son Daniel did quite well in Lowell, running a clothing store, and according to my mother he was a wonderful man, gentle and kind. He had a fine Irish tenor voice and sang at funerals. And then my father—he was a good man, a great reader, once wanted to be a priest but I'm glad he didn't. He would have loved to be here with me. And my mother, I tell you, if she could have gotten on a plane she'd have made me come here long ago." I imagine what it would be like to be here with my parents, visiting the graveyard and then adjourning to O'Brien's pub for dinner and discussing the day.

I pause before plunging into the next generations and look around the

334

graveyard. Some people are wading through the underbrush up the hill, off to visit a grave that has a marker, and at the top of the hill I see a car stop and the driver get out, cross over to the wall and gaze at the cemetery for a while before making the Sign of the Cross and driving on.

"The three of us are fine, and so are Maureen's kids and grandkids," I tell them, and find myself on the verge of adding the expected refrain, "thanks be to God," even though that way of speaking is really foreign to me. But I've heard so many references to God over the last few days, naturally woven into conversation—*thanks be to God, God willing, God bless, God rest their souls*—as well as hearing the Angelus bells on Irish radio and television (broadcast at noon and six o'clock), that the word "God" is on the tip of my tongue.

A FAMILY OF tourists or pilgrims has entered the cemetery and stands reading the marker, but I'm just about done so they won't have to hear me speaking to the field of grass. I'd been wondering what my ancestors' reaction might be to knowing they have Jewish and Muslim descendants, along with some lapsed Catholics, but the feeling I'm getting from the green lawn is that they don't care. They're just glad to know that some members of their family have survived.

"I'm glad to see where you live," I tell the green lawn. "I'm driving to Dublin now, but I'll be back and I'll bring some more of your relatives. God bless."

I WALK OUT PAST the famine markers, past the gate that says "Abbey-strowry Cemetery." The sun is setting out over the Atlantic, and the clouds passing over the Ilen River, just across the road from the cemetery, are lighting up pink. The *Irish Times* weather forecast for tomorrow is "Cloud with Sunny Spells," a prediction you'd never see in the States. It means that you can expect a mix of clouds and rain and breakthroughs of sun, what we'd call "partly cloudy with chance of showers," but I like their way of putting it better.

Acknowledgments

WRITING IS OFTEN A LONELY PROCESS. Some writers claim to be so internally motivated that they would write even without readers, producing dozens of books even if marooned on desert islands. I am not one of them. When I began writing about family and depression twelve years ago, I was not at all sure that my essays and stories would ever be published, and in fact was not thinking about publication. Yes, I wanted to write, but part of that motivation came from all the friends and colleagues who read my work and encouraged me over the years. I could not have completed this book without these readers, whose support was particularly important during the times when I doubted the worth of my project. I want to thank Malaga Baldi, Brenda Bretz, Kate Burnett, Mary Clayton, Grace D'Alo, Mara Donaldson, Amy Farrell, Jackie Fear-Segal, Peggy Garrett, Jay Hill, Sharon Hirsh, Cathy Hughes, Carol Ann Johnston, Mary Kelley, Pat Keough, Chris Mathna, Niall McMonagle, Susan Monsky, Jane Müller-Peterson, Wolfgang Müller, Cary Nicholas, Jeannie Nicholas, Miles Orvell, Polly Peterson, Ted Pulcini, Janice Radway, Meredith Rialls, Anne Roper, Susan Rose, Ellen Rosenman, Lois Rudnick, Maggy Sears, Maida Solomon, Nancy Somers, Jonathan Strong, Susan Thornsley, Judy Tuwaletsiwa, and Bob Winston.

Writing groups have also been important to me; when you meet with other people who are also writing, this solitary endeavor becomes communal. You feel that you are part of a shared enterprise and that writing is—if not exactly *normal*—at least something that other people do. For this intangible gift, as well as for making good suggestions and reinforcing my super-ego (those writing group due dates helped a lot) I want to thank the Essential Experience of Philadelphia writing group, my Cambridge writing group, the Dead Birds Society, my Tuesday night Women's Memoir Group in Carlisle, and the Friday Morning Breakfast Group (the latter not a writing group, but populated by women friends who kept checking up on me, asking for progress reports after we'd ordered our eggs and pancakes).

I want to thank the National Endowment for the Humanities, Dickinson College, the MacDowell Colony, and the Dorland Mountain Arts Colony for giving me grants and residencies that were crucial to my creative life. My colleagues and friends at Dickinson gave me another sustaining gift: thank you for your faith in me as I ventured, often unsure, into new forms of writing and teaching.

I am grateful to the Boston chapter of the Manic-Depressive and Depressive Association for providing me encouragement, companionship, and a few much-needed laughs during my year in Boston. I have been faithful to the group's commitment to confidentiality, telling only my story of group meetings, not revealing anyone else's. In portraying group discussions I have invented dialogue and speakers, based on my remembered emotional truth, not on the conversations that took place.

I have been blessed with editorial support that has helped me to turn my much revised manuscript into an even more revised (and better) one. Thanks to Anne duBuisson Anderson for her cogent editorial suggestions that improved the structure of the book and to my outside readers for the University of Chicago Press, whose comments helped me rethink how to interweave my father's story with my own. I am grateful to Jean Weaver and her staff in Dickinson's Instructional Technology for scanning and improving the illustrations—often in the context of short notice and authorial anxiety. I could not have found a better editor than Doug Mitchell or a better home for my book than the University of Chicago Press, whose editorial and production staff have been superb: you all have understood the soul of my writing as well as handling, with grace and elegance, the transition of my manuscript into the public world.

All this support has been immeasurably important to me, both personally and professionally. But this book is, most of all, a gift from my family. Maureen, my dearest sister, what can I say? Without your love, support, and commitment I would not have a book (or as happy a life). Even when things have been tough, we've always been able to laugh, and that has sustained me both in living and in writing. Kevin, my dearest brother: you are the other family historian and, I have always felt, the one who carries my father's spirit into this generation. Your love and concern and humor have been sustaining—and I love those clippings from the *Boston Globe* you send me (here you have taken on our mother's role).

And let me not fail to mention, Maureen, that if you had not escaped the family mausoleum in 1957, bringing down parental wrath, we would now not have this amazing family. Maureen, David, Beth, Ted, and John, my wonderful nieces and nephews—thank you for helping me discover how being an aunt is one of the best things in my life. Years ago, if people asked me whether I had a family, I'd probably have answered no, since that question seems to demand that you have children in order to say yes. Now I would say yes immediately: you are my family, and I am so lucky to have you. And thanks to Maureen and Ted for expanding our family and bringing Adil Karamali and Valerie Courville, my nephew- and niece-in-law, into my life.

Sometimes in the midst of a busy semester I'll say to some unsuspecting friend "We need to have *more fun!*" I never say that when I'm around my great-niece and nephews—Jahan, Amar, and Zain Karamali and Dylan Courville. When we're together it's really not possible to have more fun. (Although now that my book is done, maybe we can find a way to have even *more*? Come up with a plan.)

I know that were my parents still living I would not have written this book. In part I needed the freedom to write without imagining them as readers, but even more, I think, it was their loss that underlay this book: I needed to discover a way, through memory and imagination, heart and soul, to find them again, and to understand them more deeply. They were the deepest source for this book, as they were for my life. I miss them.